The Sporting

BASEBALL

The Sporting News

BASEBALL Trivia 2

Co-Editor-Writer
JOE HOPPEL

Co-Editor-Researcher
CRAIG CARTER

President-Chief Executive Officer
RICHARD WATERS

Editor
TOM BARNIDGE

Director of Books and Periodicals
RON SMITH

Published in the United States by THE SPORTING NEWS Publishing Co.,
1212 North Lindbergh Boulevard, St. Louis, Missouri 63132.

ISBN: 0-89204-242-7
10 9 8 7 6 5 4 3 2 1

First Edition

TABLE OF
CONTENTS

Cover and inside illustrations by Bill Wilson of The Sporting News.

INTRODUCTION

The Sporting News Baseball Trivia Book made its debut in 1983, arriving as a one-of-a-kind reference source and trivia "who's who."

As the popularity of the book met high expectations, two inevitable questions were asked: What will The Sporting News do for an encore? When will a second Trivia Book be published?

The answers to those questions were supplied by baseball itself and the legions of loyal fans who treat both its feats and foibles with a fascination that borders on fanaticism.

Baseball, by nature of its pace, intricacies, nuances and statistical bent, seems to supply more memorable moments in a single season than other sports provide in a decade. A baseball fan demands access to this wealth of information. Certainly, no other sport documents its goings-on— the dramatic, coincidental, strange, funny, ironic and poignant occurrences —quite like baseball. And, just as certainly, no other observer craves such documentation quite like a baseball fan.

Clearly, with the passing of four years, it is time for The Sporting News Baseball Trivia Book 2.

Let's see. In the seasons that have passed since the publication of the first Baseball Trivia Book, we've come to know all about pine tar. And Fred Lynn walloping the first bases-loaded home run in All-Star Game history . . . Dave Winfield conking a sea gull . . . Bob Horner becoming the second player in major league history to slug four homers in one game in a losing cause . . . two minor league teammates hitting for the cycle in the same game . . . Roy Hobbs swinging a potent bat for Manager Pop Fisher's New York Knights . . . Mike Scott pitching the majors' first title-clinching no-hitter . . . Charlie Hough striking out three batters in one inning of an All-Star Game and still not retiring the side . . . a ground ball eluding Bill Buckner . . . and on it goes.

The Sporting News Baseball Trivia Book 2 chronicles all of the aforementioned events—zeroing in on their principal and peripheral characters —and that's just for starters. Indeed, the all-new "Trivia 2" dates to 1876 in its review of both the headline-making and little-publicized moments that have earned special places in baseball lore. Plus, we've broken new ground with the inclusion of such chapter topics as movies (remember Ronald Reagan as Grover Cleveland Alexander?), families, the minor leagues and trades.

For the record, there are two key guidelines: 1. We consider 1900 as the start of baseball's modern era. 2. The Sporting News doesn't accord "big league" status to the 1914-15 Federal League, whose playing ranks appeared considerably inferior to those leagues we do recognize as "major" (National League, American League, 1882-1891 American Association, 1884 Union Association and 1890 Players League).

Finally, all entries in The Sporting News Baseball Trivia Book 2 reflect records and situations as they were through the 1986 season.

United States President William Howard Taft became the first Chief Executive to throw out the first ball at a major league season opener, setting the stage for the Senators-Philadelphia A's Washington Inaugural in 1910.

CHAPTER 1
OPENING DAY

HANK AARON

The major leagues' all-time home run leader, he hit only one opening-day homer in his nine seasons with the Atlanta Braves—the April 4, 1974, smash at Cincinnati's Riverfront Stadium that tied him with Babe Ruth (714 homers) on the career list.

Aaron hit only one other opening-day home run in the big leagues, connecting for the Milwaukee Braves against the Chicago Cubs on April 17, 1956, in Milwaukee. He finished his 23-season career in the majors with 755 homers.

ATLANTA BRAVES

National League team that lost nine straight opening-day games from 1972 through 1980, tying the big-league record for beginning-of-the-season futility that had been established by the New York Giants at the turn of the century. The Giants' string of losses in season openers began in 1893 and ran through 1901.

9

ATLANTA BRAVES

Holders of the modern major league record for consecutive victories at the beginning of the year, having started the 1982 National League season with 13 straight triumphs. From April 6 through April 21, the Braves beat Houston six times, Cincinnati five times and San Diego twice. Atlanta, though, went from a 13-0 record to a 13-5 mark; the five-game losing streak began with a 2-1 loss to the Reds on April 22.

The Oakland A's, who ran off an 11-0 record at the outset of the 1981 season, hold the A.L. record for consecutive victories at the start of a season.

EARL AVERILL

The only member of baseball's Hall of Fame to hit a home run in his first big-league at-bat on opening day. Playing for the Indians in an April 16, 1929, game at Cleveland, center fielder Averill broke into the majors by homering in the first inning off Detroit's Earl Whitehill. Cleveland went on to a 5-4 victory in 11 innings, and Averill went on to an outstanding career (238 homers, a .318 lifetime batting average).

Hoyt Wilhelm is the only other Hall of Famer who homered in his first major league at-bat, regardless of the juncture of the season. Pitcher Wilhelm connected for the New York Giants in an April 23, 1952, game against the Boston Braves (and never hit another homer in a big-league career that spanned 21 seasons).

BALTIMORE ORIOLES

The first team in big-league history to turn a triple play on opening day. With Washington's Roy Sievers on second base and Bob Allison on first and Hoyt Wilhelm pitching for Baltimore in the fifth inning of an April 9, 1959, game at Griffith Stadium, Senators catcher Ed Fitz Gerald hit a line drive that Orioles first baseman Bob Boyd speared for the first out. Boyd fired the ball to shortstop Chico Carrasquel, who doubled up Sievers at second, and Carrasquel's throw back to Boyd caught Allison off first base. Despite the triple play, the Orioles fell to the Senators, 9-2.

Only two other major league clubs have made triple plays in season openers—the 1978 Houston Astros (against Cincinnati) and the 1981 St. Louis Cardinals (versus Philadelphia). Like the '59 Orioles, the '78 Astros and '81 Cardinals were first-day losers despite their defensive gems. Houston lost to Cincinnati, 11-9, and St. Louis was beaten by Philadelphia, 5-2.

YOGI BERRA, GARY CARTER

The only players in big-league history to smash home runs in four consecutive season-opening games. Berra clubbed homers for the New York Yankees on each opening day from 1955 through 1958, while Carter homered for Montreal in all of the Expos' season openers from 1977 through 1980.

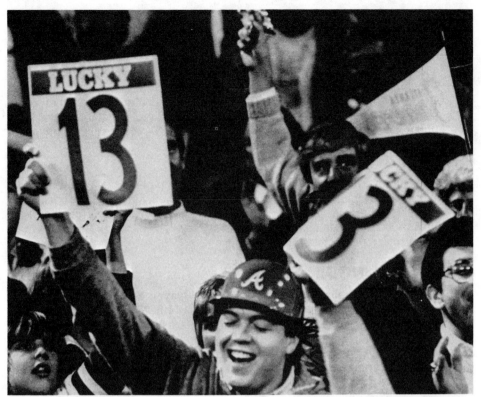

Jubilant Atlanta fans had plenty of reason to celebrate in 1982 when the Braves dispatched Cincinnati for their 13th straight victory, a modern major league record for season-opening success.

BERT BLYLEVEN

Pitcher who at the age of 30 had started season openers for four major league clubs. Blyleven was the opening-day starter for the Minnesota Twins from 1972 through 1976, for the Texas Rangers in 1977, for the Pittsburgh Pirates in 1979 and 1980 and, five days past his 30th birthday, for the Cleveland Indians in 1981.

Blyleven was the opening-day pitcher for Cleveland again in 1985.

BOSTON BRAVES

Winners of their 1946 season opener, but one aspect of the 5-3 triumph over Brooklyn didn't sit too well with more than 300 of the 18,261 spectators at Braves Field. Shortly before the April 16 opening-day game, Braves management decided to spruce up the stands with a fresh coat of paint. Cold and damp weather prevented the paint from drying by game time in some sections of the grandstand, though, and a throng of customers showed up at the club offices after the game complaining about paint stains on clothing. The following day, the Braves ran a notice in the Boston newspapers offering apologies to fans and agreeing to pay cleaning bills.

BOSTON RED SOX

The only team to hit three consecutive home runs in an opening-day major league game. In the second inning of an April 19, 1948, game at Boston's Fenway Park, Stan Spence, Vern Stephens and Bobby Doerr homered in succession for the Red Sox off Philadelphia pitcher Phil Marchildon. The homers weren't enough, however, as Boston fell, 5-4, to the A's in 11 innings.

PETE BURNSIDE

The winning pitcher in the longest opening-day game in big-league history. Working four innings of relief for the Tigers in their April 19, 1960, opener in Cleveland, Burnside was credited with the victory as Detroit downed the Indians, 4-2, in 15 innings. Jim (Mudcat) Grant, who pitched 3⅓ innings in a relief role, took the loss for Cleveland.

CHICAGO, CINCINNATI

Cities whose National League teams have played a major league-record number of opening-day games against each other. A Chicago-Cincinnati matchup has been the first game of the N.L. season for *both* clubs 30 times. (Such a pairing has proved the initial game of the season for the Cubs 32 times. In 1951 and 1953, the Cubs opened play against the Reds—but Cincinnati had started its season a day earlier against Pittsburgh and Milwaukee, respectively.)

CHICAGO CUBS

National League club that, in 10 opening-day games from 1944 through 1953, employed 10 different starting pitchers. In order, the Cubs called on Hank Wyse, Paul Derringer, Claude Passeau, Hank Borowy, Russ Meyer, Dutch Leonard, Johnny Schmitz, Frank Hiller, Paul Minner and Bob Rush. Chicago won seven of the 10 games, with Wyse, Derringer, Schmitz, Hiller and Rush notching victories and Passeau and Minner getting no-decisions in games won by Chicago relievers Ray Prim and Joe Hatten. Borowy, Meyer and Leonard were charged with losses in their season-opening starts.

CINCINNATI REDS

National League team that opened the season at home for 76 consecutive years, 1890 through 1965, a major league record. The Reds compiled a 32-44 mark in those opening-day games before starting the 1966 season at Philadelphia following the rainout of a scheduled three-game series at Crosley Field against the New York Mets. Cincinnati, the city that fielded baseball's first professional team in 1869, resumed its opening-at-home tradition in 1967, and through 1986 the Reds had played only one season opener—the '66 game—outside Cincinnati in 97 years.

CINCINNATI REDS

The only major league club to hit home runs in 10 straight opening-day games, connecting in season openers from 1963 through 1972. Fourteen

Reds accounted for a total of 17 homers in those games, with Deron Johnson, Tony Perez and Bobby Tolan leading the way with two each.

JOHN CLARKSON, WALTER JOHNSON

The only pitchers in major league history to win five consecutive opening-day games for one team. Clarkson won season-opening starts for Boston's National League club from 1888 through 1892, and Johnson was victorious for the American League's Washington Senators in openers from 1913 through 1917.

DAIN CLAY, HOD LISENBEE

Cincinnati players whose combined efforts on opening day in 1945 proved noteworthy in the Reds' 7-6, 11-inning triumph over Pittsburgh. Clay, the Reds' center fielder, cracked a bases-loaded home run off the Pirates' Fritz Ostermueller in the fifth inning of the April 17 season opener and delivered a game-winning single in the 11th. The grand slam was Clay's only homer of the year—he had a major league-leading 656 at-bats in '45—and the first of only three home runs in his four-season big-league career. Lisenbee, a 43-year-old relief pitcher, worked two hitless innings and was credited with the victory—his 37th and last triumph in an eight-year career in the majors.

HARRY COVELESKI

The only pitcher in big-league history to collect four hits in an opening-day game. Detroit's Coveleski rapped two singles, a double and a triple on April 12, 1916, at Chicago, and pitched a three-hitter as the Tigers blanked the White Sox, 4-0.

FRANK (POP) DILLON, JIM GREENGRASS

The only players in big-league history to hit four doubles in an opening-day game. Dillon, playing for the Tigers in an April 25, 1901, game in Detroit, collected his doubles in a 14-13 victory over the Milwaukee Brewers. Greengrass' four-double spree came on April 13, 1954, and helped the Cincinnati Reds to a 9-8 triumph against another Milwaukee team—the Braves—at Crosley Field. (Because seats were set up on the field at Cincinnati to accommodate an overflow crowd, ground-rule doubles were plentiful in the '54 opener. In fact, there were 12 ground-rule doubles in the game and 13 doubles overall.)

DON DRYSDALE

The only pitcher in major league history with two lifetime home runs on opening day. On April 11, 1959, at Wrigley Field, Drysdale provided the Los Angeles Dodgers with their only run in a 6-1 loss to the Chicago Cubs when he homered off Bob Anderson. Six years later (April 12, 1965), Drysdale slugged a two-run homer off New York's Al Jackson as Los Angeles scored a 6-1 victory over the Mets at Shea Stadium.

CHUCK ESSEGIAN

Playing his first regular-season game after establishing a World Series record the previous fall with two pinch-hit home runs for the Los Angeles Dodgers, he got the Dodgers' 1960 season off to a dramatic start on April 12. Cast in his familiar role of pinch-hitter, Essegian went to the plate with the score tied, 2-2, and two out in the 11th inning at the Los Angeles Memorial Coliseum and drilled a game-winning homer off Cubs reliever Don Elston. The Dodgers' 3-2 victory over Chicago featured a complete-game, 14-strikeout performance by Dodgers pitcher Don Drysdale and came before a season-opening crowd of 67,550.

AL EVANS

Reflecting the personnel changes that gripped major league baseball during World War II and the postwar period, catcher Evans was the lone player to start for the Washington Senators on opening day in both 1945 and 1946. In its '45 season opener, Washington started Joe Kuhel at first base, George Myatt at second base, Harlond Clift at third base, Gil Torres at shortstop, George Case in left field, Walt Chipple in center field, George Binks in right field, Evans behind the plate and Dutch Leonard on the mound. The Senators' first-day lineup in '46 had Mickey Vernon at first, Jerry Priddy at second, Sherry Robertson at third, Cecil Travis at short, Jeff Heath in left, Stan Spence in center, Buddy Lewis in right, Evans catching and Roger Wolff pitching.

BOB FELLER, LEON (RED) AMES

Pitchers who, respectively, tossed the only complete-game no-hitter on opening day in big-league history and threw no-hit ball through nine innings in a season opener only to lose in extra innings. Cleveland's Feller held the White Sox hitless in a 1-0 Indians triumph on April 16, 1940, at Chicago. Ames, working for the New York Giants, yielded his first hit to Brooklyn in the 10th inning of an April 15, 1909, opener that was 0-0 through 12 innings. Brooklyn wound up with seven hits and a 3-0, 13-inning victory over Ames at NewYork.

4-0

The opening-day record in 1969 of the four expansion teams that entered the major leagues that year. The Montreal Expos won their first National League game, beating the New York Mets, 11-10, while the San Diego Padres broke into the N.L. with a 2-1 victory over the Houston Astros. The American League's two new clubs, the Seattle Pilots and Kansas City Royals, won over California and Minnesota, respectively. The Pilots slipped past the Angels, 4-3, and the Royals edged the Twins by the same score in a 12-inning game.

The six other modern expansion teams went 3-3 in their franchise-opening games. Opening-day winners in their first seasons were the Los Angeles Angels (1961), Houston Colt .45s (1962) and Toronto Blue Jays (1977); losers

Cleveland Indians great Bob Feller receives a pat on the back from teammate Hal Trosky after completing his 1940 opening-day no-hitter against the
Chicago White Sox.

their first time out were the second Washington Senators team ('61), the New York Mets ('62) and the Seattle Mariners ('77).

14-3, 16-7

If getting off on the right foot is crucial, then the Houston Astros may have had misgivings about the 1982 and 1983 seasons—as evidenced by these 11- and nine-run losses that the National League team suffered at the beginning of '82 and '83. The Astros lost to the St. Louis Cardinals in their April 6, 1982, season opener as the Cards broke loose for 18 hits and 14 runs. Then, on April 5, 1983, the Los Angeles Dodgers went on a 15-hit, 16-run spree against Houston. Adding insult to injury, both first-game trouncings came in Houston's home ball park, the Astrodome.

The Astros went on to finish fifth in the National League West in '82 with a 77-85 record, but they ended up third in the West Division in '83 with an 85-77 mark.

NELLIE FOX

The last player to get five hits in a season-opening major league game. Playing for the White Sox on April 10, 1959, at Detroit, Fox rapped three singles and a double before connecting for a game-winning home run in the 14th inning as Chicago downed the Tigers, 9-7. Fox, who had seven at-bats in the contest, slugged his homer with a man on base.

GARY GAETTI

While no major leaguer has hit three home runs in a season-opening game, Gaetti came close to accomplishing the feat on April 6, 1982. Playing for the Twins against Seattle in the first American League game contested at the Metrodome in Minneapolis, Gaetti hammered two home runs after being tagged out at the plate in the first inning while trying to stretch a triple into an inside-the-park homer. He also singled in the game. Despite Gaetti's 4-for-4 effort and four runs batted in, Minnesota lost to the Mariners, 11-7.

LOU GEHRIG, TED WILLIAMS

Gehrig's 17-year big-league playing career ended two weeks into the 1939 season and Williams' 19-season stay in the majors began in '39, so chances that the future Hall of Famers played against each other might appear slim. However, Yankee first baseman Gehrig and Red Sox outfielder Williams did go head-to-head—once. While storms postponed the scheduled Yankees-Red Sox season opener on April 18, 1939, at Yankee Stadium and also wiped out April 19 action, the teams finally got their seasons under way on April 20 in New York, and the Yanks' Red Ruffing outdueled Boston's Lefty Grove, 2-0. Williams cracked a double in four at-bats in his major league debut; Gehrig went 0 for 4, lining into two double plays, but stretched his consecutive-game streak to 2,123. Gehrig played in only seven more games that spring before leaving the New York lineup for good.

AL (LEFTY) GERHEAUSER

The last man to make his major league debut as a starting pitcher in an opening-day game. Gerheauser was the Phillies' starter in the club's 1943 opener, played April 24 at Brooklyn. He allowed seven hits and five runs in four innings, striking out two and walking three, as Philadelphia lost to the Dodgers, 11-4. Gerheauser went on to post a 10-19 record in '43 and a 25-50 mark in five big-league seasons.

PETE GRAY

One-armed outfielder whose big-league debut came on opening day, 1945, at Sportsman's Park in St. Louis. Playing for the Browns, Gray went 1 for 4 at the plate against Detroit—he singled off reliever Les Mueller—as St. Louis defeated the Tigers, 7-1, in an April 17 game. The '45 season was Gray's only year in the majors, and he wound up hitting .218 in 77 games.

GUY HECKER

He made his major league debut on opening day, 1882, as a first baseman—and collected four hits. Then, in the next four years, he served as the season-opening pitcher for his big-league club. Hecker's team was Louisville and his league was the American Association, which at the time was a "major league." Hecker singled four times on May 2, 1882—the first day of play in the Association's 10-year history—as Louisville lost, 9-7, at St. Louis. In his opening-day pitching starts from 1883 through 1886, Hecker fashioned a 3-1 record for Louisville.

Getting four hits in a major league debut on opening day was achieved five other times in "pre-modern" baseball history—and one of those performances also came on the American Association's first afternoon of action. Charlie Morton of Pittsburgh broke into the majors with four hits in a May 2, 1882, Association opener at Cincinnati.

SPOOK JACOBS

The only player in modern big-league history to collect four hits in an opening-day game that marked his debut in the majors. Jacobs, a second baseman, broke into the big leagues for the A's on April 13, 1954, in a game against the Red Sox at Philadelphia. He delivered four singles in five at-bats as Philadelphia defeated Boston, 6-4, in the final season opener for the A's as a Philadelphia-based club (the franchise was moved to Kansas City in 1955 and then to Oakland in 1968).

SPUD JOHNSON

He went 9 for 9 at the plate in his first two opening-day games in the majors, breaking into the big leagues with four hits in four at-bats for Columbus of the American Association in its April 18, 1889, game against Baltimore and then going 5 for 5 in Columbus' April 17, 1890, contest against Toledo. (No other player in major league history has totaled nine hits in two straight season openers.) Johnson, who played only three years in the major leagues, was 2 for 4 for Cleveland in that National League club's April 22, 1891, season opener against Cincinnati, giving him 11 hits in 13 at-bats (.846) on opening day.

WALTER JOHNSON

The Washington great who pitched seven opening-day shutouts in his 21-season major league career, all of which was spent with the Senators. Johnson was the Senators' starting pitcher 14 times overall on opening day, and he fashioned a 9-5 record in those games.

Johnson's best opening-day performance was his first, which came on April 14, 1910, in Washington. Johnson tossed a one-hitter that day in the Senators' 3-0 American League victory over the Philadelphia A's. On the same afternoon in Chicago, Frank Smith of the White Sox allowed the Browns only one hit as the Sox beat St. Louis, 3-0, in another A.L. opener.

MIKE (KING) KELLY

The first player in major league history to hit a home run on opening day, connecting on the first afternoon of play in the National League's fifth season. Kelly's homer, which came with Cap Anson on base in the second inning, helped the Chicago White Stockings to a 4-3 triumph over the Red Stockings on May 1, 1880, at Cincinnati. The second homer in opening-day history was struck in the same game—by Cincinnati's player-manager, John Clapp, who socked a two-run shot in the eighth inning.

SANDY KOUFAX

Winner of three Cy Young Awards, recipient of one Most Valuable Player honor and author of four no-hitters in the majors—but an opening-day pitcher in the big leagues only once. Koufax's lone season-opening start came on April 14, 1964, at Dodger Stadium, and the lefthander pitched Los Angeles to a 4-0 victory over St. Louis. Koufax held the Cardinals to six hits.

ERNIE KOY, EMMETT MUELLER

Principals in the lone instance in history when two players hit home runs in their first major league at-bats in the same game. On opening day of the 1938 season at Philadelphia's Baker Bowl, Brooklyn left fielder Koy made his big-league debut at the plate with two out in the top of the first inning and rapped a bases-empty homer off Phillies pitcher Wayne LaMaster. Then, leading off the bottom of the first against the Dodgers' Van Lingle Mungo, Phils second baseman Mueller tied the score, 1-1, with a home run in his first time up in the majors. Koy went 3 for 5 overall for the Dodgers, who won, 12-5; Mueller was 2 for 3 for Philadelphia.

SIXTO LEZCANO

The only player in big-league history to hit bases-loaded home runs in two opening-day games—and he slugged only three grand slams in his 12-year

Phillies second baseman Emmett Mueller (left) and Brooklyn outfielder Ernie Koy celebrated their 1938 major league arrivals by hitting first-inning home runs in the same game on their first big-league at-bats.

major league career. As a member of the Milwaukee Brewers, Lezcano socked bases-full homers on the first day of the season in 1978 and 1980.

Lou Gehrig, the majors' all-time leader in grand slams with 23, never hit a bases-loaded homer on opening day. In fact, the longtime Yankee star never hit a grand slam in the month of April.

HERMAN LONG

The first player in major league history to slug two home runs in an opening-day game, connecting for Boston of the National League on April 19, 1890, in a 15-9 victory over Brooklyn.

ROGER MARIS

Acquired from the Kansas City Athletics in December 1959, the majors' future single-season home run champion made his debut with the New York Yankees on opening day, 1960—and slugged two homers at Boston's Fenway Park. Maris, in fact, went 4 for 5 with four runs batted in as the Yankees downed the Red Sox, 8-4, in an April 19 game.

BILLY MARTIN, RUSS MORMAN

The only men to collect two hits in one inning in their first major league games—and Martin performed his feat in his first two trips to the plate in the majors as the Yankees battled the Red Sox in a 1950 season opener. After replacing Jerry Coleman at second base for New York in the sixth inning of an April 18 game at Boston, Martin made his first big-league plate appearance in the eighth inning and doubled home a run against Boston starter Mel Parnell. Martin batted again in the eighth—the Yankees enjoyed a nine-run inning—and delivered a two-run single off Al Papai. New York, which had trailed, 9-0, after four innings, won the slugfest, 15-10. Morman homered and singled for the Chicago White Sox in the fourth inning of his first big-league game, an August 3, 1986, contest against the Detroit Tigers at Comiskey Park. He had singled in his first major league at-bat in the second inning.

JOHN MAYBERRY

The last of only five players in big-league history to collect four or more hits in consecutive season-opening games. Mayberry went 4 for 4 for Toronto in the Blue Jays' 1979 opener, played April 5 in Kansas City. In the Jays' first game of 1980, contested April 9 in Seattle, Mayberry socked two home runs and had four hits overall in five at-bats. Despite Mayberry's slugging, Toronto lost its '79 and '80 openers by scores of 11-2 and 8-6.

Also getting four or more hits in consecutive opening-day major league games were: Spud Johnson, Columbus, American Association, 1889 and 1890; Joe Gedeon, St. Louis Browns, 1918 and 1919; Buck Weaver, Chicago White Sox, 1919 and 1920, and Ira Flagstead, Boston Red Sox, 1925 and 1926.

WILLIE MAYS

The only player in major league history to hit home runs in each of his club's first four games of a season. Playing for San Francisco in 1971, Mays homered at San Diego on April 6, 7 and 8 as the Giants won two of three season-opening games from the Padres. In San Francisco's fourth game of the season, an April 10 contest at St. Louis, Mays connected again as the Giants won for the third time.

JIM McCORMICK, RICK REUSCHEL

The only pitchers in big-league history to lose opening-day games in four consecutive years for the same team. McCormick, pitching for Cleveland of the National League, lost season openers from 1879 through 1882, while Reuschel was a first-day loser for the Chicago Cubs from 1978 through 1981.

MILWAUKEE BREWERS

Members of the American League when the circuit opened its first big-league season in 1901, the Brewers got everyone's attention by mounting a 13-3 lead after 7½ innings in their debut in the majors—and then really made headlines. Negative headlines. Detroit, Milwaukee's opponent in the April 25, 1901, game, scored once in the bottom of the eighth inning and 10 times in the last of the ninth for a stunning 14-13 victory. The Tigers' Frank (Pop) Dillon hit two doubles in the ninth—the second proving to be the game-winning hit—and had four doubles overall that afternoon in Detroit.

The Brewers' opening-day collapse was a hint of things to come. Milwaukee went on to finish last in the American League's maiden season, compiling a 48-89 record. By 1902, Milwaukee was out of the league and St. Louis was in (with the Browns).

MONTREAL EXPOS

An expansion club that began play in 1969, this team has never opened the National League season at home.

BOBBY MURCER

The only player in big-league history to slug a bases-loaded home run on opening day as a pinch-hitter. Playing for the New York Yankees against Texas on April 9, 1981, Murcer was called upon to bat for designated hitter Dennis Werth in the seventh inning and walloped a grand slam off Rangers pitcher Steve Comer. The Yankees beat Texas, 10-3, at Yankee Stadium.

BOBO NEWSOM

Opening-day winning pitcher for the St. Louis Browns in 1938 and 1939 and opening-day losing pitcher against the Browns in 1940 and 1941. In a '38 opener, the Browns' Newsom beat Cleveland, 6-2; in the first game of the '39 season, he pitched the St. Louis club to a 5-1 victory over the Chicago White Sox. Traded to Detroit in May 1939, Newsom started season-opening games for the Tigers in '40 and '41 and lost to the Browns by 5-1 and 8-1 scores.

NEW YORK YANKEES, CHICAGO WHITE SOX

The last major league teams to open their seasons with a doubleheader, doing so on April 11, 1982. The White Sox had been snowed out three straight days in Chicago, where they were supposed to open the season against the Boston Red Sox; the Yankees experienced the same misfortune in New York, where they were scheduled to begin the season against the Texas Rangers. (While both matchups were two-game sets, attempts to make up postponements on scheduled off-days also were snowed out.) Then, the White Sox and Yanks were to meet in a weekend series at Yankee Stadium —but snow postponed the Friday and Saturday games. Finally, the teams got their '82 seasons under way on Sunday, April 11, with the playing date rescheduled as a doubleheader to make up one of the postponements. The White Sox won the opener, 7-6, in 12 innings and took the nightcap, 2-0.

The Boston Red Sox, also snow victims for five straight days at the outset of the '82 season, got started with a doubleheader, too. Boston was a 2-0 winner and a 5-3 loser at Baltimore on April 10, originally a single-game date. The Orioles had opened their season five days earlier.

The White Sox were the last big-league team to open a season with a scheduled doubleheader, scoring 6-5 and 12-4 victories at Oakland on April 7, 1971. The A's had started their season two days earlier in Washington.

NEW YORK YANKEES, PHILADELPHIA A'S

The first clubs to combine for seven home runs in a season-opening major league contest, a first-game total that has been matched only twice. On April 12, 1932, at Philadelphia, the Yankees' Babe Ruth and Sammy Byrd each hit two homers and Lou Gehrig powered another in New York's 12-6 triumph over the A's, who got homers from Al Simmons and Jimmie Foxx.

The Boston Red Sox (Lenny Green, two, and Felix Mantilla, Tony Conigliaro and Lee Thomas) and Washington Senators (Don Lock and Ken McMullen) slammed seven home runs in a 1965 season opener, and the Red Sox (Carl Yastrzemski and Butch Hobson) and Milwaukee Brewers (Sixto Lezcano, two, and Ben Oglivie, Don Money and Paul Molitor) totaled seven homers in a 1980 opening-day game.

Besides the 1932 Yankees, 1965 Red Sox and 1980 Brewers, only two other big-league teams have walloped five homers in an opening-day game—the 1936 Chicago Cubs and the 1964 San Francisco Giants. Frank Demaree homered twice and Gabby Hartnett, Billy Herman and Chuck Klein each connected once for the Cubs against the St. Louis Cardinals in 1936, while Willie Mays slugged two homers and Orlando Cepeda, Jim Ray Hart and Tom Haller each homered once for the Giants against the Milwaukee Braves in 1964.

NEW YORK YANKEES, WASHINGTON SENATORS

Only once in an opening-day major league game have both teams hit as many as three home runs—and the Yankees and the Senators accomplished the feat on April 17, 1956, at Washington. Mickey Mantle socked two homers for New York and Yogi Berra contributed one for the Yankees, who won, 10-4; Karl Olson homered twice for the Senators and Dick Tettlebach connected once. Tettlebach's blast was the only home run of his big-league career, while Olson hit only six major league home runs.

19-1

The biggest opening-day romp in modern major league history, with the New York Yankees beating the Washington Senators by that 18-run margin at Yankee Stadium in the Yanks' first game of the 1955 season. (The Senators had opened their season two days earlier in Washington with a 12-5 rout of the Baltimore Orioles.) Whitey Ford pitched a two-hitter for the Yankees in the April 13 game and also contributed three singles and four runs batted in. Mickey Mantle and Bob Cerv also had four RBIs apiece. Yogi Berra, Bill Skowron and Mantle hit homers for the Yanks, who scored two or more runs in every inning from the third through the eighth against the Senators, who employed four pitchers (one of whom, reliever Vince Gonzales, was appearing in his only major league game).

19-17

The highest-scoring season opener (36 total runs) in big-league history. The date was April 19, 1900, and the city was Boston—and the local National League team thrilled the crowd by tying Philadelphia, 17-17, with a nine-run outburst in the bottom of the ninth inning. But Philadelphia, which at one point led, 16-4, scored twice in the 10th inning and emerged as the opening-day winner.

The Cleveland Indians and St. Louis Browns fell one run short of the combined opening-day scoring record when they played a 21-14 season opener (won by Cleveland) on April 14, 1925—but the Indians-Browns game may have been more notable because of slick-fielding George Sisler's four errors at first base for St. Louis than for the day's offensive fireworks.

OPENING-DAY PITCHERS

A team-by-team listing of pitchers most prominent in the opening-day history of baseball's old and current franchises:

NATIONAL LEAGUE

Club	Games Started	Wins	Losses
Atlanta Braves	Phil Niekro-8	Rick Mahler-3	Phil Niekro-6
Boston Braves	Kid Nichols-6 Vic Willis-4 Dick Rudolph-4 Al Javery-4 Johnny Sain-4	John Clarkson-5 Kid Nichols-5 Cy Young-3	Dick Rudolph-3 Al Javery-3 Johnny Sain-3
Brooklyn Dodgers	William Kennedy-6 Nap Rucker-4 Van Mungo-4 Carl Erskine-4	William Kennedy-4 Bill Donovan-2 Leon Cadore-2 Dutch Ruether-2 Jesse Petty-2 Van Mungo-2 Curt Davis-2	Nap Rucker-3
Chicago Cubs	Fergie Jenkins-7	Lon Warneke-4	Rick Reuschel-4
Cincinnati Reds	Pete Donohue-5 Mario Soto-5	Mario Soto-4	Art Fromme-3 Bucky Walters-3
Houston Astros	J.R. Richard-5	Larry Dierker-4	Don Wilson-2 J.R. Richard-2 Joe Niekro-2 Nolan Ryan-2

Club	Games Started	Wins	Losses
Los Angeles Dodgers	Don Drysdale-7 Don Sutton-7	Don Drysdale-5	Don Drysdale-2 Claude Osteen-2 Don Sutton-2 F'ndo Valenzuela-2
Milwaukee Braves	Warren Spahn-8	Warren Spahn-3	Warren Spahn-3
Montreal Expos	Steve Rogers-9	Steve Rogers-2	Steve Rogers-4
New York Giants	Carl Hubbell-6	Mickey Welch-4 C. Mathewson-3 Bill Voiselle-3	Amos Rusie-4 Leon Ames-3 Carl Hubbell-3 Larry Jansen-3
New York Mets	Tom Seaver-11	Tom Seaver-6	Roger Craig-2 Al Jackson-2
Philadelphia Phillies	Steve Carlton-14	Robin Roberts-5	Steve Carlton-9
Pittsburgh Pirates	Bob Friend-7	D. Phillippe-3 Howie Camnitz-3 Babe Adams-3 Rip Sewell-3	Frank Killen-4 Wilbur Cooper-3
St. Louis Cardinals	Bob Gibson-10	Flint Rhem-3	Jack W. Taylor-2 John Lush-2 Jesse Haines-2 Dizzy Dean-2 Mort Cooper-2 Harry Brecheen-2 Bob Gibson-2 Bob Forsch-2
San Diego Padres	Randy Jones-4	Clay Kirby-2 Randy Jones-2	Many With 1
San Fran. Giants	Juan Marichal-10	Juan Marichal-6	Juan Marichal-2 Gary Lavelle-2

AMERICAN LEAGUE

Club	Games Started	Wins	Losses
Baltimore Orioles	Jim Palmer-6	Jim Palmer-5	Mike Flanagan-2
Boston Red Sox	Cy Young-6	Babe Ruth-3 Wes Ferrell-3	Cy Young-3 Howard Ehmke-3
California Angels	Frank Tanana-4	Nolan Ryan-3	George Brunet-2 Frank Tanana-2
Chicago White Sox	Billy Pierce-7	Billy Pierce-3	Billy Pierce-3
Cleveland Indians	Bob Feller-7	Bob Feller-4	Bob Feller-3

Club	Games Started	Wins	Losses
Detroit Tigers	George Mullin-10	Jack Morris-6	George Mullin-5
Kansas City Athletics	Alex Kellner-2	Alex Kellner-2	Many With 1
Kansas City Royals	Dennis Leonard-4	Bud Black-2	Dennis Leonard-3
Milwaukee Brewers	Jim Slaton-3	Mike Caldwell-2	Many With 1
Minnesota Twins	Bert Blyleven-5	Gaylord Perry-2 Bert Blyleven-2 Frank Viola-2	Many With 1
New York Yankees	Whitey Ford-7 Mel Stottlemyre-7 Ron Guidry-7	Mel Stottlemyre-4	Ray Caldwell-3 Lefty Gomez-3 Whitey Ford-3 Mel Stottlemyre-3
Oakland Athletics	Rick Langford-5	Blue Moon Odom-2 Mike Torrez-2	Rick Langford-3
Philadelphia Athletics	Lefty Grove-4	Chief Bender-2 Eddie Plank-2 Jack Coombs-2 Lefty Grove-2 Chubby Dean-2 Phil Marchildon-2	Joe Bush-3
St. Louis Browns	Urban Shocker-4 Ned Garver-4	Urban Shocker-3 Ned Garver-3	Carl Weilman-2
Seattle Pilots	Marty Pattin-1	Marty Pattin-1	None
Seattle Mariners	Glenn Abbott-3 Mike Moore-3	Many With 1	Diego Segui-1 Glenn Abbott-1
Texas Rangers	Jon Matlack-3 Charlie Hough-3	Many With 1	Dick Bosman-2
Toronto Blue Jays	Dave Stieb-3	Jerry Johnson-1 Dave Stieb-1	Dave Lemanczyk-2 Dave Stieb-2
Washington Senators (1)	Walter Johnson-14	Walter Johnson-9	Walter Johnson-5
Washington Senators (2)	Pete Richert-2 Camilio Pascual-2 Dick Bosman-2	Bennie Daniels-1 Dick Bosman-1	Pete Richert-2 Camilio Pascual-2

NOTE: In instances where there are two numbers in a category, the smaller number represents the modern (1900 or later) record.

MEL OTT

Longtime New York Giants star and one of only 13 players to hit 500 or more home runs in his major league career, he struck his last big-league homer in an opening-day game—an April 16, 1946, clash against the Philadelphia Phillies at the Polo Grounds. Ott, the Giants' player-manager at the time, smashed a first-inning homer—the 511th of his career—off Oscar Judd and New York went on to an 8-4 victory.

Ott, who appeared in only 30 more games in 1946 and in just four in 1947 before ending the playing portion of his career, was the National League's all-time home run king until another Giant—San Francisco's Willie Mays—surpassed him 20 years later. Mays hammered No. 512 on May 4, 1966, and finished with 660 homers in his career (which concluded with nearly two seasons with the New York Mets).

MIKE PARROTT

The starting and winning pitcher for Seattle in the Mariners' 1980 season opener against Toronto—but everything was downhill from there. In fact, Parrott never won again in 1980 despite 26 additional appearances that included 15 more starts. After pitching 6⅓ innings and gaining the victory in Seattle's 8-6 triumph over the Blue Jays on April 9 at the Kingdome, Parrott lost his next four decisions in April and proceeded to go 0-2 in May, 0-3 in June, 0-2 in July, 0-0 in August (most of which he spent in the minor leagues), 0-4 in September and 0-1 in October. Parrott's 1-16 won-lost record in 1980 was accompanied by a 7.28 earned-run average.

CAMILO PASCUAL

Pitcher who lost opening-day games for both the first and second Washington Senators franchises—in fact, he dropped *two* season openers for both teams. While with the first Senators club (which moved to Minnesota in 1961 and became the Twins), Pascual lost to the New York Yankees as a starter in 1956 and to the Baltimore Orioles as a reliever in 1957; as a starter for the second Senators team (an expansion club that began play in '61), he lost to the Twins in 1968 and to the Yankees in 1969. Overall, Pascual was 1-4 on opening day for Washington's two modern major league franchises. He pitched a complete game in the Senators' 1960 season opener, beating the Boston Red Sox.

Pascual pitched for the first Senators franchise from 1954 through 1960 and then accompanied the team to Minnesota. After pitching for the Twins from 1961 through 1966, Pascual was traded to Washington and pitched for the second Senators club in 1967, 1968 and 1969. He saw brief duty with the Cincinnati Reds, Los Angeles Dodgers and Cleveland Indians at the end of his career.

HERB PENNOCK

A's pitcher who on opening day, 1915, pitched no-hit ball against the Boston Red Sox for 8⅔ innings. Boston's Harry Hooper then bounced a single over the lefthander's head, and Pennock had to settle for a one-hit, 2-0 triumph in the April 14 game at Philadelphia.

Outfielder Lou Piniella was a Kansas City Royals rookie on opening day in 1969 when he collected his first four major league hits.

Two months after his one-hitter against Boston, Pennock was claimed on waivers from Philadelphia by the Red Sox.

GAYLORD PERRY

Pitcher who didn't start an opening-day major league game until he was 31 years old—but wound up as a season-opening pitcher a total of nine times for *five* clubs. Perry started on opening day for the San Francisco Giants in 1970, for the Cleveland Indians from 1972 through 1975, for the Texas Rangers in 1976, for the San Diego Padres in 1978 and 1979 and, at age 44, for the Seattle Mariners in 1983.

PHILADELPHIA PHILLIES

The only team in modern major league history to win an opening-day game because of a forfeit. In the ninth inning of a cold April 11, 1907, game in New York (snow had to be cleared from the field prior to the contest), many fans left the stands and gathered behind the outfielders and the home-plate umpire. Apparently disinterested in the baseball goings-on—Phillies pitcher Frank Corridon was tossing a one-hitter and holding a 3-0 lead—fans remaining in the stands and those positioned on the field began a cushion-and-snowball exchange and plate umpire Bill Klem, believing the crowd was breaking out of control, proclaimed the game a forfeit, with the Phillies listed as 9-0 winners.

Shortly before the start of the 1907 season, New York's police commissioner decided not to deploy officers inside the ball park. Instead, he asked that owners of entertainment enterprises supply their own security—and the Giants' in-house security staff obviously couldn't handle the New York crowd for the '07 opener.

PHILADELPHIA PHILLIES

The only team in big-league history to play season-opening tie games in consecutive years. The Phillies battled the Dodgers to a 5-5 deadlock in their 1923 season opener at Brooklyn and they tied the Boston Braves, 6-6, in 11 innings in their 1924 opener at Philadelphia. Darkness stopped both games.

LOU PINIELLA

Outfielder who on opening day, 1969, collected the first four hits of his major league career. Hitless in brief appearances with the Baltimore Orioles in 1964 (one at-bat) and Cleveland Indians in 1968 (five at-bats), Piniella lashed a double and three singles in five at-bats for the expansion Kansas City Royals, who were making their American League debut in a game against the Minnesota Twins. Piniella's first-inning double accounted for the first hit in Royals history and his sixth-inning single tied the score, 3-3. The Royals went on to win, 4-3, in 12 innings in an April 8 game at Kansas City that marked the major league managerial debut of the Twins' Billy Martin.

An expansion-draft selection of the American League's other new team of 1969, the Seattle Pilots, Piniella had been traded to the Royals a week before the '69 season opener.

PITTSBURGH PIRATES

After opening the season at home in their first five years of play (1887 through 1891) and six of their first seven seasons of existence, the Pirates played their season openers on the road for 60 consecutive years (1894 through 1953), a major league record. Long considered a "cold weather" city in terms of schedule-making (and early-season games therein), Pittsburgh played 20 of its 33 season openers on the road from 1954 through 1986.

PITTSBURGH PIRATES, ST. LOUIS CARDINALS

Participants in the major leagues' first season-opening game played at night. The Pirates and the Cardinals squared off in St. Louis on the evening of April 18, 1950, and the Cards—getting six-hit pitching from Gerry Staley and home runs from Red Schoendienst and Stan Musial—scored a 4-2 victory.

MIKE POWERS

Philadelphia A's catcher whose death two weeks after the beginning of the 1909 season may have been linked to an injury incurred in his club's season-opening game. Powers, 38 years old, made a desperate lunging attempt to catch a foul ball on opening day, April 12, against the Boston Red Sox. After the game, which the A's won, 8-1, in the first major league game played at Philadelphia's new Shibe Park, Powers complained of severe abdominal pain. While acute indigestion was the immediate diagnosis, Powers' condition deteriorated that night when a gangrenous condition set in. The next day, surgeons removed part of Powers' intestines, but the 11-year major leaguer failed to improve. Powers died on April 26, with one doctor speculating that his death resulted from internal injuries suffered on the pop-fly lunge.

Powers appeared in 647 big-league games, playing for Louisville and Washington of the National League and for Philadelphia and New York of the American League.

CARL POWIS

Outfielder who had only two runs batted in during his major league career —but one of the RBIs was a game-winner for Baltimore on opening day, 1957, at Washington's Griffith Stadium. With the Senators and Orioles tied, 6-6, after 10 innings of the April 15 game, Baltimore's Dick Williams doubled in the 11th inning and moved to third on Al Pilarcik's sacrifice. Powis, appearing in his first major league game, lofted a sacrifice fly and Baltimore held on for a 7-6 victory.

Powis played in only 15 big-league games, all for the '57 Orioles, and batted .195 (eight hits in 41 at-bats).

ROBIN ROBERTS

Pitcher who started the most consecutive opening-day games for one team in major league history. Roberts was the Philadelphia Phillies' season-opening pitcher for 12 straight years, 1950 through 1961, and he compiled a 5-6 won-lost record in those starts (with one no-decision).

FRANK ROBINSON

The major leagues' all-time leader in opening-day home runs with eight. Robinson belted three homers in season openers for the Cincinnati Reds, three for the Baltimore Orioles and one each for the California Angels and Cleveland Indians.

No other player has walloped opening-day homers for four big-league teams.

BABE RUTH

Baseball legend forever linked to uniform number 3, but he never wore that number—or any number—in the majors until opening day of the 1929 season, his 16th year in the big leagues. While the Cleveland Indians experimented with small numbers on their sleeves in 1916 and made big-league history by introducing numbers on the backs of their home uniforms in their 1929 season opener (played two days before the twice-rained-out New York Yankees initially appeared in numbered uniforms), it was the Yankees who first wore large numbers on their backs on a permanent basis, home and away. The Yankees' numbers for the outset of the '29 season corresponded to the batting order of the team's position players, and they went like this for New York's delayed season-opening game against Boston on April 18 at Yankee Stadium:

Uniform number/Yankees' batting order
1 Earle Combs, center field
2 Mark Koenig, third base
3 Babe Ruth, right field
4 Lou Gehrig, first base
5 Bob Meusel, left field
6 Tony Lazzeri, second base
7 Leo Durocher, shortstop
8 Johnny Grabowski, catcher
14 George Pipgras, pitcher

Fred Heimach, who relieved winning pitcher Pipgras that day in the Yankees' 7-3 victory over the Red Sox, wore number 17 and was the only other New York player to appear in the game.

BABE RUTH

A .422 hitter in 18 opening-day major league games, and his first-game production included five doubles, one triple and seven home runs. Ruth had particularly memorable season openers in 1921, 1932 and 1935. In '21, he

When Babe Ruth hit his 60th home run in 1927 (left), he was identifiable only by his good looks and familiar home run trot. But by 1929, the Bambino was wearing the No. 3 that will forever remain part of his baseball mystique and he later hauled the uniform out of mothballs (below) for a post-career appearance at Yankee Stadium.

began the year with a 5-for-5 performance for the New York Yankees against the Philadelphia A's. He drilled two home runs and a single for the Yanks in the '32 opener against the A's, and in his National League debut on opening day, 1935, he singled and homered for the Boston Braves against New York Giants' pitching standout Carl Hubbell.

Not only did Ruth excel as a hitter in season inaugurals, he also was the starting and winning pitcher for the Boston Red Sox in his first three opening-day appearances in the majors (1916, 1917 and 1918).

ST. LOUIS BROWNS

Possessing a checkered history in 52 years of American League play, this team went out with a whimper by compiling 64-90 and 54-100 records in the franchise's final two seasons before moving to Baltimore in 1954—but the Browns left with an opening-day roar. In their next-to-last opening-day game, played April 15, 1952, at Detroit, the Browns shut out the Tigers, 3-0, behind the six-hit pitching of Ned Garver. Then, in an April 14, 1953, season opener at St. Louis' Sportsman's Park, the Browns walloped Detroit, 10-0, as Virgil Trucks tossed a four-hitter.

ST. LOUIS BROWNS, NEW YORK METS

Co-holders of the modern major league record for consecutive opening-day games won, nine. The American League's Browns won season openers from 1937 through 1945, while the National League's Mets were victorious on opening day from 1975 through 1983.

ST. LOUIS CARDINALS

The only club in modern major league history to lose as many as four consecutive games at the start of the season and then win a league championship. The 1985 Cardinals lost their first two games of the year to the Mets at New York, then dropped two straight to the Pirates in Pittsburgh. Overall, St. Louis dropped six of its first eight games in '85, but the Cardinals went 99-55 the rest of the way in the regular season and won the National League East by three games over the Mets. St. Louis then defeated the Los Angeles Dodgers, four games to two, in the N.L. Championship Series.

The only other team in big-league history to win a pennant after losing its first four games of the season was Boston's 1897 National League club, which actually went winless in its first six games. Boston began the year with four consecutive defeats, played a tie game and then lost again before winning 93 of its final 127 decisions and capturing the N.L. flag by two games over Baltimore.

Since divisional play was adopted in the majors in 1969, three teams besides the 1985 Cardinals have lost at least four games at the start of a season but rebounded to win division championships. However, all three clubs—the 1969 Minnesota Twins (who started off 0-4), the 1974 Pittsburgh Pirates (0-6) and the 1977 Philadelphia Phillies (0-4)—lost in Championship Series play.

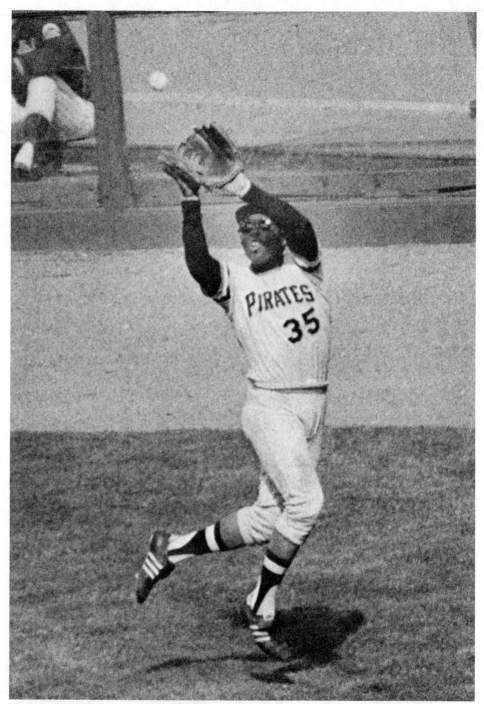

Pittsburgh catcher Manny Sanguillen became the Pirates' early-season regular right fielder In 1973 after the death of Roberto Clemente. By the time the '73 season came to an end, however, Sanguillen was back behind the plate with Richie Zisk in right.

SAN DIEGO PADRES, SAN FRANCISCO GIANTS

National League teams that on April 5, 1983, played the majors' highest-scoring season opener in more than 50 years, with the Padres seizing a 13-3 lead and holding on for a 16-13 triumph at Candlestick Park. Garry Templeton homered and drove in four runs for San Diego, which got three RBIs apiece from Terry Kennedy and winning pitcher Tim Lollar. Bob Brenly paced the Giants' attack with a home run and four RBIs, and Darrell Evans, Max Venable and Chili Davis also hit homers for San Francisco.

MANNY SANGUILLEN

The Pirates' No. 1 catcher for the four previous years, he started in right field in the club's 1973 season opener—Pittsburgh's first regular-season game since the death of Roberto Clemente, the team's longtime right-field star. Clemente, a four-time National League batting champion and lifetime .317 hitter in 18 big-league seasons, was killed in a December 31, 1972, plane crash off the coast of Puerto Rico. Sanguillen went 2 for 4 in the April 6, 1973, opener against St. Louis as the Pirates rallied from a 5-0 deficit and handed the Cardinals a 7-5 loss at Pittsburgh.

By the time the '73 season ended, Richie Zisk had the most playing time in right field for Pittsburgh. Zisk batted .324 with 10 home runs and 54 runs batted in while playing 103 games overall and getting 333 at-bats. He was the everyday right fielder in 1974 and responded by hitting .313 with 17 homers and 100 RBIs. Sanguillen, who wound up playing the outfield in 59 games in '73 (and catching in 89), returned to full-time catching duty for the Pirates in '74.

EDDIE SAWYER

Manager of the Philadelphia Phillies for the previous year and a half, he guided the Phils into the 1960 season—but quit as the club's pilot after one game. Sawyer, who also managed the Phillies in the late 1940s and early 1950s (and was at the helm of the '50 Whiz Kids), saw his 1960 team lose at Cincinnati, 9-4, on opening day. The Phillies were off the next day, April 13. On the morning of April 14, the Phils announced Sawyer had resigned; that night, with coach Andy Cohen running the team, Philadelphia won its home opener over Milwaukee, beating the Braves, 5-4, in 10 innings. Gene Mauch, ticketed to manage Minneapolis of the American Association for the third straight year, was appointed the Phils' manager and took over in game three of the '60 season.

"There wasn't any one thing (that prompted the resignation), just a lot of things," said Sawyer, explaining his actions. The quality of his team probably headed Sawyer's list of reasons; the Phils went on to compile a 59-95 record in '60 and finished last in the National League.

SEALS STADIUM

Site of a 1958 opening-day game in San Francisco that marked the debut of

A packed house at San Francisco's Seals Stadium watched on April 15, 1958, as the Giants and Dodgers participated in opening-day ceremonies for the first major league game on the West Coast.

major league baseball on the West Coast. The Dodgers and Giants, longtime Brooklyn and New York franchises, transferred to Los Angeles and San Francisco, respectively, after the 1957 National League season and met in an April 15, 1958, season opener that the Giants won, 8-0. Playing before 23,448 fans in San Francisco's former minor league ball park, the Giants got six-hit pitching from Ruben Gomez and home runs from Daryl Spencer and rookie Orlando Cepeda in the landmark game.

SEATTLE MARINERS

American League expansion team that has never finished better than 10 games below .500 in a season since joining the majors in 1977—but boasts eight victories in 10 opening-day games. Eight different Seattle pitchers— Glenn Abbott (1978), John Montague (1979), Mike Parrott (1980), Floyd Bannister (1982), Bryan Clark (1983), Mike Stanton (1984), Mike Moore (1985) and Pete Ladd (1986)—have been credited with the season-opening triumphs.

The Toronto Blue Jays, an A.L. expansion club that has posted four winning seasons and captured one divisional championship since entering the big leagues along with the Mariners in '77, have lost eight of their 10 opening-day contests.

Pitcher Diego Segui made his mark in Seattle baseball history by pitching in the first game for both the Pilots (left) and the Mariners. The Pilots were moved to Milwaukee after one season and became the Brewers.

TOM SEAVER

The major leagues' all-time leader in opening-day pitching starts with 16. Seaver, career winner of more than 300 games while pitching for the New York Mets (two stints), Cincinnati Reds, Chicago White Sox and Boston Red Sox, was the season-opening pitcher for the Mets for 10 straight seasons, 1968 through 1977, and again in 1983. He also drew the first-game assignment for the Reds in 1978, 1979 and 1981, and for the White Sox in 1985 and 1986. Seaver has seven opening-day victories, only two losses and seven no-decisions.

DIEGO SEGUI

He pitched in the first game of both Seattle franchises in the big leagues, working in relief in the Pilots' season-opening game against California in 1969 and starting and losing in the Mariners' 1977 opener against the Angels.

SHEA STADIUM

Site of an April 6, 1974, opening-day major league game in which New York—the Yankees, that is—scored a 6-1 victory. The Yankees, uprooted from Yankee Stadium in 1974 and 1975 because of a massive renovation of their half-century-old ball park, played their home games at the Mets' stadium in those two years and opened the '74 season by beating Cleveland at Shea. Mel Stottlemyre stopped the Indians on seven hits, and Graig Nettles socked a two-run home run for the Yankees. Only 20,744 fans turned out at Shea for the Yanks' American League season opener.

The Mets opened the '74 season on the road, while in 1975 the National League club began the year at Shea Stadium and the Yankees started the season away from home.

JIMMY SHECKARD

The lone player in big-league history to hit three triples in an opening-day game, accomplishing the feat for Brooklyn on April 18, 1901, at Philadelphia. Sheckard scored four runs that day as Brooklyn defeated the Phillies, 12-7.

Sheckard's penchant for triples didn't stop on opening day. He went on to lead the National League in three-base hits in 1901 with 21.

LOU STRINGER

Infielder who made his major league debut on opening day, 1941, as the starting shortstop for the Chicago Cubs—and proceeded to make four errors that afternoon. The Cubs opened the season April 15 at Wrigley Field, and Chicago overcame Stringer's miscues and downed the Pittsburgh Pirates, 7-4. Stringer contributed offensively, rapping a single and a double and scoring two runs.

A second baseman in four minor league seasons (1937 through 1940), Stringer was returned to his old position three weeks into the 1941 season after the Cubs traded Billy Herman, their longtime second baseman, to the Brooklyn Dodgers. Stringer ended up playing 137 games at second base for the Cubs in '41.

CLYDE SUKEFORTH

Brooklyn coach who was thrust into the Dodgers' managerial job for the first two games of the 1947 season—and thus was managing Brooklyn when Jackie Robinson became the first black player in modern major league baseball. Robinson made his debut with the Dodgers on April 15, 1947, six days after Commissioner Happy Chandler had suspended Dodgers Manager Leo Durocher for the '47 season because of "conduct detrimental to baseball." Sukeforth handled the team April 15 and again on April 17, fashioning a 2-0 record (the Dodgers scored 5-3 and 12-6 victories over the Boston Braves) before scout Burt Shotton took over the club for the balance of the season.

WILLIAM HOWARD TAFT

The 27th President of the United States—and the first Chief Executive to

Because of Brooklyn Manager Leo Durocher's one-season suspension, coach Clyde Sukeforth (center) was interim manager on opening day in 1947 when Jackie Robinson (right) became the first black player in modern major league history.

throw out the first ball at a major league season opener. Taft made his tradition-starting toss on April 14, 1910, in Washington before the Senators-Philadelphia A's game. Washington pitcher Walter Johnson, about to begin his fourth big-league season, caught Taft's throw and then shut out the A's, 3-0. Johnson allowed only one hit, a double by Frank Baker.

RON TAYLOR

Canadian who gave up what proved to be a game-deciding home run in the first major league game involving a Canadian-based team. Pitching in relief for the New York Mets on opening day, 1969, Taylor, a native of Toronto, yielded a three-run homer to Coco Laboy of Montreal in a four-run eighth inning that boosted the expansion Expos into an 11-6 lead. Montreal weathered a four-run Mets rally in the ninth and won, 11-10, at Shea Stadium in an April 8 game.

BILL TERRY

The first player in major league history to smash a bases-loaded home run on opening day. Terry walloped his grand slam for the New York Giants on April 12, 1927, at Philadelphia, and the fifth-inning blast off Hal Carlson helped the Giants to a 15-7 rout of the Phillies.

FRANK THOMAS

He played in the last game in New York Giants history and the first game in New York Mets history. On September 29, 1957, at the Polo Grounds, Thomas played first base for Pittsburgh against New York in the Giants' last game as a New York-based club (the team moved to San Francisco in 1958). Then, on April 11, 1962, Thomas was the left fielder for the Mets as that expansion club made its debut at St. Louis against the Cardinals.

JOE TORRE

Braves player who hit two home runs in his team's season-opening game in 1965 and duplicated the feat in 1966. Torre turned the trick for the Milwaukee Braves on April 12, 1965, at Cincinnati and repeated the accomplishment exactly a year later in Atlanta when the transplanted Braves made their debut in the Georgia city. His two-homer performance in the '66 opener came against Pittsburgh.

Only one other player in big-league history has enjoyed two two-homer games in season openers—and he also was a member of the Braves. And, like Torre, Eddie Mathews unloaded for Milwaukee at Cincinnati (April 13, 1954) and then at home (Milwaukee, in Mathews' case, on April 15, 1958) against Pittsburgh.

23-2

The score by which Buffalo of the Players League won its season-opening game over Cleveland on April 19, 1890. Buffalo's run total and its 21-run victory margin established opening-day major league records that still stand, and the club proceeded to win its next three games as well. A juggernaut in the making? Guess again. Buffalo finished the season with a 36-96 record.

GALE WADE

The opening-day center fielder for the Chicago Cubs in 1955 and 1956—but a member of the starting lineup in only seven other major league games. Wade, a rookie, started the first three games of the '55 National League season, going 1 for 12 at the plate, and soon was returned to the minor leagues. Recalled, he started four more games for Chicago in September. In

1956, Wade was the Cubs' center fielder for the first two games of the year, contests in which he went 0 for 8, and then saw brief service as a pinch-runner, pinch-hitter and defensive replacement before being reassigned to the minors. Overall, Wade appeared in 19 big-league games—all for the Cubs in '55 and '56—and batted .133 (6 for 45) with one home run.

GERALD (GEE) WALKER

The lone player in major league history to hit for the cycle on opening day. Playing for the Tigers against the Indians on April 20, 1937, at Detroit, outfielder Walker began his assault with a second-inning home run and followed, in order, with a triple, double and single. His 4-for-4 performance helped the Tigers edge Cleveland, 4-3.

LON WARNEKE

Chicago Cubs pitcher who opened his club's 1934 season on April 17 by tossing a one-hitter against the Reds in Cincinnati and followed up that masterpiece with a one-hitter on April 22 against the Cardinals in St. Louis. Warneke won his consecutive one-hitters by scores of 6-0 and 15-2, allowing a one-out ninth-inning single to Reds outfielder Adam Comorosky in the first game and a fifth-inning double to St. Louis first baseman Rip Collins in his second start of the year.

WASHINGTON

Traditional major league opening-day site that played host to its last season opener on April 5, 1971, when the Senators' Dick Bosman shut out the Oakland A's, 8-0, on six hits before 45,061 fans at Robert F. Kennedy Stadium. Frank Howard and Mike Epstein each drove in two runs for the Senators, who moved to Arlington, Tex., in 1972 and became the Texas Rangers. Washington, which had lost its last 14 games of the 1970 season, beat Oakland's Vida Blue, who was making his first opening-day start in the big leagues. Blue, sporting a 3-1 career record in the majors entering the game, went on to post 24 victories in '71 and he captured Most Valuable Player and Cy Young Award honors in the American League that year.

Army Master Sgt. Daniel Pitzer, a former prisoner of war in Vietnam, threw out the ceremonial first ball at Washington's last opening-day game.

WASHINGTON SENATORS, DETROIT TIGERS

Co-holders of the longest losing streak, 13 games, at the beginning of a major league season, Washington having established the record in 1904 and Detroit tying the mark in 1920. The start proved particularly disastrous for the Senators, who went on to compile one of the worst records (38-113, .252) in big-league history. The 1920 Tigers finished 61-93 but, unlike the '04 Senators, escaped last place (ending up seventh, 13 games ahead of the Philadelphia A's).

TED WILLIAMS

Boston Red Sox star who played in 14 opening-day games in his big-league career—and hit safely in all of them. In fact, Williams went 22 for 49 (.449) in season-opening games, with seven doubles, one triple, three home runs, 14 runs batted in and nine runs scored. Williams saw action in 19 major league seasons from 1939 through 1960, with military service cutting into his career.

AL WOODS

The last player to hit a pinch home run in his first major league at-bat in an opening-day game, accomplishing the feat on April 7, 1977. Batting for Toronto right fielder Steve Bowling in the fifth inning of the first game in Blue Jays history, Woods walloped a two-run homer off Chicago White Sox reliever Francisco Barrios. Toronto went on to win, 9-5, at Exhibition Stadium.

Only two other players have hit pinch homers in their first big-league at-bats on opening day—Eddie Morgan of the St. Louis Cardinals in 1936 and Chuck Tanner of the Milwaukee Braves in 1955.

Following is a list of all players who have homered in their first big-league at-bats on opening day:

Mike Griffin, Baltimore, American Association, April 16, 1887
Johnny Bates, Boston, National League, April 12, 1906
Earl Averill, Cleveland, American League, April 16, 1929
*Eddie Morgan, St. Louis, National League, April 14, 1936
Ernie Koy, Brooklyn, National League, April 19, 1938
Emmett Mueller, Philadelphia, National League, April 19, 1938
George Vico, Detroit, American League, April 20, 1948
Wally Moon, St. Louis, National League, April 13, 1954
*Chuck Tanner, Milwaukee, National League, April 12, 1955
*Al Woods, Toronto, American League, April 7, 1977
Will Clark, San Francisco, National League, April 8, 1986

   *Pinch-hitter

WRIGLEY FIELD

Site of the last tie game to occur on opening day in the major leagues. In an April 12, 1965, season opener matching the Chicago Cubs against the St. Louis Cardinals, the visiting Cards struck for five first-inning runs and led, 9-6, entering the bottom of the ninth. However, the Cubs' Ernie Banks drilled a three-run homer off Barney Schultz that sent the game into extra innings. Both teams scored in the 11th inning, after which the 10-10 game was halted because of darkness.

The '65 Cubs-Cardinals opener featured the managerial debut of the Cards' Red Schoendienst. It also marked the first major league appearance of pitcher Steve Carlton, who faced one batter in an 11th-inning relief role for

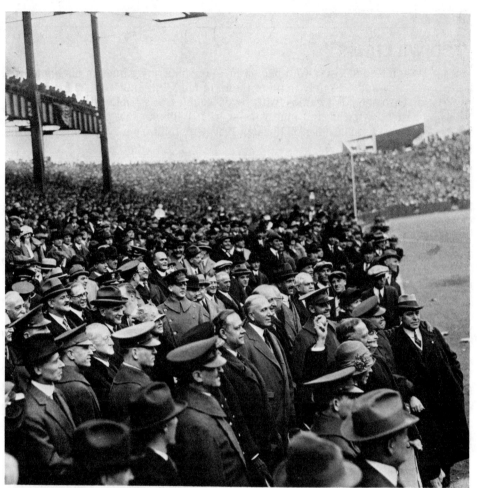

New York Gov. Al Smith was the center of attention on April 18, 1923, when he threw out the first ball for the first major league game at Yankee Stadium.

St. Louis. The 20-year-old Carlton walked the Cubs' George Altman and was promptly removed. (Schoendienst went on to manage the Cardinals to two National League pennants and one World Series title, while Carlton proceeded to win more than 320 games as a member of the Cards, Philadelphia Phillies, San Francisco Giants and Chicago White Sox.)

YANKEE STADIUM

"The House That Ruth Built" was host to its first American League game on April 18, 1923—a season opener that, fittingly, starred Yankee slugger Babe Ruth himself. Ruth, whose gate appeal and accompanying revenue-producing power had led, in large part, to the construction of Yankee Stadium, drilled a three-run home run in the '23 opener at New York, connecting in the third inning off Boston's Howard Ehmke. Pitcher Bob Shawkey and the Yankees went on to a 4-1 victory over the Red Sox before a crowd reportedly exceeding 74,000.

HANK AARON

The leading career home run hitter in Braves history. Aaron walloped 733 homers for the Braves' franchise, connecting for 398 while the club was based in Milwaukee and 335 after the team was transferred to Atlanta. Aaron hit 22 homers in two seasons with the Milwaukee Brewers, finishing with a big-league record of 755 home runs.

Eddie Mathews ranks second on the Braves' all-time homer list, totaling 493. Mathews hit 25 homers for the Boston Braves, 452 for the Milwaukee Braves and 16 for the Atlanta Braves.

HANK AARON, DICK ALLEN

The only visiting players to hit home runs at both Cincinnati ball parks in 1970, a season in which the Reds played their first 36 home games at Crosley Field and their last 45 in new Riverfront Stadium. Playing for the Atlanta Braves, Aaron socked two homers in both Crosley Field and Riverfront

Stadium. Allen, of the St. Louis Cardinals, walloped one homer at Crosley and two at Riverfront.

Six Reds players—Johnny Bench, Lee May, Tony Perez, Pete Rose, Bobby Tolan and Bernie Carbo—homered in each stadium, with Bench leading the way with 15 in each park.

HANK AARON, BABE RUTH, WILLIE MAYS

Major league baseball's top three career home run hitters with totals of 755, 714 and 660, they concluded their long big-league careers in the same cities in which they began them—but with different franchises. Aaron reached the majors in 1954 with the Milwaukee Braves and bowed out in 1976 as a member of the Milwaukee Brewers. Ruth broke into the big leagues in 1914 with the Boston Red Sox and wound up his playing career in 1935 with the Boston Braves. And Mays started out with the New York Giants in 1951 and finished up with the New York Mets in 1973.

HANK AARON, CHARLIE WHITE

Milwaukee Braves rookies who hit their first major league home runs in the same game, April 23, 1954, at St. Louis. Aaron, who hit a bases-empty shot off Cardinals starter Vic Raschi in the fourth inning, went on to slug 754 more homers in his big-league career. White, who connected with no one on base against Cot Deal in the 13th inning, never hit another homer in the majors. The Braves beat the Cards that night, 7-5, in 14 innings.

JOE ADCOCK

Milwaukee Braves slugger who, the day after slamming a landmark home run at the Polo Grounds in New York, was removed for a pinch-hitter in the eighth inning of a 0-0 game with the Giants. On April 29, 1953, Adcock became the first hitter in a regular-season major league game to reach the Polo Grounds' distant center-field bleachers since the bleachers were remodeled (and the distance to the fence lengthened) in 1923. Adcock's homer against the Giants carried an estimated 475 feet. But, with the bases loaded in the eighth the next afternoon, Milwaukee Manager Charley Grimm sent up George Crowe to bat for Adcock (who was hitless in three at-bats). Sal Maglie induced Crowe to ground out, ending the inning, and New York wound up a 1-0 winner when Bobby Thomson—no stranger to heroics at the Polo Grounds—socked a one-out homer in the ninth off Vern Bickford.

JOE ADCOCK

Drilling home runs against Don Newcombe, Erv Palica, Pete Wojey and Johnny Podres on July 31, 1954, at Brooklyn, Milwaukee's Adcock equaled the major league record of four home runs in one game—a feat that had last been accomplished nearly four years earlier in the same ball park, Ebbets Field, by the Dodgers' Gil Hodges in a game that also involved the Braves (then based in Boston). Adcock embellished his accomplishment with a double off Palica, establishing a big-league record for total bases in one

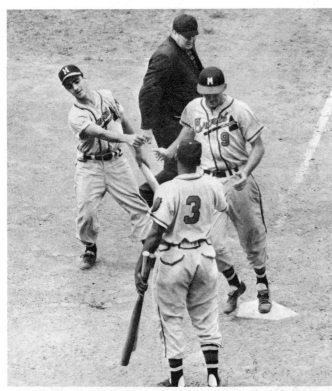

Slugger Joe Adcock gets a warm reception (left) from the Milwaukee bat boy and teammate Jim Pendleton after crossing the plate on the last of his four home runs against the Brooklyn Dodgers on July 31, 1954. Adcock doubled in two at-bats the next day against the Dodgers before being struck on the head (below) by a Clem Labine pitch and having to leave the game.

game, 18. The Braves thrashed the Dodgers, 15-7, as Adcock drove in seven runs.

The night before his home run barrage, Adcock singled, doubled and homered against Brooklyn. The day after the four-homer performance, he doubled in two at-bats before leaving the game after being hit in the head by a pitch from Dodgers reliever Clem Labine. Adcock was back in the Braves' lineup the next day.

AMERICAN LEAGUE

The league that since 1919 has possessed the majors' single-season home run leader. In 1919, Babe Ruth of the Boston Red Sox belted 29 home runs, breaking the major league season mark of 27 established by Ned Williamson of Chicago's National League club in 1884. Ruth eventually raised his record total to 60 with the New York Yankees until the mark was exceeded in 1961 by another Yankee, Roger Maris. Following is a chronology showing the one-season record-holders for each league since the inception of the N.L. in 1876 and the A.L. in 1901 (capitalized names indicate that the player's total was a major league record):

NATIONAL LEAGUE	YEAR	AMERICAN LEAGUE
GEORGE HALL, Philadelphia, 5	1876	
CHARLEY JONES, Boston, 9	1879	
BUCK EWING, New York, 10	1883	
NED WILLIAMSON, Chicago, 27	1884	
	1901	Nap Lajoie, Philadelphia, 14
	1902	Socks Seybold, Philadelphia, 16
	1919	BABE RUTH, Boston, 29
	1920	BABE RUTH, New York, 54
	1921	BABE RUTH, New York, 59
Rogers Hornsby, St. Louis, 42	1922	
	1927	BABE RUTH, New York, 60
Chuck Klein, Philadelphia, 43	1929	
Hack Wilson, Chicago, 56	1930	
	1961	ROGER MARIS, New York, 61

EARL AVERILL, HAL TROSKY

Cleveland teammates in the 1930s who rank 1-2 on the Indians' lifetime home run list. Averill hit 226 home runs for the Tribe and Trosky connected for 216.

Right behind Trosky on the Indians' homer chart are Larry Doby (215) and Andre Thornton (214).

BALTIMORE ORIOLES

Team whose pitching staff allowed a league-low three home runs to Roger Maris in 1961 when the Yankee outfielder set a major league record with 61 homers. While Oriole pitchers were stingy in the home run department in their battles with Maris, they did figure in two of Maris' dramatic blasts as

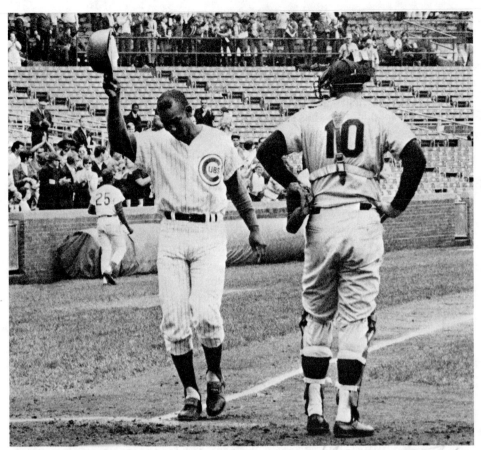

Ernie Banks offered a tip of the cap to Cubs fans in 1970 after hitting the 500th home run of his illustrious career.

Milt Pappas gave up No. 59 and Jack Fisher was tagged for No. 60. Baltimore's Chuck Estrada yielded No. 7 to Maris, who found Chicago White Sox pitching the easiest home run mark. Maris drilled 13 homers off White Sox pitchers in '61.

ERNIE BANKS

The Chicago Cubs' all-time leader in home runs with 512. Banks topped the 40-homer mark in five of his first seven full seasons in the majors (but never again reached 40), attaining his big-league high of 47 in 1958.

Second on the Cubs' career homer list is Billy Williams, who slammed 392 for the National League club.

JESSE BARFIELD

The all-time American League leader in home runs hit in Canada. Barfield has clubbed 75 homers in Canada, all for Toronto at the Blue Jays' Exhibition Stadium.

JESSE BARFIELD

Although never attaining 400 official at-bats in one major league season until 1985, he has become the leading home run hitter in Toronto Blue Jays history. Barfield has hit 128 homers as a Blue Jay, while Toronto's No. 2 man, Lloyd Moseby, has slugged 102.

JOHNNY BENCH

The top home run hitter in Cincinnati Reds history, smashing 389 homers for the National League club. Entering the 1979 season, Bench trailed Frank Robinson on the Reds' homer list, 324 to 310. Bench, though, seized the Reds' career lead during his 22-homer season of '79, then hit 24 homers in 1980, eight in 1981, 13 in 1982 and 12 in 1983, his final big-league season.

BABE BIRRER

Relief pitcher who worked four scoreless innings for Detroit against Baltimore on July 19, 1955, and won headlines—for his hitting. Birrer went 2 for 2 that afternoon and cracked a three-run homer on each trip to the plate. After taking over for starter Frank Lary in the top of the sixth inning and protecting the Tigers' 5-4 lead, Birrer homered off Orioles reliever George Zuverink with two men on base in the bottom half of the inning and then repeated the long-ball feat against Art Schallock in the eighth. Birrer's second homer accounted for the final three runs of the game as the Tigers trounced the Orioles, 12-4, in Detroit.

Birrer pitched in the majors in 1955, 1956 and 1958, compiling a 4-3 record while appearing in a total of 56 games for Detroit, Baltimore and the Los Angeles Dodgers. In 27 at-bats, he collected seven hits for a .259 average. Birrer's career homer and runs-batted-in totals? HRs: 2. RBIs: 6.

BOSTON RED SOX

The team most frequently victimized by Babe Ruth when the Yankee slugger hit 60 home runs in 1927. Red Sox pitchers gave up 11 homers to Ruth. The Chicago White Sox, on the other hand, were the toughest for Ruth to measure; their pitchers allowed only six homers to the Babe in '27.

GEORGE BRETT

Kansas City third baseman whose first home run of the 1986 season, a third-inning shot off Ed Whitson of the New York Yankees in the Royals' second game of the year, gave him the undisputed lead in club career homers. Entering the '86 season, Brett had shared the Royals' top spot with Amos Otis; at the conclusion of the year, Brett's total had climbed to 209, compared with Otis' 193.

CLAY CARROLL

A major league pitcher for 15 seasons, he allowed only two bases-loaded home runs in 1,353 innings of work—and those grand slams were struck by

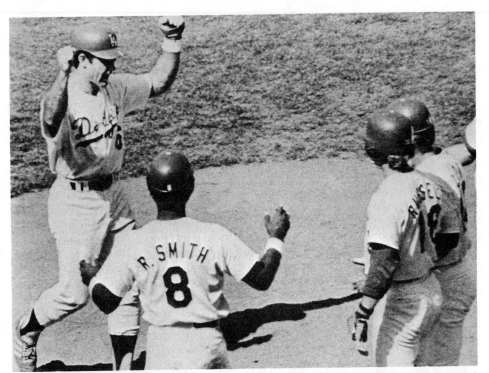

Dodgers first baseman Steve Garvey arrives home after slugging his second grand slam of the 1977 season against the Cardinals and pitcher Clay Carroll. Those two slams were the only ones Carroll allowed in 15 major league seasons.

the same player in the same year (Carroll's 14th big-league season) and in the same ball park. Los Angeles' Steve Garvey connected for bases-full homers at Dodger Stadium against St. Louis' Carroll on June 22, 1977, and again on August 28. The homers, Garvey's first two grand slams in the majors, helped the Dodgers to 12-1 and 11-0 victories over the Cardinals.

GARY CARTER

The major leagues' career leader in home runs hit in Canada. Carter, who played for the Montreal Expos from 1974 through 1984 before being traded to the New York Mets, has hammered 115 homers in Canada (111 as an Expo, four as a Met). After socking his first 15 Canadian homers at Montreal's Jarry Park, he has connected for his last 100 at the Expos' Olympic Stadium.

Only six other players have hit 50 or more big-league home runs in Canada: Andre Dawson (95), Jesse Barfield (75), Ron Fairly (68), Lloyd Moseby (56), Bob Bailey (52) and John Mayberry (51).

GARY CARTER, JESSE BARFIELD

Players who share the big-league record for the most home runs hit in Canada in one season. Carter, playing for the Expos, slammed 22 homers at

49

Montreal's Olympic Stadium in 1977; Barfield, as a member of the Blue Jays, connected for 22 at Toronto's Exhibition Stadium in 1983.

ORLANDO CEPEDA

Veteran slugger who in 1966 hit one home run at St. Louis' old Busch Stadium, formerly Sportsman's Park, and eight at the new Busch Stadium, which became the Cardinals' home about a month into the '66 season. Cepeda, traded from San Francisco to St. Louis on May 8, 1966, was a member of the Giants when he homered at the old stadium in '66 and played for the Cardinals when he hit eight homers that year at the new ball park. While no one hit as many as two homers at both Busch Stadiums that season, nine players besides Cepeda connected for at least one home run at both St. Louis parks. Those nine were Lou Brock, Curt Flood, Tim McCarver, Mike Shannon and Charley Smith, all of the Cardinals; Willie Stargell and Jim Pagliaroni of the Pittsburgh Pirates; Dick Allen of the Philadelphia Phillies, and Eddie Bressoud of the New York Mets.

CINCINNATI REDS

The victimized team each time a National League club has hit five home runs in one inning—and such an outburst has occurred three times in league history.

The New York Giants were the first big-league team to wallop five homers in one inning, with Harry Danning, Frank Demaree, Burgess Whitehead, Manny Salvo and Joe Moore connecting after the first two Giants batters had been retired in the fourth inning of a June 6, 1939, game against the Reds. The homers by Whitehead, pitcher Salvo (his inside-the-park smash was the only homer of his major league career) and Moore came in succession and featured an eight-run inning that gave the Giants a 14-0 lead at the Polo Grounds. New York ended up a 17-3 winner and finished with 20 hits, seven of which were homers.

Ten years later, on June 2, 1949, the Phillies clouted five eighth-inning homers against Cincinnati—Andy Seminick drilled two of them—in a 12-3 victory at Philadelphia. The Phils, who got three home runs from Seminick in the game, scored 10 runs in the eighth, with Del Ennis, Willie Jones and pitcher Schoolboy Rowe also homering in the inning. The Reds were victimized again on August 23, 1961, when San Francisco's Orlando Cepeda, Felipe Alou, Jim Davenport, Willie Mays and John Orsino hit homers in a 12-run ninth-inning explosion at Crosley Field that turned a pitchers' duel into a 14-0 Giants triumph (with Juan Marichal winning, Joey Jay losing).

The fourth and last five-homer inning by a major league team—and the first such inning in American League history—occurred on June 9, 1966, when Minnesota's Rich Rollins, Zoilo Versalles, Tony Oliva, Don Mincher and Harmon Killebrew lashed seventh-inning homers against the Kansas City Athletics. The shots by Oliva, Mincher and Killebrew came in succession, and the five homers produced six runs and a 9-4 Twins victory at Bloomington, Minn.

HORACE CLARKE

A 10-year major leaguer who hit only 27 home runs in 1,272 games, but whose first two big-league homers came with the bases loaded. Playing for the New York Yankees, Clarke hit his first homer in the majors off Cleveland's Floyd Weaver on September 21, 1965. The grand slam helped the Yankees to a 9-4 victory at Yankee Stadium. On July 16, 1966, Clarke rapped a bases-full homer off the Athletics' Jack Aker, and the 10th-inning blast enabled New York to score a 9-5 triumph at Kansas City. None of Clarke's subsequent 25 homers came with the bases loaded.

ROCKY COLAVITO

The last American Leaguer to hit four home runs in one game (only three A.L. players have achieved the feat), and his big night on June 10, 1959, was particularly remarkable because it came in a ball park that, previous to Colavito's rampage, had not yielded more than three homers to a *team* in one major league game. In fact, in more than five seasons of big-league service, Baltimore's Memorial Stadium had yielded three homers to one club only six times preceding Colavito's heroics. Playing for Cleveland, Colavito slammed a third-inning homer off the Orioles' Jerry Walker, fifth- and sixth-inning shots off Arnold Portocarrero and a ninth-inning drive against Ernie Johnson as the Indians scored an 11-8 victory. Colavito's homers accounted for six RBIs. Cleveland hit six homers overall in the game, with Minnie Minoso and Billy Martin also connecting.

NATE COLBERT

Powered by 38-homer seasons in 1970 and 1972, Colbert remains the San Diego Padres' No. 1 career home run hitter more than a decade after playing his final game for one of the major leagues' youngest franchises. A Padre from the club's inception in 1969 through 1974, he hit 163 homers for San Diego. Second on the Padres' lifetime home run chart is Dave Winfield with 154.

DALE COOGAN

Pittsburgh first baseman who hit his only big-league home run on June 24, 1950, at Brooklyn's Ebbets Field—but was playing in the minor leagues by the time that night's Pirates-Dodgers game was completed. Coogan, only 19 years old, drilled a three-run homer off Ralph Branca in the first inning of a wild game that was halted by curfew, stoppage coming in the eighth inning with Brooklyn leading, 19-12. The game—won by the Dodgers, 21-12—was completed on August 1, a night on which the demoted Coogan was playing for Indianapolis of the American Association.

HENRY COTTO

Outfielder who through 1986 had hit two home runs in the majors—one on the final day of the 1985 season and the other on the last day of the '86 season. Playing for the New York Yankees on October 6, 1985, Cotto helped

Phil Niekro to his 300th career pitching victory by hitting his first big-league homer and driving in four runs as the Yanks drubbed the Toronto Blue Jays, 8-0. On October 5, 1986, Cotto slammed a homer against the Boston Red Sox in a 7-0 New York romp.

PAT CRAWFORD, LESTER BELL

Players who slugged pinch-hit, bases-loaded home runs in successive innings of a May 26, 1929, Giants-Braves contest, the only game in big-league history in which two pinch grand slams have been struck. With the score tied, 2-2, in the bottom of the sixth inning at the Polo Grounds, Crawford triggered a nine-run New York inning by belting a bases-full home run off Harry Seibold while batting for Giants pitcher Dutch Henry. With the bases loaded in the top of the seventh, Bell was sent up as a pinch-hitter for Boston relief pitcher Art Delaney and promptly smashed a homer off reliever Carl Hubbell. The Giants beat the Braves, 15-8.

JOE CUNNINGHAM

Holder of the modern record for most home runs in a player's first two games in the major leagues, having hit three for the St. Louis Cardinals against Cincinnati and Milwaukee on June 30 and July 1, 1954. Brought up from Rochester of the International League by the Cardinals, Cunningham slammed a three-run, fifth-inning homer off the Reds' Art Fowler on June 30 for his first big-league hit and later contributed a two-run single as the Cards drubbed the Reds, 11-3, at Crosley Field. The next day, at County Stadium, the rookie first baseman homered twice off Warren Spahn—first with the bases empty and then with two men on—and St. Louis bombed the Braves, 9-2. Cunningham drove in a total of nine runs in his first two games in the majors.

TOMMY DAVIS

The first of only four major leaguers to hit home runs at both Colt Stadium, Houston, and Sick's Stadium, Seattle, outdoor ball parks that predated the domed stadiums currently used in those big-league cities. As a member of the Los Angeles Dodgers, Davis homered once in 1962 and twice in 1964 at Houston's outdoor park (where the National League's expansion Colts played from '62 through '64 before becoming the Astros and moving into the Astrodome). And as a member of the Seattle Pilots (an American League expansion team that played only one season in the Pacific Northwest before moving to Milwaukee), Davis homered against the Chicago White Sox on April 13, 1969, in the third big-league game played at the Pilots' outdoor stadium. It was one of three homers that Davis hit at Sick's Stadium, a ball park that saw just one year of major league service. The American League's Mariners (Seattle's second expansion team) have played in the Kingdome since joining the A.L. in 1977.

Also slugging home runs at both Colt Stadium and Sick's Stadium were Leo Cardenas (two at Colt Stadium, one at Sick's), Frank Howard (three at Colt Stadium, four at Sick's) and Jim Pagliaroni (two at Colt Stadium, five at Sick's).

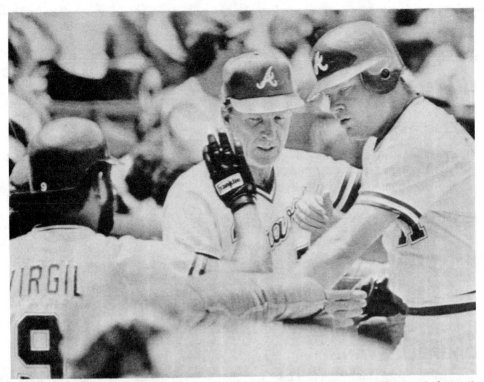

Atlanta first baseman Bob Horner is welcomed back to the Braves' dugout by Manager Chuck Tanner and catcher Ozzie Virgil after hitting the second of his record-tying four homers in a July 6, 1986, game against Montreal.

ANDRE DAWSON

Outfielder who in 1986 supplanted Gary Carter as the Montreal Expos' career home run leader. Dawson, trailing Carter, 215 to 205, on Montreal's homer list entering the '86 season, had nine home runs for the year going into the Expos' June 1 game against Houston at the Astrodome. Dawson rapped a bases-empty homer off the Astros' Bob Knepper in the fourth inning, tying Carter, and then seized the Expos' lifetime homer lead by socking a three-run shot off Knepper in the sixth. By season's end, Dawson had belted 225 homers overall for Montreal.

ED DELAHANTY, BOB HORNER

Two of the 11 major leaguers to hit four home runs in a game—and the only players to accomplish the feat as members of losing teams. Delahanty walloped four homers for the Philadelphia Phillies in a July 13, 1896, game in Chicago, but the Phils lost, 9-8. Adonis Bill Terry yielded all four homers to Delahanty, who also singled in the National League game. Atlanta's Horner slugged three home runs off Montreal's Andy McGaffigan and connected for a ninth-inning shot against Expos reliever Jeff Reardon on July 6, 1986; the Braves, though, were 11-8 losers despite Horner's four homers and six runs batted in. Horner hit bases-empty homers in the second, fourth and ninth innings and blasted a three-run drive in the fifth inning at Atlanta.

JOE DiMAGGIO, JOE GORDON

The last major league players to out-homer a league rival—a rival *team*, that is. In 1948, DiMaggio pounded 39 home runs for the New York Yankees and Gordon drilled 32 for the Cleveland Indians; the Washington Senators, collectively, hit 31. Cleveland's Ken Keltner equaled the Senators' team total.

The last major leaguer to match the home run production of a team from his league was Ted Williams of the Boston Red Sox. Williams' 43 homers in 1949 equaled the season output of the Chicago White Sox.

EBBETS FIELD, SHIBE PARK

The only ball parks where four-homer games were achieved by as many as two big-league players, with Gil Hodges of the Dodgers (1950) and Joe Adcock of the Milwaukee Braves (1954) enjoying record-equaling home run salvos at Brooklyn's Ebbets Field and Lou Gehrig of the New York Yankees (1932) and Pat Seerey of the Chicago White Sox (1948) hitting four homers in games played at Philadelphia's Shibe Park.

DARRELL EVANS

The oldest single-season home run champion in major league history. Playing for the Detroit Tigers at age 38, Evans cracked an American League-leading 40 homers in 1985. The homer crown was a first for Evans.

DARRELL EVANS

The only player to wallop 40 or more home runs in a season in both the National League and the American League. Evans smashed 41 homers for the Atlanta Braves in the 1973 N.L. season and clubbed 40 for the A.L.'s Detroit Tigers in 1985.

HOOT EVERS

His game-winning, inside-the-park home run for the Tigers in the ninth inning of a June 23, 1950, game at Detroit against the New York Yankees capped a 10-9 contest in which 11 homers—a major league record—were struck and all 19 runs were scored on homers. The losing Yankees cracked six homers—two by Hank Bauer and one apiece by Yogi Berra, Jerry Coleman, Joe DiMaggio and pinch-hitter Tommy Henrich. Evers, whose ninth-inning drive came with one runner on base, had homered earlier in the game for Detroit. The Tigers also got homers from Vic Wertz, Jerry Priddy and pitcher Dizzy Trout, who socked a grand slam.

The 11-homer record has been equaled five times since the 1950 Tigers-Yankees game. Eleven home runs were last hit in a big-league game on May 17, 1979, when the Philadelphia Phillies outlasted the Chicago Cubs, 23-22, in 10 innings.

Darrell Evans enjoyed a big 1985 season for Detroit, becoming the oldest player in major league history to win a home run title and the only player to hit 40 or more homers in both the American and National leagues.

RON FAIRLY

The top home run hitter in the history of Jarry Park, which served as the Montreal Expos' home field from their inception in 1969 through 1976. Fairly, who joined the Expos in June 1969 and played for Montreal through 1974, hit 58 homers at Jarry Park, all as a member of the Expos. He also played at Jarry Park as a member of the Los Angeles Dodgers and St. Louis Cardinals.

GEORGE FOSTER

The only major leaguer from a non-domed-stadium team to lead his league in indoor home runs in a season, topping the National League with four at Houston's Astrodome in 1979 while playing for the Cincinnati Reds. Denny Walling had a Houston-high three homers at the Astrodome in '79.

PAUL FOYTACK

The only pitcher in big-league history to allow four consecutive home runs in one inning. Working in relief for the Los Angeles Angels in the second game of a July 31, 1963, doubleheader at Cleveland, Foytack retired the first two Indians batters in the sixth inning before Woodie Held, Pedro Ramos, Tito Francona and rookie Larry Brown rocked the 32-year-old veteran for homers. The home run was the second of the game for Ramos, Cleveland's starting and winning pitcher, while Brown's homer was his first in the majors.

Ten other major league pitchers have been tagged for four homers in an inning, the last of whom was Cincinnati's Mario Soto. In the fourth inning of an April 29, 1986, Reds-Expos game in Cincinnati, Soto yielded home runs to Andre Dawson, Hubie Brooks, Tim Wallach and Mike Fitzgerald (a two-run shot).

LOU GEHRIG

The first American Leaguer to hit four home runs in one game. On June 3, 1932, in Philadelphia, Gehrig socked three homers off the Athletics' George Earnshaw and another off Roy Mahaffey as the New York Yankees outscored the A's, 20-13. Bidding for a record fifth homer in the ninth inning, Gehrig saw his long smash hauled down by center fielder Al Simmons and settled for a four-homer, six-RBI day. Despite Gehrig's homers, which came in succession, the Yankees needed a six-run ninth inning—highlighted by Tony Lazzeri's grand slam—to ensure the victory.

LOU GEHRIG

New York Yankees star who smashed 14 home runs against the Cleveland Indians in 1936, the most in one season against one club in major league history. Gehrig walloped four of his homers against Lloyd Brown and three off Johnny Allen en route to matching his big-league high of 49 home runs in one season (achieved two years earlier).

BOBBY GRICH

The top career home run hitter in California Angels history. Through the 1986 season, Grich had smacked 154 homers for California.

Ranking No. 2 in Angels lifetime homers with 141 is Don Baylor, who is one ahead of Brian Downing.

GEORGE HALL

The only player to hit all of his lifetime major league home runs in one league-leading season. Hall was the first home run champion in big-league history, hitting five homers for Philadelphia in the National League's first season, 1876. Hall played only one other season of big-league ball, in 1877 with Louisville.

Only two other major leaguers failed to hit another home run after enjoying homer-leading seasons. Cincinnati's Fred Odwell, who managed one homer in his rookie season of 1904, topped the National League with nine in 1905 but was unable to hit a home run in either of his final two big-league seasons, 1906 and 1907. Boston's Dave Brain, who entered the 1907 National League season with 17 career homers, slugged a league-high 10 homers in '07 but failed to connect in 1908, his last year in the big leagues.

TOBY HARRAH

The top home run producer for Texas since the second Washington Senators franchise relocated to Arlington, Tex., in 1972 and was renamed the Texas Rangers. Harrah, who hit two homers for Washington in 1971, had slugged 122 in a Rangers uniform through 1986.

No. 2 in lifetime Ranger homers is Larry Parrish with 110.

TOBY HARRAH, LARRY SHEETS, JIM DWYER

Players who hit bases-loaded home runs in the August 6, 1986, Texas-Baltimore game, the only contest in major league history in which three grand slams have been struck. Texas, paced by Harrah's bases-full homer off Baltimore starting pitcher Ken Dixon in the second inning, took a 6-0 lead into the bottom of the fourth, an inning in which the Orioles scored nine times and became only the fifth team in big-league history to hit two bases-loaded home runs in one inning as Sheets connected off Rangers starter Bobby Witt and Dwyer delivered against Jeff Russell. Baltimore added two more runs in the sixth inning, but Texas regained the lead with a six-run rally in the eighth and scored a 13-11 victory at Baltimore's Memorial Stadium.

DAVE HENDERSON

The No. 1 career home run hitter in Seattle Mariners history, having slugged 79 homers for the franchise. Jim Presley ranks second with 65.

CHUCK HINTON

California Angels right fielder who was the first player to hit an American League home run at Milwaukee's County Stadium. Home park for the National League's Milwaukee Braves from 1953 through 1965 and for the American League's Milwaukee Brewers beginning in 1970, County Stadium was *first* used for American League regular-season games in 1968 and 1969 when the Chicago White Sox played a total of 20 "home games" there. In the first of those games, contested on May 15, 1968, Hinton hit a ninth-inning homer off Chicago's Wilbur Wood.

GIL HODGES

Of the 11 major leaguers to hit four home runs in one game, the one to collect the most runs batted in during the contest and the first to connect against four different pitchers. Brooklyn's Hodges knocked in nine runs in his four-homer game, rapping two-run homers off Boston's Warren Spahn, Bob Hall and Johnny Antonelli and a three-run shot off Norman Roy on August 31, 1950. Hodges also singled as the Dodgers lambasted the Braves, 19-3, in a night game at Brooklyn.

DICK HUGHES

The only pitcher to surrender three home runs in one inning of a World Series game. Pitching for the St. Louis Cardinals in Game 6 of the 1967 Series, Hughes gave up a leadoff homer to Boston's Carl Yastrzemski in the fourth inning. After retiring the next two Red Sox batters, Hughes yielded consecutive homers to Reggie Smith and Rico Petrocelli in the October 11 game at Fenway Park. Boston's three-homer inning, unmatched in Series history, helped the Red Sox to an 8-4 victory.

DON HURST

Phillies first baseman who in 1929 went 6 for 21 at the plate in a six-game stretch from July 28 through August 2—and all six hits were home runs. Hurst's at-bats/hits figures for the six contests were (in succession): 4-1, 4-2, 4-1, 3-1, 2-0 and 4-1. Hurst was on the way to a 31-homer, 125-runs-batted-in season for Philadelphia.

REGGIE JACKSON, SAL BANDO

Standout players for the dominant Oakland A's teams of the mid-1970s, they are the top career home run hitters in Oakland history. Jackson walloped 253 homers for the Oakland club and Bando cracked 192.

REGGIE JACKSON

The only player in major league history to slug 100 or more home runs for three franchises. Jackson hit 254 of his 548 career homers while with the A's (one when the club was based in Kansas City, 253 after the team moved to Oakland), 144 for the New York Yankees and 123 for the California Angels.

Jackson also homered 27 times as a member of the Baltimore Orioles.

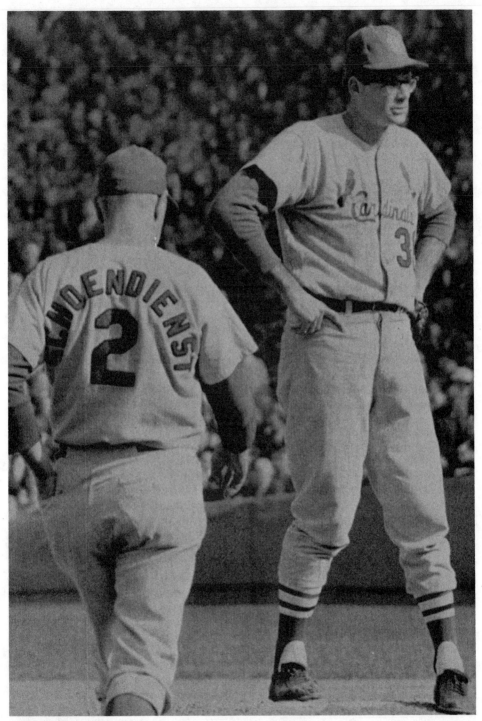

**Cardinals pitcher Dick Hughes stares in disbelief as Manager Red Schoen-
dienst approaches the mound to make a pitching change in the sixth game
of the 1967 World Series. Boston jumped on Hughes for three fourth-inning
home runs.**

AL KALINE

Although hitting only four home runs in his first full year in the majors and never reaching the 30-homer mark in one season, he became the leading home run hitter in Detroit Tigers history. Kaline played 22 seasons for the Tigers and rapped 399 homers.

Norm Cash, with 373 homers as a Tiger, is No. 2 on Detroit's long-ball chart.

HARRY KELLEY

The most-victimized pitcher during Rudy York's record home run spree in August 1937. Detroit's York, establishing a major league mark for most home runs in a month, blasted 18 homers in August of '37 and connected three times off the Philadelphia Athletics' Kelley, twice against Pete Appleton of the Washington Senators and Bill Trotter of the St. Louis Browns and once each off 11 other American League pitchers. Kelley allowed York's first homer of the month on August 4 and yielded No. 11 and No. 12 to the Tigers' slugger in the first game of an August 24 doubleheader.

GEORGE KELLY

The first major leaguer to wallop home runs in three consecutive innings, smashing homers for the New York Giants in the third, fourth and fifth innings of a September 17, 1923, game against the Cubs at Chicago. Kelly's slugging helped the Giants to a 13-6 victory.

Only three other big-league players have hit homers in three straight innings. On July 2, 1930, at New York, Carl Reynolds of the Chicago White Sox homered in each of the first three innings of a game against the Yankees that Chicago dominated, 15-4. Another White Sox player accomplished the feat on July 18, 1948, as Pat Seerey—en route to a four-homer performance in an 11-inning, 12-11 Chicago victory—smashed home runs in the fourth, fifth and sixth innings against the A's at Philadelphia. And, 30 years later, Larry Parrish turned the trick. Parrish drilled homers for Montreal in the third, fourth and fifth innings of a July 30, 1978, contest in Atlanta. The Expos romped, 19-0.

HARMON KILLEBREW

Minnesota Twins slugger whose 1963 home run total of 45 stands as a big-league high for a player finishing a season with fewer than 100 runs batted in. Killebrew collected 96 RBIs in '63.

Six other big-leaguers have missed the 100-RBI mark despite hitting 40 or more homers in a season. Those six are: Dave Johnson, Atlanta Braves, 1973 (43 homers, 99 RBIs); Mickey Mantle, New York Yankees, 1958 (42, 97) and 1960 (40, 94); Rico Petrocelli, Boston Red Sox, 1969 (40, 97); Hank Aaron, Braves, 1973 (40, 96); Darrell Evans, Detroit Tigers, 1985 (40, 94), and Duke Snider, Brooklyn Dodgers, 1957 (40, 92).

HARMON KILLEBREW

The leading home run hitter for Minnesota since the old Washington Senators franchise moved to Bloomington, Minn., in 1961 and was renamed the Twins. Killebrew, who had 84 career homers while playing for the Senators, crashed 475 in a Twins uniform.

Second on Minnesota's lifetime homer list is Tony Oliva, who hit 220 homers as a Twins player.

DAVE KINGMAN

A member of the New York Mets in 1975, 1976 and part of 1977 and again in 1981, 1982 and 1983, he holds the franchise's lifetime-homer record. Kingman clubbed 154 homers as a Met, 36 more than totaled by No. 2 man Ed Kranepool.

DAVE KINGMAN

The only player to homer for a team in each of the major leagues' four divisions in one season. In fact, Kingman is the only man to play for teams in all four divisions in one year. Kingman started the 1977 season with the National League East's New York Mets, for whom he hit nine home runs in 58 games. In June, he was traded to San Diego of the N.L. West and went on to smack 11 homers for the Padres in 56 games. Sold to the American League West's California Angels in September, Kingman connected for two homers in 10 games before being sold again—this time to the New York Yankees of the A.L. East. As a Yankee, Kingman rapped four home runs in eight games.

CHUCK KLEIN

The first National Leaguer in the 20th Century to slug four home runs in one game and the first major leaguer to achieve the feat in an extra-inning game. Klein's fourth homer of the day, a bases-empty shot off Bill Swift, broke a 6-6 tie in the 10th inning and sparked the Philadelphia Phillies to a 9-6 triumph over the Pittsburgh Pirates on July 10, 1936. Klein, a Phillies star in the late 1920s and early 1930s before being traded to the Chicago Cubs, had been reacquired by the Phils only seven weeks before his four-homer performance, which occurred in Pittsburgh. Klein drove in six runs against the Pirates.

TED KLUSZEWSKI

Veteran first baseman who hit home runs for the Los Angeles Angels in each of the first two innings of play in the American League expansion team's history. The Angels made their debut on April 11, 1961, in Baltimore and Kluszewski hammered a two-run homer off Orioles starter Milt Pappas in the first inning. Then, in the second inning, he powered a three-run shot off rookie reliever John Papa, who was facing his first batter in the big leagues. The Angels downed the Orioles, 7-2.

HAL LEE, GEORGE PUCCINELLI

Two of the four players who walloped pinch-hit home runs in the July 21, 1930, doubleheader between Brooklyn and St. Louis—and the pinch homers were the first major league hits for Brooklyn's Lee and St. Louis' Puccinelli. In the opening game of the doubleheader at Ebbets Field, Brooklyn scored a 9-8 victory when Harvey Hendrick smashed a pinch three-run homer in the ninth inning. Jim Bottomley had put the Cardinals ahead, 5-4, with a two-run pinch homer in the seventh inning, and the Cards' Puccinelli, hitless in two previous big-league at-bats, had broken a 5-5 tie with a three-run pinch homer in the eighth. Lee, 0 for 16 at the plate in the majors, clubbed a three-run pinch homer in the second inning of the nightcap, but St. Louis romped to a 17-10 victory.

The four pinch homers established a major league record for a doubleheader, a mark that has never been equaled.

MICKEY LOLICH

The only man in big-league history to hit a home run in World Series play but never one in a regular-season game. Pitcher Lolich, who posted a lifetime batting average of .110 (90 for 821) while playing for the Detroit Tigers, New York Mets and San Diego Padres in a 16-season career in the majors, blasted his lone big-league homer in his first at-bat in World Series competition, connecting for the Tigers in the third inning of Game 2 of the 1968 World Series. Lolich's bases-empty smash came off St. Louis Cardinals pitcher Nelson Briles.

LOS ANGELES ANGELS

The winning team in all four 1-0 games decided by home runs in the American League during the 1964 season, with the homers giving Dean Chance three victories and Fred Newman one. Chance, on the way to the '64 Cy Young Award, benefited from a July 11 homer by Joe Adcock against the Chicago White Sox, a July 15 smash by Bob Perry against Detroit and an August 18 drive by Vic Power against the Tigers. Felix Torres' homer on July 17 against the Minnesota Twins made a winner out of Newman, who received two-inning relief help from Bob Lee.

BOBBY LOWE

The first player in major league history to hit four home runs in one game. Playing for Boston's National League team on May 30, 1894, Lowe slammed four consecutive homers off Cincinnati's Elton Chamberlain and led Boston to a 20-11 victory in the second game of a morning-afternoon doubleheader. Lowe smashed two homers in his team's nine-run third inning and also contributed a single in the game, which was played in Boston.

BOBBY LOWE

Of the 11 major leaguers to have hit four home runs in a single game, the one with the lowest lifetime homer total. Lowe, who played for Boston,

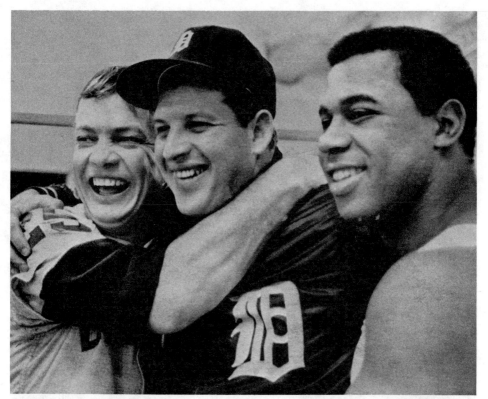

Detroit pitcher Mickey Lolich (center) enjoyed his unlikely role as a home run hitter, posing with teammates Norm Cash (left) and Willie Horton after the Tigers had defeated St. Louis in Game 2 of the 1968 World Series.

Chicago and Pittsburgh in the National League and for Detroit in the American League, finished his 18 seasons in the big leagues with 70 homers.

MICKEY MANTLE

Holder of the record for most home runs in a season by a major league batting champion. Mantle won the American League batting crown in 1956 with a .353 average and clouted 52 home runs for the New York Yankees that year.

Jimmie Foxx is the only other player in big-league history to hit 50 or more home runs and win a batting title in the same year. Foxx walloped 50 homers for the Boston Red Sox in 1938 and led the American League in hitting with a .349 mark.

ROGER MARIS, HACK WILSON

The leading single-season home run hitters in American League and National League history—Maris struck an A.L.-record 61 homers for the New York Yankees in 1961 and Wilson slugged an N.L.-high 56 for the Chicago Cubs in 1930—but neither hit as many as 40 homers in another big-league season. Maris and Wilson hit 39 home runs in their second-best long-ball

This aerial view of Milwaukee's County Stadium shows the routes of Willie Mays' four home runs in an April 30, 1961, game between the San Francisco Giants and Milwaukee Braves.

seasons, and both achieved their No. 2 homer totals in years (1960, 1929) immediately preceding their record accomplishments.

LEE MAY, GARY WARD, KENT HRBEK

They share the major league record for the most indoor home runs, 18, in one season. May walloped 18 homers at the Astrodome for the National League's Houston Astros in 1974. Ward, playing for the American League's Minnesota Twins in 1982, cracked 16 at the Metrodome and two at Seattle's Kingdome. And Hrbek, as a member of the 1986 Twins, hit 18 at the Metrodome (while going homer-less at the Kingdome).

WILLIE MAYS

San Francisco slugger who, two days after Milwaukee's Warren Spahn had pitched a no-hitter against the Giants, jolted Braves pitching for a record-tying four home runs in one game during the first month of the 1961 season. Mays' four-homer spree came on April 30 at Milwaukee's County Stadium and paved the way for a 14-4 Giants victory. Lew Burdette was the victim of Mays' first two homers, in the first and third innings, while Seth Morehead allowed No. 3 (a three-run smash) in the sixth inning and Don McMahon surrendered No. 4 in the eighth inning. Mays, who collected eight runs batted in, was on deck when the Giants were retired in the ninth inning.

WILLIE MAYS

The highest-ranking player on the majors' career home run list to have struck four homers in one game. Mays is No. 3 in the big leagues with 660 lifetime homers.

BILL MELTON

Despite playing only six full seasons for the Chicago White Sox, he ranks as the No. 1 lifetime home run hitter in the American League club's history. Melton, the 1971 A.L. homer champion, walloped 154 career homers for the White Sox, 14 more than Harold Baines has clouted for Chicago.

HUBERT H. HUMPHREY METRODOME

Of the big leagues' three domed stadiums, the one that has yielded the most home runs in one season. The indoor record was established in 1986, the fifth year that the ball park served as the Minnesota Twins' home field, when 223 homers were struck at the Metrodome (116 by the Twins, 107 by their opponents).

PETE MILNE

New York Giants outfielder who hit one home run in his major league career—a pinch-hit, inside-the-park grand slam. With Brooklyn leading New York, 8-6, in the seventh inning of an April 27, 1949, game at the Polo Grounds, the Giants closed within one run on two walks and Jack Lohrke's single. Walker Cooper's infield hit filled the bases and Milne was called upon to bat for relief pitcher Andy Hansen. Milne, facing Brooklyn reliever Pat McGlothin, lashed a drive to left-center field and Dodgers center fielder Duke Snider dived for the ball. The ball got past Snider, however, and rolled to the wall; Milne circled the bases without a play at the plate. The home run capped the day's scoring as the Giants held on for an 11-8 victory.

Milne played for the Giants in 1948, 1949 and 1950 and appeared in a total of 47 games.

MILWAUKEE BRAVES

The first team in major league history to slug four consecutive home runs in one inning, accomplishing the feat on June 8, 1961, at Cincinnati. In the seventh inning of the Braves-Reds game at Crosley Field, Eddie Mathews (with a man on base), Hank Aaron, Joe Adcock and Frank Thomas rifled consecutive homers. Despite the onslaught, the Braves lost to Cincinnati, 10-8.

The Cleveland Indians and the Minnesota Twins have equaled the Braves' achievement. In the sixth inning of the second game of a July 31, 1963, doubleheader at Cleveland, the Indians' Woodie Held, Pedro Ramos, Tito Francona and Larry Brown stroked consecutive homers against the Los Angeles Angels on the way to a 9-5 victory. And the Twins socked four straight home runs in the 11th inning of a May 2, 1964, game at Kansas City. The homers—by Tony Oliva, Bob Allison, Jimmie Hall and Harmon Killebrew—powered Minnesota to a 7-3 triumph over the Athletics.

MILWAUKEE BREWERS

The only team in major league history to hit bases-loaded home runs in three straight games—and the Brewers got the 1978 season off to a rousing start by accomplishing the feat at County Stadium in the first series of the year. On April 7, 1978, Sixto Lezcano belted a grand slam as Milwaukee opened its season by walloping Baltimore, 11-3, in George Bamberger's debut as the Brewers' manager. On April 8, Gorman Thomas homered with the bases full as the Brewers humbled the Orioles, 16-3. And, on April 9, Cecil Cooper connected with the bases loaded as Milwaukee punished Baltimore, 13-5.

The Brewers hit six home runs overall in the three games against the Orioles and outscored Baltimore, 40-11.

STAN MUSIAL

The majors' career home run leader among players who never won a league homer title. Musial socked 475 home runs for the St. Louis Cardinals, yet he never finished higher than runner-up in a battle for the National League homer crown. Musial belted a career-high 39 homers in 1948, but Ralph Kiner of the Pittsburgh Pirates and Johnny Mize of the New York Giants shared the N.L. championship with 40. In 1949, Musial smacked 36 homers—his second-best season total—but finished a distant second to Kiner, who hit 54.

STAN MUSIAL

Easily the St. Louis Cardinals' career home run leader. His 475 homers for the Cards are 220 ahead of St. Louis' No. 2 man, Ken Boyer.

TONY OLIVA

The first player in major league history to hit a home run in the role of designated hitter. The designated-hitter rule was introduced in the American League in 1973, and season-opening games on April 6 included a night contest at Oakland matching the A's against the Minnesota Twins. Oliva, Minnesota's "DH," rapped a two-run homer in the first inning off Jim (Catfish) Hunter and the Twins went on to an 8-3 triumph.

LARRY PARRISH

The most recent of five players to slug three home runs in a game in both the National League and the American League. Parrish had three-homer games for the N.L.'s Montreal Expos in 1977, 1978 and 1980 before connecting for three home runs in one contest for the A.L.'s Texas Rangers in 1985.

Babe Ruth, Johnny Mize, Claudell Washington and Dave Kingman also have recorded three-homer performances in both leagues.

GAYLORD PERRY, NOLAN RYAN

Pitchers who gave up regular-season home runs to Hank Aaron in both the National League and the American League. Perry, who won 314 games in the majors, and Ryan, the big leagues' all-time strikeout king, were not alone in this victimized-by-Aaron category. Mike Cuellar, Pat Dobson, Nelson Briles and Dave Roberts also surrendered regular-season homers to Aaron in both leagues.

Don Larsen also allowed home runs to the majors' career long-ball king as an N.L. and A.L. pitcher, but Aaron was batting as a National Leaguer both times—once in the regular season and once in the World Series.

PHILADELPHIA ATHLETICS

The opposing *team* that, by finishing with 56 home runs, came closest to Babe Ruth's homer total of 60 in the 1927 American League season. The Yankees' Ruth, while personally out-homering all seven other American League teams, posted a total more than double that of the club figures compiled by Cleveland (26), Boston (28) and Washington (29). New York hit 158 homers overall, with Lou Gehrig's 47 accounting for nearly half of the Yanks' other 98 homers.

PHILADELPHIA PHILLIES

National League team that has accounted for three of the 11 four-homer performances by big-league players. Ed Delahanty was the first Phillies player to accomplish the feat, slugging four home runs against Chicago on July 13, 1896. Forty years later, on July 10, 1936, the Phils' Chuck Klein walloped four homers in a game against Pittsburgh. And, 40 years after Klein's bombardment, Philadelphia's Mike Schmidt—playing against the Cubs on April 17, 1976—drilled four homers in one contest.

BILL PHILLIPS

The only pitcher in big-league history to allow two bases-loaded home runs in one inning. Working for Pittsburgh in an August 16, 1890, National League game against Chicago, Phillips yielded fifth-inning grand slams to third baseman Tom Burns and catcher Malachi Kittredge. The homers highlighted a 13-run Chicago inning in a game that Pittsburgh lost, 18-5.

PINE TAR GAME, PART I

With two out in the top of the ninth inning and Kansas City trailing New York, 4-3, in a July 24, 1983, American League game at Yankee Stadium, the

The great Pine Tar controversy began when umpire Tim McClelland, under the watchful eye of Yankees Manager Billy Martin, measured George Brett's bat (above) against home plate to see if the amount of pine tar exceeded the major league rule limit. It did, and Brett and Kansas City Manager Dick Howser reacted vehemently (right) when Brett was declared out and his ninth-inning, game-winning home run was disallowed.

Royals' U.L. Washington singled off Yankees reliever Dale Murray. George Brett was the next batter, and Yankees Manager Billy Martin replaced Murray with bullpen ace Goose Gossage. Brett promptly drilled a Gossage delivery into the right-field stands, thrusting the Royals into a 5-4 lead. After Brett circled the bases following his dramatic smash, Martin, acting at coach Don Zimmer's urging, asked the umpires to check Brett's bat. The umpires discovered that pine tar extended beyond the 18-inch limit allowed above the knob, and they subsequently signaled Brett out. End of game. Apparently. New York 4, Kansas City 3. Brett went into a rage over the no-homer ruling, and the Royals protested the umpires' decision. Kansas

City claimed that a clarification of the rules—particularly in regard to "intent"—would lead to a restoration of Brett's home run.

Supporting Cast:

● **Bud Black.** Royals starting pitcher who worked six innings and allowed all four New York runs.

● **Joe Brinkman.** Crew chief of the umpires who worked the Pine Tar Game.

● **Lee MacPhail.** American League president who took the Royals' protest under advisement.

● **Tim McClelland.** Plate umpire and the target of Brett's furious protest. After examining the bat and making the initial measurement of the tar, McClelland conferred with his three associates, at which time Brinkman took charge and made a second measurement.

● **Gaylord Perry.** Royals pitcher who didn't appear in the game, but who sneaked behind the home-plate chaos and spirited away the bat, only to have it intercepted by a uniformed guard.

● **Shane Rawley.** New York's starting pitcher. He yielded 10 hits and three runs in 5⅓ innings.

On July 28, MacPhail upheld the Royals' protest, saying that the intent of the rules was to penalize a player for using a bat "altered to improve the distance factor." Brett's motive clearly was to get a better grip on his bat, not better distance on the batted ball. MacPhail stressed that the problem was not with the umpires' handling of the situation, but with ambiguous playing rules that needed to be "rewritten and clarified." He ordered a resumption of the game with the Royals ahead, 5-4, with two out in the top of the ninth inning. The continuation would come during the regular season if "practicable," or after the season if the game's outcome would affect either A.L. divisional race.

PINE TAR GAME, PART II

Resumption of the July 24 Royals-Yankees game proved "practicable" on August 18, originally an open date for both clubs. The Yankees were between dates of a home stand, while the Royals were en route to Baltimore. With a gathering of 1,245 fans on hand, George Frazier took the mound for the Yankees. Before Frazier threw a pitch, though, the Yankees made appeal plays at first and second base, claiming Brett had missed first base, at least, on his home run trot 25 days earlier. Crew chief Dave Phillips came prepared, flashing a notarized letter from the July 24 umpiring crew that said Brett had touched every base.

Supporting Cast:

● **Mike Armstrong.** The winning pitcher in the Pine Tar Game, having worked the seventh and eighth innings for Kansas City. Gossage took the loss.

● **Ron Guidry, Don Mattingly.** Guidry, New York's standout lefthanded pitcher, was the Yankees' center fielder when the game resumed; Mattingly, a lefthanded first baseman, was the Yanks' second baseman. New

York employed the strategy because of manpower needs, in light of the possibility of extra innings.

● **Hal McRae.** Royals designated hitter who was the first man to bat August 18. He struck out against Frazier, ending the top of the ninth inning.

● **Greg Pryor.** Royals reserve infielder who took over for Brett at third base in the bottom of the ninth. Brett and Manager Dick Howser had been ejected from the game July 24 because of their heated arguing over the no-homer ruling.

● **Dan Quisenberry.** Kansas City reliever who wrapped up the Pine Tar Game in the Yankees' ninth by getting Mattingly to fly to center field, Roy Smalley to fly to left field and Oscar Gamble to ground out to second base.

The game's outcome didn't affect either A.L. divisional race. The Yankees finished third in the East, seven games behind division titlist Baltimore, and the Royals ended up second in the West, 20 games behind Chicago.

BOOG POWELL

Since the Baltimore Orioles (the former St. Louis Browns) began play in the American League in 1954, no one has hit more home runs for the Orioles than Powell. The massive first baseman clubbed 303 homers for Baltimore.

Entering the 1986 season, Powell's longtime teammate, Brooks Robinson, was No. 2 in lifetime Oriole homers with 268. However, Eddie Murray jumped into the Orioles' runner-up spot in '86 after a 17-homer output gave him 275 career home runs in a Baltimore uniform.

DOUG RADER

The first player to slug home runs in all three ball parks that have housed Canada's big-league teams. After hitting six homers at Montreal's Jarry Park earlier in his career, Rader hit one at the Expos' second home, Olympic Stadium, on May 21, 1977, while playing for the San Diego Padres. Sold to Toronto 2½ weeks later, Rader completed the all-Canada homer feat by connecting off Baltimore's Ross Grimsley on June 17, 1977, at the Blue Jays' Exhibition Stadium.

DOUG RADER, RUSTY STAUB, CLIFF JOHNSON

The only major leaguers to hit home runs in Canada in both the National League and the American League in the same season. In 1977, Rader hit one homer at Montreal for the N.L.'s San Diego Padres and four in Toronto for the A.L.'s Blue Jays. Staub socked one in Toronto for the Detroit Tigers in 1979 and two at Montreal for the Expos in '79. And Johnson belted one at Toronto for the Cleveland Indians in 1980 and one in Montreal for the Chicago Cubs that year.

BOB RODGERS

The only Angels player to hit home runs in all three home ball parks of the American League's Los Angeles/California franchise. Rodgers collected two homers at Wrigley Field, Los Angeles, which served as the Angels' home in the expansion team's first season of play, 1961. From 1962 through 1965, when the Angels played at Chavez Ravine (Dodger Stadium), Rodgers hit two homers in his home park. And from 1966 until his major league career ended in 1969, Rodgers totaled seven homers at the club's third home, Anaheim Stadium.

BABE RUTH

Renowned slugger who hit all 714 of his major league home runs in the United States (the big leagues' expansion into Canada came 34 years after he retired), but whose lone minor league homer was struck in Canada. On September 5, 1914, Ruth pitched a one-hitter for Providence of the International League and slugged a three-run homer off Ellis Johnson in a 9-0 triumph at Toronto. Ruth, who appeared in 2,503 major league games, played in only 46 minor league contests.

EDDIE SANICKI

Called up from Toronto of the International League by the Philadelphia Phillies in mid-September of 1949, outfielder Sanicki broke into the majors by going 3 for 13 at the plate in the final three weeks of the National League season—and all three of his hits were home runs. On September 14, Sanicki made his first plate appearance in the big leagues a memorable one by drilling a three-run homer off the Pirates' Rip Sewell in Pittsburgh. Five days later in St. Louis, he hit a two-run shot off the Cardinals' Howie Pollet. And on September 28, in Philadelphia, Sanicki slugged a bases-empty home run off Sheldon Jones of the New York Giants. Sanicki, who boasted a .923 slugging percentage in his '49 stint in the majors, also played briefly for the Phillies in 1951.

HANK SAUER

A player with 288 lifetime home runs in the majors, he twice hit three home runs in one game—and Phillies starter Curt Simmons was the victim of both onslaughts, yielding all six homers. Sauer, playing for the Cubs, slammed three home runs off lefthander Simmons on August 28, 1950, as Chicago prevailed, 7-5, in the first game of a doubleheader at Wrigley Field. On June 11, 1952, again at Wrigley Field, Sauer repeated the three-homer salvo against Simmons and the Cubs edged Philadelphia, 3-2. Simmons was the losing pitcher in both games.

MIKE SCHMIDT

The 10th major leaguer to smack four home runs in one game—and he didn't hit his first homer on the record-tying afternoon of April 17, 1976, until the fifth inning. The Phillies' Schmidt further embellished his performance by connecting for three of his homers off a brother combination and winning the game against the Cubs with a two-run shot in the 10th inning. Philadelphia, which twice in the game had trailed by 11 runs, scored another run in the 10th and held on for an 18-16 triumph at Chicago's wind-

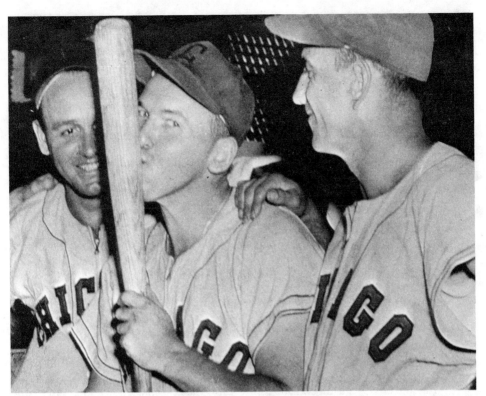

Pat Seerey and his bat were the center of attention on July 18, 1948, after the Chicago White Sox player had blasted four home runs in a game against the Philadelphia A's.

swept Wrigley Field. With his team behind, 13-2, Schmidt went to work in the fifth inning by hammering a two-run homer off Chicago starter Rick Reuschel and then, in the seventh, he solved Reuschel for a bases-empty home run. With Mike Garman pitching for the Cubs in the eighth, the Phillies' third baseman hit a three-run smash. Finally, with the score tied, 15-15, in the 10th, Schmidt connected for a two-run blast off Paul Reuschel, Rick's older brother, capping an eight-RBI, 5-for-6 day (the Phils' standout singled in the fourth inning).

MIKE SCHMIDT

Infielder who in his eighth full major league season (1980) became the Phillies' all-time homer champion. Del Ennis' 259 home runs held up as the team mark from 1956 until mid-1980, but Schmidt slugged his 259th homer as a Phils player on July 23, 1980, and hit No. 260 (and No. 261) two days later. Through the 1986 season, Schmidt had belted a club-record 495 homers.

PAT SEEREY

Chicago White Sox player whose power-hitting display in the first game of a July 18, 1948, doubleheader marked the second straight time in major league history that a four-homer performance had been capped by a game-

73

winning, extra-inning home run. Seerey's bases-empty blast off Athletics pitcher Lou Brissie, his fourth homer of the game, gave the White Sox a 12-11 victory in 11 innings at Philadelphia. Seerey, who totaled seven RBIs in the contest, had been obtained from the Cleveland Indians a month and a half earlier.

Before Seerey's dramatic long-ball outburst—which included homers in three consecutive innings—the last four-homer game in the majors had been recorded by the Philadelphia Phillies' Chuck Klein, whose final homer of the day proved decisive in a 10-inning game in 1936.

ART SHAMSKY

Cincinnati Reds outfielder who hammered three home runs in an August 12, 1966, game at Crosley Field against the Pittsburgh Pirates—and he didn't enter the game until the eighth inning. Inserted into the lineup during defensive maneuvering in the top of the eighth, when the Reds trailed the Pirates, 7-6, Shamsky came to bat in the bottom of the inning and laced a two-run home run off Pittsburgh relief pitcher Al McBean. Pittsburgh tied the score, 8-8, in the ninth and seized a 9-8 edge in the 10th when Willie Stargell homered. However, Shamsky countered with a bases-empty shot off Roy Face in the bottom of the 10th. The Bucs regained the lead in the 11th when Bob Bailey doubled home two runs, but Shamsky continued his dramatics with a two-run homer off Billy O'Dell in the bottom of the 11th. Pittsburgh scored three runs in the 13th, though, and emerged a 14-11 winner in a game that featured 11 homers, a total that tied the big-league record for two teams in one game. Among the home runs—besides Shamsky's three clutch blows—were two by the Pirates' Bailey and one by Pittsburgh's Jerry Lynch, whose 18th and last career pinch homer (still tops in the National League) thrust the Pirates into a tie in the ninth inning.

After sitting out the Reds' August 13 game against Pittsburgh, Shamsky was called upon as a pinch-hitter on August 14 and tagged Vern Law for a two-run homer (and thus equaled a major league record with his fourth consecutive home run).

DUKE SNIDER

The most prolific home run hitter in Dodgers history, having totaled 389 homers for the National League team. Snider poled 316 homers for the Brooklyn Dodgers and 73 for the Los Angeles Dodgers.

No. 2 in lifetime Dodger home runs is Gil Hodges, who smashed 361 (298 for Brooklyn and 63 for Los Angeles).

WILLIE STARGELL

While Pittsburgh's Ralph Kiner led the National League in home runs or shared the league lead in that department for seven consecutive seasons, it is two-time N.L. homer king Stargell who ranks as the Pirates' all-time home run leader. Stargell, in fact, hit 174 more homers in a Pirates uniform than Kiner did. Stargell played 21 years and 2,360 games for the Pirates, drilling 475 home runs. Kiner, a Pirate for seven-plus seasons and 1,095 games, hit 301 homers for the Bucs and ranks No. 2 on Pittsburgh's lifetime home run list.

WILLIE STARGELL, ROBERTO CLEMENTE

Pirate standouts who were the most prolific of the nine players who walloped home runs at both Pittsburgh ball parks in 1970. Stargell hit four homers at Forbes Field, which closed its gates on June 28, 1970, and nine at Three Rivers Stadium, which became the Pirates' new home on July 16. Clemente slammed three homers at both Forbes Field and Three Rivers. No other National Leaguer hit as many as two homers at both stadiums in '70, but seven other players did slug at least one homer at both parks that season. Those seven were Pittsburgh's Richie Hebner, Al Oliver, Bob Robertson and Manny Sanguillen, Willie Smith and Billy Williams of the Chicago Cubs and Jim Wynn of the Houston Astros.

DICK STUART

The first player in major league history to achieve 30-homer seasons in both the National League and the American League. After cracking 35 home runs for the N.L.'s Pittsburgh Pirates in 1961, Stuart drilled 42 homers for the A.L.'s Boston Red Sox in 1963 (and 33 more for Boston in 1964).

Eleven other players have joined Stuart in recording 30-homer seasons in both leagues: Dick Allen, Bobby Bonds, Jeff Burroughs, Darrell Evans, Frank Howard, Dave Kingman, Greg Luzinski, Frank Robinson (the only man with four or more 30-homer years in both leagues, totaling seven in the National and four in the American), Reggie Smith, Jason Thompson and Dave Winfield.

ED SUMMERS

A Detroit Tigers pitcher who fashioned a 68-45 record in the majors, he hit two home runs as a big-leaguer—and both came off the same pitcher in the same game. Summers, a lifetime .162 hitter, not only pitched the Tigers to a 10-3 victory over the A's on September 17, 1910, at Detroit, but homered twice that day off Philadelphia's Harry Krause.

GORMAN THOMAS

The No. 1 home run hitter in Milwaukee Brewers history. Thomas has rapped 208 lifetime homers for the Brewers.

Second in Brewer career homers is Cecil Cooper, who had homered 195 times for Milwaukee through the 1986 season.

JIM TOBIN

The only pitcher in modern major league history to hit three home runs in one game. In a May 13, 1942, contest at Boston against the Chicago Cubs, the

Braves' Tobin clubbed bases-empty homers in the fifth and seventh innings and then broke a 4-4 tie in the eighth with his third consecutive home run, a two-run shot. Tobin pitched a five-hitter as Boston won, 6-5.

The day before his three-homer salvo, Tobin was used as a pinch-hitter against the Cubs—and socked a two-run homer.

BOB WATSON, DUANE WALKER

The only players to hit indoor home runs in both major leagues in the same season. In 1979, Watson connected once at the Astrodome for the National League's Houston Astros and once at Seattle's Kingdome for the American League's Boston Red Sox. In 1985, Walker hit one homer at Houston's Astrodome for the N.L.'s Cincinnati Reds and one at Minnesota's Metrodome for the A.L.'s Texas Rangers.

DEL WILBER

The only player in big-league history to hit three bases-empty home runs in a game in which no other runs were scored by either team. In the second game of an August 27, 1951, doubleheader at Philadelphia, Phillies lefthander Ken Johnson shut out the Reds, 3-0, and batterymate Wilber cracked three homers off Cincinnati's Ken Raffensberger.

Only five other major leaguers have homered three times in a game in which their teams scored only three runs. Clyde McCullough and Hank Sauer accomplished the feat for the Chicago Cubs (McCullough in a 4-3 loss in 1942 and Sauer in a 3-2 victory in 1952), Boog Powell and Eddie Murray turned the trick for the Baltimore Orioles (Powell in a 3-1 triumph in 1964 and Murray in a 4-3 setback in 1980) and Gus Bell hit three solo homers for the Cincinnati Reds in a 5-3 defeat in 1955.

TED WILLIAMS, CARL YASTRZEMSKI

Superstar outfielders who rank No. 1 and No. 2 on the Red Sox's lifetime home run list, having smashed a total of 973 homers for Boston. Williams, who began his big-league career in 1939 and ended it in 1960, hit 521 homers for the Red Sox. Yastrzemski, who made his debut with the Boston club the year after Williams departed, drilled 452 homers for Boston until retiring at the end of the 1983 season.

GENE WOODLING

New York Yankees outfielder who in 1951 hit home runs off Cleveland's Early Wynn on June 24, July 24 and August 24.

JIM WYNN

The major leagues' all-time leader in indoor home runs with 97. Wynn slugged all of his domed-stadium homers while playing as a National Leaguer at Houston's Astrodome, hitting 93 as a member of the Houston Astros (with whom he played 11 seasons) and four while with the Los Angeles Dodgers.

Only six other players have totaled 50 or more big-league homers indoors: American League leader Tom Brunansky (68), Kent Hrbek (67), Cesar Cedeno (66), Doug Rader (65), Gary Gaetti (57) and Bob Watson (53). Brunansky, of the Minnesota Twins, has achieved his A.L.-pacesetting figure with 59 homers at Minnesota's Metrodome and nine at Seattle's Kingdome.

JIM WYNN

The No. 1 home run hitter in the history of Houston's major league franchise, hammering a total of 223 homers for the Colt .45s and the Astros. Wynn slammed four homers for the Colts in 1963, Houston's second season in the majors, and hit five in 1964. In 1965, when the Houston club moved into the Astrodome and changed its nickname to the Astros, Wynn became an everyday player in the big leagues and responded by hitting 22 homers. He walloped 192 more homers for Houston, for whom he played through 1973. The "Toy Cannon" hit 37 home runs in 1967 and 33 in 1969.

Cesar Cedeno ranks No. 2 on Houston's long-ball chart with 163 career homers.

YANKEES, GIANTS

The only major league teams for whom *two* players have struck 500 home runs. Babe Ruth hit a club-record 659 homers as a Yankee and Mickey Mantle contributed 536 for the Yanks. Willie Mays socked a franchise-record 646 homers for the Giants (187 when the club was based in New York and 459 after the team switched to San Francisco), while Mel Ott smashed 511 home runs for the New York Giants.

RUDY YORK

The only man in the history of the majors to belt two bases-loaded home runs in one game off one pitcher. Playing for the Boston Red Sox against the Browns on July 27, 1946, at St. Louis, York hit a grand slam off Browns reliever Tex Shirley in the second inning and then clubbed another basesfull shot off Shirley in the fifth. Boston thrashed St. Louis, 13-6.

Six other big-leaguers have hit two grand slams in one game, connecting off different pitchers. They are Tony Lazzeri of the New York Yankees (1936), Jim Tabor of the Red Sox (1939), Jim Gentile and Frank Robinson of the Baltimore Orioles (1961, 1970), Tony Cloninger of the Atlanta Braves (1966) and Jim Northrup of the Detroit Tigers (1968).

RICHIE ZISK

The first player to hit home runs in Canada in both the National League and the American League. After hitting four N.L. homers at Montreal's Jarry Park earlier in his career, Zisk connected for the Chicago White Sox at

Slugger Richie Zisk, pictured in 1973 when he played for the Pittsburgh Pirates, went on to become the first player to homer in Canada in both the American and National leagues.

Toronto in an April 7, 1977, game that marked the Blue Jays' A.L. debut. Zisk's smash off Bill Singer at Exhibition Stadium was the first A.L. home run ever hit in Canada.

RICHIE ZISK

The first player to hit home runs in all three of the major leagues' indoor ball parks. After homering at the Astrodome and the Kingdome earlier in his career, Zisk homered for the Seattle Mariners against the Minnesota Twins' Roger Erickson at the Metrodome on April 7, 1982, to complete the three-stadium feat.

HANK AARON

The last player to hit an All-Star Game home run in his home park. Representing the Atlanta Braves in the 1972 All-Star contest at Atlanta Stadium, Aaron connected off Cleveland's Gaylord Perry with one man on base in the sixth inning. The homer thrust the National League into a 2-1 lead in a game that the N.L. won, 4-3, in 10 innings. A complete list of players who have slugged All-Star Game homers in their home parks follows:

1939/Joe DiMaggio, New York Yankees/Yankee Stadium
1946/Ted Williams, Boston Red Sox (2 homers)/Fenway Park
*1948/Stan Musial, St. Louis Cardinals/Sportsman's Park
1951/Vic Wertz, Detroit Tigers/Briggs Stadium
1951/George Kell, Detroit Tigers/Briggs Stadium
1954/Al Rosen, Cleveland Indians (2 homers)/Cleveland Stadium
1954/Larry Doby, Cleveland Indians/Cleveland Stadium
**1959/Jim Gilliam, Los Angeles Dodgers/Memorial Coliseum
1969/Frank Howard, Washington Senators/Robert F. Kennedy Stadium
1972/Hank Aaron, Atlanta Braves/Atlanta Stadium

*The St. Louis Browns, host team for the 1948 All-Star Game, shared their ball park with the Cardinals.
**Second All-Star Game of the season.

HANK AARON

The first of only three major leaguers to play for the same manager for both National League and American League teams in All-Star Game competition. Aaron played for Alvin Dark as a National Leaguer in 1963 and as an American Leaguer in 1975.

Nolan Ryan pitched for the 1973 A.L. and 1985 N.L. All-Star teams, both of which were managed by Dick Williams. And Dave Winfield played for Sparky Anderson on the 1977 N.L. squad and the 1985 A.L. club.

SPARKY ANDERSON

The only man in All-Star Game history to suffer losses as both a National League and American League manager. Anderson compiled a 3-1 record as a National League manager and has a 0-1 mark as an American League pilot. His N.L. loss was by a 6-4 score in 1971 and his A.L. defeat was a 6-1 setback in 1985.

Only two other managers have guided N.L. and A.L. clubs in the All-Star Game. Al Dark won his lone game as an N.L. manager and lost his only A.L. managerial assignment. Dick Williams was 1-0 in the N.L. and 0-3 in the A.L.

WALLY BERGER

The only starting player in the 1934 All-Star Game who has not reached the Hall of Fame. Berger, center fielder for the Boston Braves, batted fifth for the National League All-Stars in the '34 game and went 0 for 2. He played 11 seasons in the major leagues, batting a composite .300 for the Braves, New York Giants, Cincinnati Reds and Philadelphia Phillies and socking 242 home runs. Berger was the N.L. homer champion in 1935 and topped the 100-runs-batted-in mark in four big-league seasons.

Starting lineups for the 1934 All-Star Game with American Leaguers on the left and National Leaguers on the right:

Charlie Gehringer, second base/ Frankie Frisch, second base
Heinie Manush, left field/ Pie Traynor, third base
Babe Ruth, right field/ Joe Medwick, left field
Lou Gehrig, first base/ Kiki Cuyler, right field
Jimmie Foxx, third base/ Wally Berger, center field
Al Simmons, center field/ Bill Terry, first base
Joe Cronin, shortstop/ Travis Jackson, shortstop
Bill Dickey, catcher/ Gabby Hartnett, catcher
Lefty Gomez, pitcher/ Carl Hubbell, pitcher

Boston Braves center fielder Wally Berger (center), shown crossing bats with National League teammates Kiki Cuyler (left) and Joe Medwick before the 1934 All-Star Game in New York, was the only member of either the A.L. or N.L. starting lineup who failed to make baseball's Hall of Fame.

YOGI BERRA, ELSTON HOWARD

The only two players from the same major league club to catch in one All-Star Game. The New York Yankees' Berra entered the first All-Star Game of 1961 in the ninth inning as a pinch-hitter for starting American League catcher John Romano of the Cleveland Indians. After taking over behind the plate in the bottom of the ninth, Berra was replaced by Yankee teammate Howard with two out in the inning. Howard finished the game, which the National League won, 5-4, in 10 innings.

BRAVES FIELD

Scheduled site of the 1953 All-Star Game, with the National League's Boston Braves due to serve as hosts. However, the Braves franchise shifted to Milwaukee in March 1953 and the Cincinnati Reds, next up among N.L. cities in the All-Star rotation, took over as hosts. The N.L. won the '53 All-Star Game, 5-1, at Crosley Field.

Braves Field was the site of one All-Star Game, the 1936 classic, won by the National League, 4-3.

CHRIS BROWN

The last of only three players to end an All-Star Game by hitting into a double play. Batting against Baltimore's Don Aase with Pittsburgh's Tony Pena on second base and Cincinnati's Dave Parker on first and one out in the ninth inning of the 1986 game, San Francisco's Brown grounded to Kansas City second baseman Frank White, who stepped on second to retire Parker and then threw to first baseman Don Mattingly of the New York Yankees for the last out of the game. The American League won, 3-2.

Also hitting into All-Star Game-ending double plays were the Yankees' Joe DiMaggio (1950) and Bobby Richardson (1963), whose grounders were induced by the Reds' Ewell Blackwell and the Los Angeles Dodgers' Don Drysdale, respectively. The National League won, 4-3, in 14 innings in 1950, and prevailed by a 5-3 score in 1963.

JIM BUNNING

The only major leaguer to pitch three perfect innings *twice* in All-Star Game history. Representing the Detroit Tigers, Bunning accomplished the feat as the American League's starting pitcher in 1957 and as the A.L.starter again in the second game of 1961. He pitched in eight All-Star Games overall.

Seven other pitchers have worked three perfect innings in an All-Star Game. The complete list follows:

1957/Jim Bunning, A.L./First through third
1958/Billy O'Dell, A.L./Seventh through ninth
*1959/Don Drysdale, N.L./First through third
*1961/Warren Spahn, N.L./First through third
**1961/Jim Bunning, A.L./First through third
1966/Denny McLain, A.L./First through third
1967/Gary Peters, A.L./Sixth through eighth
1980/Steve Stone, A.L./First through third
1986/Roger Clemens, A.L./First through third
    *First All-Star Game of the season.
    **Second All-Star Game of the season.

ROD CAREW

The lone player in All-Star Game history to bat against the same pitcher 10 or more years apart. Carew, representing the Minnesota Twins, grounded out to Cincinnati Reds shortstop Leo Cardenas while batting against the New York Mets' Tom Seaver in the seventh inning of the 1968 game. In the 1981 contest, Carew was wearing a California Angels uniform and Seaver was representing the Cincinnati Reds when, in the second inning, Carew grounded out to the veteran pitcher.

STEVE CARLTON

The only major leaguer to pitch in two All-Star Games indoors. Carlton, representing the St. Louis Cardinals, pitched one inning in the 1968 game at Houston's Astrodome and, as a member of the Philadelphia Phillies, worked one inning at Seattle's Kingdome in 1979.

Only eight other players have appeared in two indoor All-Star Games. Carl Yastrzemski (Boston Red Sox) also played in the 1968 and 1979 contests, while Gary Carter (Montreal Expos, New York Mets), Keith Hernandez (St. Louis Cardinals, Mets), Dave Parker (Pittsburgh Pirates, Cincinnati Reds), Jim Rice (Red Sox), Mike Schmidt (Philadelphia Phillies), Frank White (Kansas City Royals) and Dave Winfield (San Diego Padres, New York Yankees) played in the '79 game and in the '86 classic at the Astrodome.

BILL CAUDILL

Pitcher who has struck out every batter he has faced in All-Star Game competition—and the relief specialist has pitched against three batters. Working the seventh inning of the 1984 game, Caudill, representing the Oakland A's, fanned Tim Raines of the Montreal Expos, Ryne Sandberg of the Chicago Cubs and Keith Hernandez of the New York Mets.

Bobby Shantz also struck out all three batters that he faced in his All-Star Game career. The Philadelphia Athletics' Shantz fanned Whitey Lockman of the New York Giants, Jackie Robinson of the Brooklyn Dodgers and Stan Musial of the St. Louis Cardinals in the fifth inning of the 1952 classic.

Only two other pitchers have struck out "all" of their All-Star Game opponents—Cy Blanton of the Pittsburgh Pirates, 1937, and Jesse Orosco of the New York Mets, 1983. Blanton faced just one hitter in his All-Star Game career, Joe DiMaggio, and he fanned the New York Yankees' star in the fourth inning of the '37 game. And Orosco has pitched against only Ben Oglivie, fanning the Milwaukee Brewers' power hitter in the seventh inning of the '83 classic.

CHICAGO WHITE SOX

The first team in All-Star Game history to have three players make pitching appearances in one All-Star Game. The White Sox's Sandy Consuegra, Bob Keegan and Virgil Trucks provided the breakthrough in the 1954 classic, but the results weren't exactly scintillating. While Trucks pitched a scoreless ninth for the American Leaguers (he walked one batter), Consuegra and Keegan were battered in their stints. Consuegra was clubbed for five hits and five runs (all earned) in one-third inning of relief, and Keegan yielded three hits and two runs (both earned) in two-thirds of an inning. Despite the ineffectiveness of Consuegra and Keegan, the A.L. squad scored an 11-9 victory.

Five other teams have seen three of their pitchers take the mound in one All-Star Game—and two of those clubs turned the trick in the same game. In the 1973 classic, Claude Osteen, Don Sutton and Jim Brewer of the Los Angeles Dodgers pitched for the National League and Jim (Catfish) Hunter, Ken Holtzman and Rollie Fingers of the Oakland A's hurled for the A.L. In the second All-Star Game of 1959, pitchers Jerry Walker, Hoyt Wilhelm and Billy O'Dell of the Baltimore Orioles worked for the A.L.; in 1960, Bob Friend, Roy Face and Vernon Law of the Pittsburgh Pirates pitched for the N.L. in that season's first All-Star Game; in 1985, the Detroit Tigers' Jack Morris, Dan Petry and Willie Hernandez were called upon by the A.L.

ROBERTO CLEMENTE

The only player to strike out four times in an All-Star Game. In the National League's 15-inning, 2-1 triumph over the American League in 1967, the Pittsburgh Pirates' star struck out in the third, sixth, ninth and 11th innings against Dean Chance, Gary Peters, Al Downing and Jim (Catfish) Hunter, respectively. Clemente collected an infield single in the first inning and grounded out in the 14th.

CLEVELAND INDIANS

The last team failing to have a player appear in an All-Star Game that the franchise hosted. No member of the Indians—pitcher Jim (Mudcat) Grant was the lone Cleveland player to make the American League squad— played in the 1963 All-Star Game, contested at Cleveland Stadium.

In 1962, Senators pitcher Dave Stenhouse, the lone Washington player named to the A.L. team, did not appear in that season's first All-Star Game, played at District of Columbia Stadium; in 1950, pitcher Ray Scarborough, the only White Sox player selected for the A.L. squad, did not get into the classic at Chicago's Comiskey Park; in 1937, pitcher Wes Ferrell, catcher Rick Ferrell and second baseman Buddy Myer, Washington's three representatives, were not used in the game played at the Senators' Griffith Stadium; in 1936, outfielder Wally Berger, the lone Braves choice, did not play for the National League in the contest at Boston's Braves Field. (First baseman George McQuinn, the St. Louis Browns' lone selection for the 1940 game at St. Louis' Sportsman's Park, did not appear in the '40 contest. However, the Cardinals, not the Browns, were the host team for that game.)

CLEVELAND STADIUM

The most frequent All-Star Game site, having played host to four midsum-

The Cooper boys, Mort (left) and Walker, are the only brothers to form a starting battery in All-Star Game history. Mort pitched to Walker in both the 1942 and 1943 classics.

mer classics. All-Star Games were played at Cleveland's lakefront ball park in 1935, 1954, 1963 and 1981.

COMISKEY PARK, BRIGGS STADIUM

Home ball parks of the American League's Chicago White Sox and Detroit Tigers, they were sites of the 1950 and 1951 All-Star Games, marking the first time that one league had played host to the midsummer classic in consecutive years. The '51 game, scheduled to be hosted by the Philadelphia Phillies, was moved to Detroit to help celebrate the 250th anniversary of the Michigan city's founding. Accordingly, the Phillies staged the 1952 game.

MORT COOPER, WALKER COOPER

The only brother combination to form a starting battery in All-Star Game history. Both members of the St. Louis Cardinals, the Coopers were National League starters in both 1942 and 1943. Pitcher Mort worked three innings in the '42 game and $2\frac{1}{3}$ innings in the '43 classic and was the losing pitcher in each contest. Catcher Walker went 1 for 2 at the plate in each game.

JOE CRONIN, BILL TERRY

The only two men to play for and manage an All-Star Game squad in one year—and both performed the feat in 1934. Cronin, representing the Washington Senators, managed the American League All-Stars and played the entire game at shortstop. He collected a single and a double in five at-bats. The New York Giants' Terry managed the National League club and played the entire game at first base. He went 1 for 3. Cronin's American Leaguers won, 9-7.

TONY CUCCINELLO

Brooklyn Dodgers infielder who was the last batter in major league baseball's first All-Star Game. Cuccinello, pinch-hitting for New York Giants pitcher Carl Hubbell in the ninth inning of the 1933 game at Chicago's Comiskey Park, struck out against Lefty Grove of the Philadelphia A's. The American Leaguers downed the National Leaguers, 4-2.

WILLIE DAVIS, TIM McCARVER, VINCE DiMAGGIO

Of the major leaguers with as many as three hits in All-Star Game play, the only players with lifetime 1.000 batting averages in the midsummer classic. Davis, center fielder for the Los Angeles Dodgers, singled in his lone at-bat in the 1971 game and homered and singled in the 1973 contest. Catcher McCarver, representing the St. Louis Cardinals, singled in his only at-bat in the 1966 game and singled and doubled in 1967. Pittsburgh Pirates outfielder DiMaggio singled, tripled and homered in his only three All-Star at-bats, all coming in 1943.

Other players with 1.000 lifetime batting averages in All-Star Games: 2 for 2—Eddie Kazak, Garry Templeton; 1 for 1—Bruce Bochte, Hank Borowy, Jim Davenport, Murry Dickson, Bob Dillinger, Brian Downing, Hank Foiles, Goose Goslin, Bert Haas, Glenn Hubbard, Eddie Kasko, Jack Kramer, Emil (Dutch) Leonard, Danny Litwhiler, Charley Maxwell, Lee Mazzilli, Ken McBride, Ray Narleski, Bobo Newsom, Tom Paciorek, Johnny Podres, Dick Sisler, Tony Taylor, Ozzie Virgil Jr., Bucky Walters, Don Wert and Max West.

DOMINIC DiMAGGIO, JOE DiMAGGIO

The only brothers to hit safely in the same All-Star Game—and they achieved the feat twice. In the 1941 game, Boston Red Sox outfielder Dom DiMaggio singled in his only at-bat and New York Yankees outfielder Joe DiMaggio collected a double in four at-bats. In the 1949 contest, Dom singled and doubled in five at-bats and Joe singled and doubled in four at-bats.

JOE DiMAGGIO

The first rookie to play in an All-Star Game. DiMaggio, who made his big-league debut on May 3, 1936, was the American League's starting right fielder a little more than two months later in the majors' fourth All-Star

Game. The New York Yankees' newcomer batted third and played the entire game, going 0 for 5 at the plate and making an error.

JOE DiMAGGIO

New York Yankees star who played in every inning of every All-Star Game for seven straight seasons, 1936 through 1942.

The only other major leaguer to play as many as six consecutive complete All-Star Games was Detroit Tigers second baseman Charlie Gehringer, who played every inning of the first six contests in history, 1933 through 1938.

LEO DUROCHER

Brooklyn Dodgers shortstop who circled the bases on a bunt play in the 1938 All-Star Game. Batting in the seventh inning with the National League ahead, 2-0, and Cincinnati's Frank McCormick on first base, Durocher bunted against Boston Red Sox pitcher Lefty Grove. The Red Sox's Jimmie Foxx, playing third base, fielded the ball and threw it past first base and into right field. New York Yankees outfielder Joe DiMaggio retrieved the ball and threw toward the plate. McCormick scored on the play—and so did Durocher, as DiMaggio's throw sailed beyond the plate. Durocher was credited with a single and Foxx and DiMaggio were charged with errors. The "gift" runs helped the N.L. to a 4-1 triumph.

FENWAY PARK

The scheduled site for the 1945 All-Star Game, a contest that was canceled because of wartime travel restictions. Seven midsummer interleague exhibition games replaced the All-Star clash, with the White Sox playing the Cubs at Chicago's Comiskey Park, the Giants meeting the Yankees at New York's Polo Grounds, the Indians facing the Cincinnati Reds at Cleveland Stadium, the Braves opposing the Red Sox at Boston's Braves Field, the Browns squaring off against the Cardinals at St. Louis' Sportsman's Park, the A's battling the Phillies at Philadelphia's Shibe Park and the Senators going against the Brooklyn Dodgers at Washington's Griffith Stadium. The Detroit Tigers were denied permission to travel to Pittsburgh to play the Pirates. Proceeds from the seven exhibitions—American League teams won five of the games—went to the War Service Relief Fund.

Fenway Park played host to the 1946 All-Star Game.

CARLTON FISK

Of All-Star Game participants who never played on the winning side in baseball's showcase game, the one to endure the most defeats—nine. American League catcher Fisk represented the Boston Red Sox in the 1972, 1973, 1976, 1977, 1978 and 1980 All-Star Games and the Chicago White Sox in the 1981, 1982 and 1985 classics, all of which the A.L. All-Stars lost. Fisk's first All-Star Game marked the beginning of an 11-game A.L. losing streak, a skid in which Fisk suffered all but one of his All-Star losses.

Fisk also was selected for the American League squad in 1974, but was replaced because of an injury.

BOB FRIEND, VERNON LAW

Pittsburgh teammates who started and won the first and second All-Star Games, respectively, of 1960. The Pirate righthanders pitched a total of 5⅔ innings (Law also worked in relief in the first game), yielding no runs and only two hits.

Pittsburgh relief ace Roy Face pitched 1⅔ innings of hitless and scoreless ball in the first All-Star Game of 1960, meaning that Pirate pitchers worked a total of 7⅓ innings in the '60 All-Star contests and gave up no runs and only two hits.

FRANKIE FRISCH

The first of only four players to lead off the first inning of an All-Star Game with a home run. The St. Louis Cardinals' Frisch, the first man to bat for the National League in the bottom of the first of the 1934 classic, drilled a homer off Lefty Gomez of the New York Yankees.

Lou Boudreau of the Cleveland Indians (1942), Willie Mays of the San Francisco Giants (1965) and Joe Morgan of the Cincinnati Reds (1977) also have struck first-inning, leadoff homers in All-Star Game competition, with each smash coming in the top half of the inning. Boudreau connected against Mort Cooper of the Cardinals, Mays off Milt Pappas of Baltimore and Morgan versus Jim Palmer of the Orioles.

STEVE GARVEY

Of players whose teams never lost an All-Star Game in which they appeared, the one with the best record—10-0. First baseman Garvey represented the National League's Los Angeles Dodgers in the All-Star Game from 1974 through 1981 and wore a San Diego Padres uniform in the 1984 and 1985 games. Garvey contributed greatly to the 10 victories, posting a lifetime .393 batting average in All-Star competition with two home runs (six extra-base hits overall) and seven runs batted in. He twice was named the All-Star Game's most valuable player.

LEFTY GOMEZ

A notoriously poor hitter (he finished his major league career with 133 hits in 904 at-bats for a .147 batting average), he nonetheless drove in the first run in All-Star Game history. With Jimmie Dykes of the Chicago White Sox on second base and Joe Cronin of the Washington Senators on first in the second inning of the inaugural All-Star Game in 1933, the New York Yankees' pitcher went to the plate against Bill Hallahan of the St. Louis Cardinals and singled home Dykes.

Chicago White Sox star Jimmie Dykes crosses the plate with the first run in All-Star Game history, courtesy of a single by a notoriously poor hitter— Yankees pitcher Lefty Gomez.

LEFTY GOMEZ

The only pitcher to win three All-Star Games, receiving credit for the American League's 4-2, 4-1 and 8-3 victories in 1933, 1935 and 1937. The New York Yankees' standout lefthander was the A.L.'s starting pitcher in five of the first six midsummer classics.

LEFTY GOMEZ

The first of six pitchers to win an All-Star Game and a World Series game in the same season. Gomez, of the New York Yankees, got the victory in the 1937 All-Star Game and then won two games against the New York Giants in the '37 World Series.

Also winning an All-Star Game and a World Series contest in the same year: Paul Derringer of the Cincinnati Reds, 1940; Frank (Spec) Shea, Yankees, 1947; Vernon Law, Pittsburgh Pirates, 1960; Sandy Koufax, Los Angeles Dodgers, 1965, and Don Sutton, Dodgers, 1977. Like Gomez, Derringer, Shea, Law and Koufax won two World Series games in the years they posted All-Star/Series "doubles." Sutton was 1-0 in the '77 Series.

RICH (GOOSE) GOSSAGE

The only player who has represented four teams in All-Star Game competition. Gossage pitched in the 1975 classic as a member of the Chicago White Sox, the 1977 game for the Pittsburgh Pirates, the 1978 and 1980 games while with the New York Yankees and the 1984 and 1985 games as a representative of the San Diego Padres.

HANK GREENBERG

Detroit first baseman who had exactly 100 runs batted in at the All-Star Game break of 1935 (at which time the Tigers had played 75 games)—but didn't make the American League's All-Star roster that year. Lou Gehrig of the New York Yankees played the entire July 8, 1935, All-Star Game at first base for the A.L. squad (whose other first baseman, Jimmie Foxx of the Philadelphia Athletics, was stationed at third base against the National Leaguers).

The only other player to have 100 or more RBIs at an All-Star Game break was Tommy Davis of the Los Angeles Dodgers. Davis had 106 RBIs entering the *second* All-Star Game of 1962, which was played on July 30. By then, the Dodgers had played 106 games.

Greenberg finished with 170 RBIs in '35; Davis totaled 153 in '62.

BILLY HERMAN

The only player to make two appearances in one All-Star Game. Herman, second baseman for the Chicago Cubs, first appeared in the 1934 All-Star Game in the third inning as a pinch-hitter for New York Giants pitcher Carl

Hubbell and popped out. Then, in the seventh inning, National League Manager Bill Terry of the New York Giants needed to replace his starting second baseman, Frankie Frisch of the St. Louis Cardinals, who was hobbled by charley-horse problems. Lacking a replacement, Terry asked permission of American League Manager Joe Cronin to insert Herman at second base, and Cronin agreed to Herman's re-entry into the game.

CHARLIE HOUGH

The only pitcher in All-Star Game history to strike out three batters in one inning without retiring the side. Representing the Texas Rangers in the 1986 classic, knuckleball specialist Hough yielded a leadoff double to San Francisco's Chris Brown in the eighth inning but proceeded to strike out the Giants' Chili Davis, Montreal's Hubie Brooks and the Expos' Tim Raines in order. End of inning with no scoring? Wrong. Davis had struck out on a wild pitch, Brown advancing to third on the play and Davis being retired on a throw to first base by Boston Red Sox catcher Rich Gedman, who was bedeviled by Hough's fluttering pitches. Brooks had fanned on a pitch that got away from Gedman, the passed ball enabling Brown to score and Brooks to reach first (as Gedman opted for a play on Brown at the plate instead of throwing to first base for a sure out on Brooks). Brooks moved to second on a balk before Raines struck out. Steve Sax of the Los Angeles Dodgers then singled home Brooks, and Dave Righetti of the New York Yankees replaced Hough for the American League. The National League failed to score again, and the A.L. held on for a 3-2 triumph.

Pitchers striking out three batters in one inning of an All-Star Game:
1934/1st/Hubbell, N.L.*/Ruth, Gehrig, Foxx
1934/2nd/Hubbell, N.L./Simmons, Cronin, Gomez
1938/7th/Grove, A.L.*/Brown, Hack, Herman
1943/5th/Vander Meer, N.L./Keltner, Wakefield, York
1943/7th/Javery, N.L./Case, Keltner, Stephens
1948/5th/Sain, N.L.**/Stephens, Doerr, Evers
1949/1st/Spahn, N.L./D. DiMaggio, Williams, Parnell
1952/5th/Shantz, A.L.**/Lockman, J. Robinson, Musial
1955/10th/Nuxhall, N.L.*/Vernon, Rosen, Sullivan
1955/12th/Conley, N.L.**/Kaline, Vernon, Rosen
1961a/10th/Miller, N.L./Wilhelm, Gentile, Maris
1961b/9th/Miller, N.L.*/Mantle, Howard, Sievers
1963/8th/Radatz, A.L./Mays, McCovey, Groat
1967/6th/Jenkins, N.L./Fregosi, Carew, Oliva
1968/7th/McDowell, A.L./Haller, Mays, McCovey
1968/8th/Seaver, N.L./Powell, Mantle, Monday
1972/9th/McGraw, N.L./Jackson, Cash, Grich
1977/1st/Palmer, A.L./Garvey, Cey, Bench
1980/6th/Reuss, N.L.**/Porter, Bell, John
1982/4th/Carlton, N.L./Cooper, Fisk, Thornton
1982/7th/Soto, N.L./White, Wilson, Bell
1983/1st/Stieb, A.L./Dawson, Murphy, Schmidt
1984/4th/Valenzuela, N.L.**/Winfield, Jackson, Brett

1984/5th/Gooden, N.L.**/Parrish, Lemon, Davis
1984/7th/Caudill, A.L.**/Raines, Sandberg, Hernandez
1986/4th/Valenzuela, N.L.**/Mattingly, Ripken, Barfield
1986/8th/Fernandez, N.L.*/Jacoby, Rice, Mattingly
1986/8th/Hough, A.L.*/C. Davis, Brooks, Raines
  aFirst game of season
  bSecond game of season
  *Consecutive
  **Only three batters of inning

REGGIE JACKSON

The major leaguer with the highest home run total at the time of the first or only All-Star Game of a season, having smashed 37 homers by the All-Star break of 1969. Jackson's Oakland A's had played 92 games when the '69 All-Star Game was played on July 23.

New York Yankee sluggers Roger Maris and Mickey Mantle established an All-Star-break high for homers in 1961, having clouted 40 by the second All-Star Game of that season (played July 31). At that juncture, the Yankees had played 101 games.

Jackson finished the 1969 season with 47 home runs; Maris slugged a major league-record 61 homers in 1961 and Mantle walloped 54 in '61.

HARMON KILLEBREW, HARVEY KUENN

When these two American Leaguers failed to play in the second All-Star Game of 1959, it marked the only time in All-Star Game history that a league did not have at least one of its "big three" offensive departmental leaders—the league pacesetter in batting average, home runs or runs batted in—play in the contest. The Washington Senators' Killebrew, whose 33 homers and 81 RBIs were leading the American League at the second All-Star break, was on the '59 A.L. squad but wasn't used in game two by Manager Casey Stengel of the New York Yankees. Kuenn, the A.L.'s top hitter with a .343 mark, was not a member of the second-game A.L. team; the Detroit Tigers' star was sidelined because of a knee injury. Despite the absence of Killebrew and Kuenn from the lineup, the A.L. All-Stars won the second classic of '59 by a 5-3 score.

HARVEY KUENN, JOE DiMAGGIO

The only two batters in history to make the last out in three All-Star Games. Representing the Detroit Tigers, Kuenn grounded into a game-ending force-out against the New York Giants' Johnny Antonelli in 1956 and fouled out against the Chicago Cubs' Don Elston to end the first All-Star Game of 1959; in 1960, as a member of the Cleveland Indians, he flied out against the Pittsburgh Pirates' Vernon Law for the last out of that season's first All-Star Game. The New York Yankees' DiMaggio popped out against the Cubs' Lon Warneke to end the 1936 game, flied out against the Giants' Carl Hubbell to

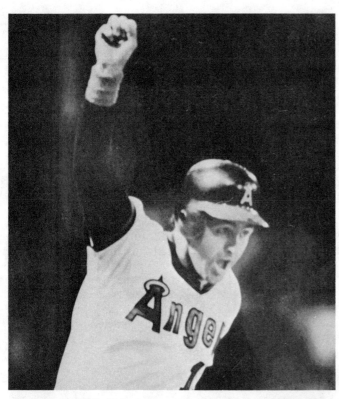

California's Fred Lynn raises a triumphant fist (left) as he circles the bases and then gets a warm reception at the plate after hitting the first bases-loaded home run in All-Star Game history, helping the American League to a 13-3 victory in the 1983 classic.

conclude the 1940 contest and grounded into a double play against the Cincinnati Reds' Ewell Blackwell to close the 1950 classic.

The only other player to bat last in three All-Star Games was Stan Musial of the St. Louis Cardinals. Musial grounded out against Joe Coleman of the Philadelphia Athletics to end the 1948 game, struck out against the Athletics' Bobby Shantz for the last out of the 1952 game (although the National League won the rain-shortened, five-inning game) and homered in the 12th inning off Frank Sullivan of the Boston Red Sox to cap the 1955 classic.

VERNON LAW, SANDY KOUFAX

The only pitchers to win an All-Star Game, a World Series game and the Cy Young Award in one season, with the Pittsburgh Pirates' Law achieving the "triple" in 1960 and the Los Angeles Dodgers' Koufax accomplishing the feat in 1965. Law posted a 20-9 record in '60, sharing the National League lead with 18 complete games; he started and won that season's second All-Star Game and then beat the New York Yankees twice in that fall's World Series. Koufax went 26-8 in '65 and topped the N.L. in numerous categories, including victories, strikeouts (382) and earned-run average (2.04); he won the All-Star Game in a relief role and notched two World Series triumphs against the Minnesota Twins.

AL LOPEZ

His 0-5 record ranks as the worst managerial mark in All-Star Game history. Lopez managed the American League All-Stars when they lost to the National Leaguers in 1955, 1960 (twice), 1964 and 1965.

LYNN'S ALL-STAR GAME 'FIRST'

The American League already had scored three runs in the third inning of the 1983 All-Star Game at Chicago's Comiskey Park, increasing its lead over the National League to 5-1. Now, Milwaukee Manager Harvey Kuenn's A.L. team had runners on second and third base in that inning and the Brewers' Robin Yount, the league's Most Valuable Player in 1982, was striding to the plate. A base hit at this juncture seemingly would ensure that the American Leaguers would get over the hump. And what a hump it was: The A.L. had lost 11 consecutive All-Star Games (and 19 of the previous 20). Yount, though, was walked intentionally, loading the bases. That brought up left-handed-hitting outfielder Fred Lynn of the California Angels. Lynn worked the count to 2 and 2, then drilled a pitch into the right-field stands. The American League rode the first grand slam in All-Star Game history to a 13-3 victory.

Supporting Cast:

● **Jim Rice.** Boston outfielder who, with the A.L. leading, 2-1, started the third-inning fireworks by homering to left field.

● **Dave Winfield.** After Kansas City's George Brett tripled and Milwaukee's Ted Simmons popped out in the third, the New York Yankees' slugger delivered a run-scoring single up the middle. A.L. 4, N.L. 1.

- **Rod Carew.** After Cleveland's Manny Trillo singled Winfield to second base and California's Doug DeCinces flied out, the Angels' Carew singled home Winfield for a 5-1 A.L. advantage. On the throw to the plate, Trillo took third base and Carew moved to second. Yount was then walked.
- **Atlee Hammaker.** Giants lefthander who had gone in to pitch for the N.L. at the beginning of the third inning. When relieved by Houston's Bill Dawley after giving up Lynn's bases-full homer, Hammaker had this log: ⅔ innings pitched, six hits and seven runs (all earned) allowed, one walk and no strikeouts. He had an N.L.-leading 1.70 earned-run average entering the game.
- **Dave Stieb.** Toronto pitcher who earned the victory, allowing no hits and one unearned run in the first three innings. He walked one batter and struck out four.
- **Mario Soto.** Having allowed the A.L. two runs (both unearned) in the first two innings, Cincinnati's Soto was saddled with the loss for St. Louis Manager Whitey Herzog's N.L. team.

CONNIE MACK

Selected to manage the 1939 American League All-Star team under special circumstances, he had to relinquish the duties and was replaced by the man who normally would have gotten the managerial assignment. While the All-Star Game managerial format normally involves using pennant-winning managers of the previous season, the scenario differed for the American League in 1939 because the junior league wanted to honor its senior manager, Mack, in baseball's centennial season. Accordingly, Mack, manager of the Philadelphia A's since the A.L.'s inception in 1901, was named to manage the A.L. club. Joe McCarthy, who guided the New York Yankees to the A.L. pennant and World Series title in 1938, wound up managing the squad, though, when illness forced Mack to miss the game.

BILL MADLOCK, JON MATLACK

The only players to share an Arch Ward Trophy, symbolic of the most valuable player in the All-Star Game and named in honor of the game's founder, a former sports editor of the Chicago Tribune. The dual honor for the National League players came in 1975 when Chicago Cubs third baseman Madlock broke a 3-3 tie in the ninth inning with a bases-loaded single and New York Mets pitcher Matlack pitched two scoreless innings of relief (during which he struck out four batters). The N.L. won, 6-3, with Matlack notching the victory.

JUAN MARICHAL

One of only five pitchers to receive the Arch Ward Trophy as the All-Star Game's most valuable player and the only Ward Trophy-winning pitcher not to be credited with a victory in his "MVP" performance. Marichal, of the San Francisco Giants, pitched one-hit, scoreless ball in the first three innings of the 1965 classic and left the game with a 5-0 lead. The American League eventually tied the score, though, before the N.L. nailed down a 6-5 triumph. Sandy Koufax of the Los Angeles Dodgers picked up the victory with one scoreless inning of relief.

Other Arch Ward Trophy-winning pitchers were the New York Mets' Jon Matlack, who shared most-valuable honors with third baseman Bill Madlock of the Chicago Cubs, 1975; Don Sutton of the Los Angeles Dodgers, 1977; LaMarr Hoyt of the San Diego Padres, 1985, and Roger Clemens of the Boston Red Sox, 1986.

WILLIE MAYS

The only player to hit two home runs off the same pitcher in All-Star Game competition. Representing the New York Giants, Mays socked a homer off Whitey Ford of the New York Yankees in the 1956 contest. Then, as a member of the San Francisco Giants, he connected against Ford in the second All-Star Game of 1960.

WILLIE MAYS

The lone player to start all eight All-Star Games from 1959 through 1962, when a two-games-a-year format was in effect.

The only other player to appear in all eight All-Star Games from '59 through '62 was Stan Musial of the St. Louis Cardinals.

WILLIE MAYS

The first of three players to win the Arch Ward Trophy as the All-Star Game's most valuable player twice, taking the honor in 1963 and 1968. In '63, the San Francisco Giants' star collected a single, walked once, stole two bases, drove in two runs, scored twice and made an outstanding catch in the National League's 5-3 triumph. He singled and scored for the N.L. in '68 in the only 1-0 game in All-Star history.

The other two-time Arch Ward Trophy winners are Steve Garvey of the Los Angeles Dodgers (1974 and 1978) and Gary Carter of the Montreal Expos (1981 and 1984).

WILLIE MAYS

Center fielder for the New York and San Francisco Giants and the New York Mets who played 11 All-Star Games in their entirety, a record, and appeared in 24 midsummer classics overall, a mark equaled by only Stan Musial of the St. Louis Cardinals and Hank Aaron of the Milwaukee and Atlanta Braves and the Milwaukee Brewers. Musial is next on the "complete game" list, having played 10 All-Star Games from start to finish, while Aaron ranks third with nine; Ted Williams of the Boston Red Sox and Brooks Robinson of the Baltimore Orioles are next on the total-games chart with 18 appearances each.

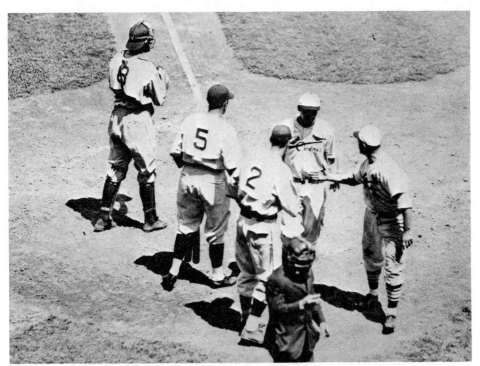

Cardinals slugger Joe Medwick, shown crossing the plate after his three-run homer in the 1934 All-Star Game at New York's Polo Grounds, put his name in the record books later that season by also homering in the World Series.

JOE MEDWICK

The first player in major league history to hit a home run in the All-Star Game and in the World Series in the same season. Playing for the St. Louis Cardinals, Medwick homered in the 1934 All-Star Game and in the first game of the '34 World Series. A list of all players hitting same-season homers in All-Star Game and World Series competition follows:

1934/Medwick, Cards/1 All-Star HR/1 Series HR
1936/Lou Gehrig, New York Yankees/1/2
1937/Lou Gehrig, New York Yankees/1/1
1939/Joe DiMaggio, New York Yankees/1/1
1952/Jackie Robinson, Brooklyn Dodgers/1/1
1955/Mickey Mantle, New York Yankees/1/1
1956/Mickey Mantle, New York Yankees/1/3
1964/Ken Boyer, St. Louis Cardinals/1/2
1965/Harmon Killebrew, Minnesota Twins/1/1
1971/Roberto Clemente, Pittsburgh Pirates/1/2
1971/Frank Robinson, Baltimore Orioles/1/2
1977/Steve Garvey, Los Angeles Dodgers/1/1

JOE MEDWICK

The only man to collect four hits in an All-Star Game and four hits in a World Series game. Medwick, of the St. Louis Cardinals, went 4 for 5 (a home run and three singles) in Game 1 of the 1934 World Series and was 4 for 5 (two singles, two doubles) in the 1937 All-Star Game.

Only two other players—Boston Red Sox sluggers Ted Williams and Carl Yastrzemski—have collected four hits in an All-Star Game. Williams belted two homers and two singles while going 4 for 4 in the 1946 contest; Yastrzemski hit three singles and a double in his 4-for-6 performance in the 1970 classic.

STU MILLER

San Francisco Giants pitcher who struck out three batters in one inning in both All-Star Games of 1961. In the 10th inning of the first game, he struck out Baltimore's Hoyt Wilhelm, the Orioles' Jim Gentile and Roger Maris of the New York Yankees—but the American League still managed to score a run on a two-out walk and a wild throw. In the ninth inning of the second game, Miller allowed a leadoff single to Al Kaline of the Detroit Tigers before striking out the Yankees' Mickey Mantle and Elston Howard and the Chicago White Sox's Roy Sievers.

Overall in the 1961 games, Miller worked 4⅔ innings, allowed one hit, one unearned run and one walk, and struck out nine batters. He was the winning pitcher in the first game, thanks to the National League's two-run 10th-inning rally that produced a 5-4 victory. The '61 contests marked Miller's only All-Star Game appearances.

JOE MORGAN

The last of seven players to end an All-Star contest with a game-winning hit. Facing Dave McNally of the Baltimore Orioles with the score tied, 3-3, and one out in the bottom of the 10th inning of the 1972 All-Star Game, the Cincinnati Reds' second baseman singled home Nate Colbert of the San Diego Padres from second base. The National League's 4-3 triumph marked the start of an 11-game N.L. winning streak.

Also ending All-Star Games with victory-producing hits were: Ted Williams, Boston Red Sox slugger whose three-run ninth-inning home run off Claude Passeau of the Chicago Cubs lifted the American League to a 7-5 triumph in 1941; the St. Louis Cardinals' Stan Musial, whose 12th-inning leadoff homer against the Red Sox's Frank Sullivan made the N.L. a 6-5 winner in 1955; Roberto Clemente, Pittsburgh Pirates standout who delivered a 10th-inning single off Hoyt Wilhelm of the Baltimore Orioles that enabled the N.L. to prevail, 5-4, in the first game of 1961; the Philadelphia Phillies' Johnny Callison, whose three-run homer off Dick Radatz of the Red Sox in the ninth inning of the 1964 game pulled the N.L. to a 7-4 victory; the Los Angeles Dodgers' Maury Wills, whose 10th-inning single off Pete Richert of the Washington Senators in 1966 slipped the N.L. past the A.L., 2-1; the Chicago Cubs' Jim Hickman, who came through with a 12th-inning single against Clyde Wright of the California Angels in the 1970 classic, the hit scoring the

Cincinnati Reds' Pete Rose—who barreled into Cleveland Indians catcher Ray Fosse—and giving the N.L. a 5-4 triumph.

STAN MUSIAL

St. Louis Cardinals first baseman who was the only non-member of the Cincinnati Reds to be elected by fans to the National League's starting lineup for the 1957 All-Star Game. Because of ballot-stuffing by Cincinnati fans, Reds players topped the voting for seven of the N.L.'s eight positions (pitching selections were made by the manager). Reds voted to starting berths were: Johnny Temple, second base; Don Hoak, third base; Roy McMillan, shortstop; Frank Robinson, left field; Gus Bell, center field; Wally Post, right field, and Ed Bailey, catcher. With the final ballots yet to be counted but the Reds fans' voting onslaught evident, Commissioner Ford Frick, thinking that more-deserving players were being victimized by the ballot avalanche, ruled that three heavy vote-getters from Cincinnati—Post, Bell and first baseman George Crowe—would not start regardless of the final ballot figures. Crowe, it turned out, finished second to Musial, anyway. Frick allowed second-place finishers Hank Aaron (Milwaukee Braves) and Willie Mays (New York Giants) to start in place of Post and Bell, respectively. Bell, named a reserve by N.L. Manager Walter Alston of the Brooklyn Dodgers, contributed a two-run pinch double in the game, which the American League won, 6-5. Starters Temple, Hoak, McMillan, Robinson and Bailey went 2 for 9 overall at the plate and played flawlessly afield.

Getting out the vote was nothing new for Cincinnati fans. In 1956, five Reds—Temple, McMillan, Robinson, Bell and Bailey—were elected as N.L. starters. All started, as scheduled, and they collected four hits in 13 at-bats (while playing errorless ball) as the N.L. scored a 7-3 triumph. Additionally, Reds first baseman Ted Kluszewski drilled two doubles in two at-bats after entering the game in the sixth inning.

STAN MUSIAL

The only player in All-Star Game history to collect two pinch hits in one year. The St. Louis Cardinals' Musial singled off Frank Lary of the Detroit Tigers while batting for the Pittsburgh Pirates' Bill Mazeroski in the eighth inning of the first All-Star Game of 1960. In the second All-Star contest of '60, played two days later, Musial was sent up in the seventh inning to hit for Stan Williams of the Los Angeles Dodgers and belted a home run off Gerry Staley of the Chicago White Sox.

NATIONAL LEAGUE

While the National League's All-Star Game players have worn uniforms of their respective teams since 1934 (and American League players have done so since the game's inception in 1933), the N.L. All-Stars wore special uniforms for the inaugural game. N.L. President John Heydler instructed A.G. Spalding & Bros. to make up a set of gray uniforms for the '33 All-Star Game with the words "National League" sewn across the shirt fronts. The senior-league players also wore caps with "NL" affixed to them.

NATIONAL LEAGUE

The winning team in all seven extra-inning contests played in All-Star Game history. The National Leaguers defeated the American Leaguers, 4-3, in 14 innings in 1950; 6-5 in 12 innings in 1955; 5-4 in 10 innings in the first game of 1961; 2-1 in 10 innings in 1966; 2-1 in 15 innings in 1967; 5-4 in 12 innings in 1970, and 4-3 in 10 innings in 1972.

NEW YORK YANKEES

The only team to have six players start in one All-Star Game. With managers responsible for choosing the starting lineups at the time, Yankees Manager Joe McCarthy selected the following American League batting order for the 1939 classic: Doc Cramer, Boston Red Sox, right field; Red Rolfe, Yankees, third base; Joe DiMaggio, Yankees, center field; Bill Dickey, Yankees, catcher; Hank Greenberg, Detroit Tigers, first base; Joe Cronin, Red Sox, shortstop; George Selkirk, Yankees, left field; Joe Gordon, Yankees, second base, and Red Ruffing, Yankees, pitcher. The A.L. won, 3-1, with Selkirk contributing a run-scoring single and DiMaggio clouting a bases-empty home run.

Apparently resenting accusations that he favored Yankee representatives in All-Star play, McCarthy didn't use any of the five New York players available to him for the 1943 game. He proved he could win without the Yankee contingent, though, as the A.L. scored a 5-3 victory in the '43 contest.

NEW YORK YANKEES

American League club that has played host to the All-Star Game three times—and gone on to win the A.L. pennant in each of those seasons. All-Star Games were played at Yankee Stadium in 1939, 1960 and 1977, years in which World Series also were contested at the Yankees' ball park.

1959-1962

The four-season span in which two All-Star Games were played each year, with the doubling-up aimed at providing additional revenue for the players' pension fund, helping needy old-time players and boosting youth baseball. The two 1959 All-Star Games were played approximately four weeks apart, while the contests in 1961 and the games in 1962 were held 20 days apart. In 1960, though, the All-Star clashes were played within two days of each other.

1965

The year in which the National League first surpassed the American League in All-Star Game triumphs. After the first All-Star Game in 1933 through the 1963 contest—a span of 34 games—the A.L. held the lead in victories. In 1964, though, the N.L. won, 7-4, and tied the series at 17-17 with one tie. The National Leaguers' 6-5 triumph in '65 thrust the senior league in front. Through 1986, the N.L. had widened the gap to 36-20-1, thanks largely to 19 victories in the 20 games that were played from 1963 through 1982.

All-Star pitchers Carl Hubbell (left) of the New York Giants and Lefty Grove of the Philadelphia A's show the contrast in uniform style in baseball's first midsummer classic in 1933. National Leaguers wore a special gray uniform while American Leaguers wore the uniforms of their respective teams.

1981

The year in which the All-Star Game marked the return of major league baseball action after a 50-day strike had forced cancellation of 712 regular-season games. Players walked off their jobs following games of June 11, 1981, and the labor dispute wasn't settled until July 31, at which time it was agreed that the All-Star Game—originally scheduled for July 14 in Cleveland—would be be played August 9 and that the regular season would resume August 10. Paced by Gary Carter's two home runs and Mike Schmidt's game-winning two-run homer in the eighth inning, the National League defeated the American League, 5-4.

1983

The only year in which at least one player from each of the current 26 big-league teams appeared in the All-Star Game. Overall, there have been eight All-Star Games in which every club in the majors has had a representative play in the contest; the seasons of those classics and the number of teams in the big leagues at the time: 1933, 16; 1944, 16; 1946, 16; 1949, 16; 1953, 16; 1961 (first game), 18; 1973, 24; 1983, 26. (The big leagues expanded from 16 to 18 clubs in 1961, from 18 to 20 in 1962, from 20 to 24 in 1969 and from 24 to 26 in 1977.)

GAYLORD PERRY, JIM PERRY

The only brothers to pitch in the same All-Star Game and the last of six brother combinations to appear in the same classic. Gaylord, of the San Francisco Giants, pitched the sixth and seventh innings of the 1970 game for the National League and Jim, of the Minnesota Twins, worked the seventh and eighth innings for the American League. Gaylord yielded four hits and two runs; Jim surrendered one hit and one run.

Other brothers appearing in the same All-Star Game were: outfielders Dominic DiMaggio (Boston Red Sox) and Joe DiMaggio (New York Yankees), 1941, 1949 and 1950; pitcher Mort Cooper and catcher Walker Cooper (both of the St. Louis Cardinals), 1942 and 1943; outfielders Dixie Walker (Brooklyn Dodgers) and Harry Walker (Cardinals, Philadelphia Phillies), 1943 and 1947; outfielders Felipe Alou (Atlanta Braves) and Matty Alou (Pittsburgh Pirates), 1968; outfielder Carlos May (Chicago White Sox) and first baseman Lee May (Cincinnati Reds), 1969.

PHILADELPHIA PHILLIES

The only team in the major leagues to go four straight All-Star Games without a representative appearing in one of the contests. No Phillies players competed in the 1968, 1969, 1970 and 1971 contests, although Philadelphia did have one representative on each National League squad—in order, pitchers Woodie Fryman, Grant Jackson, Joe Hoerner and Rick Wise.

Only two other teams have gone as many as three consecutive All-Star Games without a player getting into the classic. No Boston Bees players appeared for the N.L. from 1936 through 1938, and no Cleveland Indians representatives played in the game for the American League from the second contest in 1962 through 1964.

PITTSBURGH PIRATES

The only team to have as many as eight players appear in one All-Star Game. In the first All-Star Game of 1960, the Pirates' Bob Skinner (left field), Bill Mazeroski (second base) and Bob Friend (pitcher) started for the National League and Pittsburgh's Roberto Clemente (right field), Dick Groat (shortstop), Smoky Burgess (catcher), Roy Face (pitcher) and Vernon Law (pitcher) also got into the contest.

POLO GROUNDS

The first two-time site of the All-Star Game, having played host to baseball's second "Dream Game" in 1934 and to the 10th classic in 1942.

National League left fielder Joe Medwick was the only player to start in both the '34 and '42 games, first representing the St. Louis Cardinals and then the Brooklyn Dodgers. Three other players—all National Leaguers—appeared in both Polo Grounds contests: Billy Herman (Chicago Cubs and Dodgers), Mel Ott (New York Giants) and Arky Vaughan (Pittsburgh Pirates and Dodgers).

PAUL RICHARDS, GENE MAUCH

The only All-Star Game managers who *never* managed teams in World Series competition. Normally, a league's All-Star pilot is the man who directed his team to the pennant in the previous year. However, Casey Stengel, who managed the New York Yankees to the American League championship in 1960, was not retained by the Yanks for 1961 and was inactive that season. Accordingly, Richards, manager of the 1960 A.L. runner-up Baltimore Orioles, guided the '61 A.L. All-Stars. Johnny Keane, manager of the 1964 National League pennant-winning and World Series champion St. Louis Cardinals, resigned after the Series and became manager of the Yankees. Mauch, who had guided the Philadelphia Phillies to a second-place tie in '64, directed the N.L. squad in the 1965 All-Star Game.

BROOKS ROBINSON, CARL YASTRZEMSKI

The only players from losing All-Star teams to win most-valuable-player honors in the showcase game. Robinson, third baseman for the Baltimore Orioles, won the Arch Ward Trophy in 1966 when he singled twice and tripled for the American League in a 2-1, 10-inning loss to the National League. Boston Red Sox standout Yastrzemski hit three singles and a double in his Ward Trophy-winning performance of 1970—but the N.L. All-Stars won the '70 classic, 5-4, in 12 innings.

BROOKS ROBINSON

Longtime Baltimore Orioles third baseman who played in 15 American

League defeats in All-Star Game competition, the most losses suffered by any All-Star participant. Overall, Robinson appeared in 18 All-Star Games from 1960 through 1974, with the A.L. winning twice (1971 and the second game of 1962) and tying once (game two of 1961).

FRANK ROBINSON

The only player to hit an All-Star Game home run and a World Series homer off the same pitcher in the same year. The Baltimore Orioles' Robinson walloped a homer off Pittsburgh's Dock Ellis in the third inning of the 1971 All-Star Game and then connected against the Pirates' righthander in the second inning of the first game of the '71 Series.

STEVE ROGERS

The last of seven pitchers who have started All-Star Games in their home ball parks. Rogers, representing Montreal, started and won the 1982 game at the Expos' Olympic Stadium.

Also starting All-Star Games in their home parks were: Carl Hubbell, New York Giants, Polo Grounds, 1934; Johnny Vander Meer, Cincinnati Reds, Crosley Field, 1938; Red Ruffing, New York Yankees, Yankee Stadium, 1939; Curt Simmons, Philadelphia Phillies, Shibe Park, 1952; Don Drysdale, Los Angeles Dodgers, Memorial Coliseum, 1959 (second game); Whitey Ford, Yankees, Yankee Stadium, 1960 (second game). Vander Meer was a winner in his home-park All-Star start, Drysdale and Ford were losers and Hubbell, Ruffing and Simmons did not get decisions.

COOKIE ROJAS

One of 14 players (seven from each league) to hit a pinch homer in All-Star Game competition—and the American League reserve did it while batting for the Minnesota Twins' Rod Carew, who was on the way to his second A.L. batting championship. Rojas, who finished his 16-season career in the majors with only 54 homers (and a .263 batting average), connected off Bill Stoneman of the Montreal Expos with a man on base in the eighth inning of the 1972 classic. The homer by the Kansas City Royals' second baseman boosted the A.L. into a 3-2 lead, but the National League rebounded for a 4-3 triumph in 10 innings.

Besides Rojas, A.L. players to slam pinch homers are: Larry Doby, Cleveland Indians, 1954, against Milwaukee Braves pitcher Gene Conley; Harmon Killebrew, Twins, first game of 1961 (Mike McCormick, San Francisco Giants); Pete Runnels, Boston Red Sox, second game of 1962 (Art Mahaffey, Philadelphia Phillies); Reggie Jackson, Oakland A's, 1971 (Dock Ellis, Pittsburgh Pirates); Carl Yastrzemski, Red Sox, 1975 (Tom Seaver, New York Mets); Frank White, Royals, 1986 (Mike Scott, Houston Astros).

N.L. players hitting pinch homers: Mickey Owen, Brooklyn Dodgers, 1942 (Al Benton, Detroit Tigers); Gus Bell, Cincinnati Reds, 1954 (Bob Keegan, Chicago White Sox); Willie Mays, New York Giants, 1956 (Whitey Ford, New

Franklin D. Roosevelt became the first U.S. President to attend an All-Star Game when he threw out the first ball for the 1937 classic at Washington's Griffith Stadium.

York Yankees); Stan Musial, St. Louis Cardinals, second game of 1960 (Gerry Staley, White Sox); George Altman, Chicago Cubs, first game of 1961 (Mike Fornieles, Red Sox); Willie Davis, Los Angeles Dodgers, 1973 (Nolan Ryan, California Angels); Lee Mazzilli, Mets, 1979 (Jim Kern, Texas Rangers).

FRANKLIN D. ROOSEVELT

The first President of the United States to attend an All-Star Game. Roosevelt was present at the 1937 game, played at Griffith Stadium in Washington. There was a wild scramble for the President's ceremonial first pitch, and New York Giants outfielder Joe Moore came up with the ball.

AL ROSEN, RAY BOONE

The first players to hit consecutive home runs in an All-Star Game. Rosen, of the Cleveland Indians, smashed a three-run homer off Robin Roberts in the third inning of the 1954 classic and Boone, of the Detroit Tigers, followed with a homer against the Philadelphia Phillies' pitcher. The blasts staked the American League to a 4-0 lead in a game that the A.L. All-Stars won, 11-9.

The only other back-to-back home runs in All-Star history were struck by the A.L.'s Ted Williams (Boston Red Sox) and Mickey Mantle (New York Yankees) in the sixth inning of the 1956 game and by the National League's Steve Garvey and Jim Wynn (both of the Los Angeles Dodgers) in the second inning of the 1975 classic.

BOB RUSH

The winning pitcher in the shortest game in All-Star history, working the final two innings of the National League's 3-2 victory over the American League in 1952 in a contest that was called after five innings because of rain. Rush, the ace of the Chicago Cubs' pitching staff, gave up four hits and both A.L. runs in his stint.

Bob Lemon of the Cleveland Indians, who yielded two hits and two runs in two innings, was the losing pitcher for the A.L.

ST. LOUIS CARDINALS

The team that accounted for the entire starting infield for the National League squad in the 1963 All-Star Game. Three Cardinals—first baseman Bill White, shortstop Dick Groat and third baseman Ken Boyer—were voted to starting berths, while St. Louis' Julian Javier was named to replace Bill Mazeroski, the leading vote-getter at second base, when the Pittsburgh Pirates' standout was unable to play because of a leg injury.

SEVEN

The fewest number of teams to be represented in the starting lineups of an All-Star Game, with only Oakland (five players), New York (three) and Minnesota (one) placing players in the American League's game-opening lineup in 1975 and just Cincinnati (four players), Los Angeles (three), St. Louis (one) and Pittsburgh (one) landing players on the National League's starting unit. The '75 lineups: N.L.—Pete Rose, Reds, right field; Lou Brock, Cardinals, left field; Joe Morgan, Reds, second base; Johnny Bench, Reds, catcher; Steve Garvey, Dodgers, first base; Jim Wynn, Dodgers, center field; Roy Cey, Dodgers, third base; Dave Concepcion, Reds, shortstop, and Jerry Reuss, Pirates, pitcher. A.L.—Bobby Bonds, Yankees, center field; Rod Carew, Twins, second base; Thurman Munson, Yankees, catcher; Reggie Jackson, A's, right field; Joe Rudi, A's, left field; Graig Nettles, Yankees, third base; Gene Tenace, A's, first base; Bert Campaneris, A's, shortstop, and Vida Blue, A's, pitcher.

There were 24 teams in the major leagues in 1975.

17

The number of times that Willie Mays and Hank Aaron played on the winning side in All-Star Game history—a record total. Each player appeared in 24 All-Star Games; Aaron had a record of 17-5-1 as a National Leaguer (representing the Milwaukee and Atlanta Braves) and 0-1 as an American Leaguer (Milwaukee Brewers), while Mays went 17-6-1 as an N.L. player (New York and San Francisco Giants and New York Mets).

FRANK (SPEC) SHEA

The first rookie pitcher to win an All-Star Game. After fashioning a 15-5 record and a 1.66 earned-run average for Oakland of the Pacific Coast League in 1946, Shea compiled an 11-2 record for the New York Yankees by the All-Star Game break of 1947 and was selected to appear in the midsummer classic in his first major league season. Working the fourth through the sixth innings for the American League, Shea allowed one run and three hits (including a home run by Johnny Mize of the New York Giants) in a game that the A.L. won, 2-1.

Shea finished with a 14-5 record for the Yankees in '47.

AL SIMMONS

Chicago White Sox outfielder who received the most votes from fans in the nationwide newspaper poll that was used to select the teams for the first All-Star Game in 1933. Simmons collected 346,291 votes, outdistancing runner-up Chuck Klein of the Philadelphia Phillies by 4,008 votes. Following Klein, who attracted 342,283 votes, were: Gabby Hartnett, Chicago Cubs, 338,653; Joe Cronin, Washington Senators, 337,766, and Lefty Grove, Philadelphia A's, 327,242. The New York Yankees' Babe Ruth, nearing the end of his career at age 38, was sixth in the balloting with 320,518 votes.

Basically, fans picked the players (including the pitchers) again in 1934, the rival managers chose the rosters from 1935 through 1937, the eight managers from each league named the squads from 1938 through 1946, fans selected the eight "position" starters from 1947 through 1957 (with managers naming the remainder of the squads) and managers, coaches and players picked the position starters from 1958 through 1969 (managers again completing the teams). Fans regained the honor of choosing the position starters in 1970 (with managers selecting the rest of the players), a process that remains in effect.

BILL TERRY

Not only the National League's manager in the 1934 All-Star Game, but the N.L.'s leading batter at the '34 All-Star break with a .367 average (108 hits in 294 at-bats). Terry, manager and first baseman of the New York Giants, collected a single in three at-bats in the All-Star contest, which the N.L. lost, 9-7.

Terry finished the '34 season with a .354 batting mark, second to the .362 figure posted by N.L. batting champion Paul Waner of Pittsburgh.

TEXAS RANGERS, TORONTO BLUE JAYS

With the Oakland A's playing host to the All-Star Game for the first time in 1987, the Rangers and the Blue Jays are the only present-day major league clubs yet to stage the midsummer classic.

TICKET PRICES

Admission to the first All-Star Game in major league history, played July 6, 1933, at Comiskey Park in Chicago, cost $1.65 for a box seat, $1.10 for a grandstand location and 55 cents for a bleacher ticket.

TUESDAY

Traditionally, the day of the week on which the All-Star Game is played—but the classic has been contested on every day of the week except Friday and Saturday. Forty-four of the 57 All-Star Games have been played on Tuesday, six on Monday, five on Wednesday, one on Thursday (the first game, in 1933) and one on Sunday (in the strike-shortened season of 1981).

FERNANDO VALENZUELA

Pitching in relief in the 57th All-Star Game, he matched a record established in the second All-Star contest when he struck out five straight batters. Valenzuela, of the Los Angeles Dodgers, fanned Don Mattingly (New York Yankees), Cal Ripken Jr. (Baltimore Orioles) and Jesse Barfield (Toronto Blue Jays) in the fourth inning of the 1986 game and then struck out Lou Whitaker (Detroit Tigers) and pitcher Ted Higuera (Milwaukee Brewers) in the fifth to tie the All-Star consecutive-strikeout mark set 52 years earlier by Carl Hubbell of the New York Giants. Hubbell, like Valenzuela a screwball pitcher, struck out Babe Ruth (Yankees), Lou Gehrig (Yankees), Jimmie Foxx (Philadelphia A's), Al Simmons (Chicago White Sox) and Joe Cronin (Washington Senators) in the first two innings of the 1934 game.

ARCH WARD

Chicago Tribune sports editor who founded the All-Star Game in 1933 as the featured sports event of Chicago's Century of Progress Exposition.

Ward, also founder of the Chicago College All-Star Football Game (1934) and the All-America Football Conference (1946), died on July 9, 1955, at age 58 and was buried in Chicago on July 12, the day baseball's 22nd All-Star Game was played at Milwaukee's County Stadium. Game time was delayed one-half hour to allow baseball dignitaries time to travel from Ward's funeral to Milwaukee.

LON WARNEKE

The only pitcher to hit a triple in an All-Star Game (no pitcher has connected for a home run), achieving the feat in the sixth inning of the first All-Star classic in 1933. Warneke, of the Chicago Cubs, rapped his triple—the first All-Star extra-base hit by a pitcher—off Alvin Crowder of the Washington Senators.

Only three other pitchers have managed extra-base hits in All-Star Game history. Bucky Walters of the Cincinnati Reds (1941), Johnny Podres of the Los Angeles Dodgers (second game, 1962) and Steve Carlton of the St. Louis

Arch Ward (right) posed with American League President Will Harridge in 1940, seven years after becoming the founding father of baseball's All-Star Game.

Cardinals (1969) all struck doubles, with Carlton's blow representing the last hit by a pitcher in an All-Star Game.

LON WARNEKE

The only man to play in an All-Star Game and umpire in the classic. Representing the Chicago Cubs, Warneke pitched in the 1933, 1934 and 1936 games. He later became a National League umpire and worked the right-field line during the 1952 All-Star contest.

DON WERT

A lifetime .242 big-league hitter who batted only .200 in 1968, he nonetheless played in the All-Star Game in '68 and collected a hit in his only career All-Star at-bat. Wert, who had a .220 average at the All-Star break as the

Detroit Tigers' third baseman, entered the game in the sixth inning for the American League and doubled off Tom Seaver of the New York Mets in the eighth.

LOU WHITAKER

American League player who arrived in Minneapolis, site of the 1985 All-Star Game, without his uniform and was forced to purchase a replica jersey from a souvenir vendor. Whitaker, the A.L.'s starting second baseman, had left Detroit without his home Tigers uniform and a replacement was lost in shipment. While the souvenir jersey had the familiar old-English "D" on the front, it was numberless on the back. So, using a marking pen, Whitaker made a reasonable facsimile of his number 1 and was ready for action.

Whitaker played error-free ball at second base in the '85 All-Star Game but was hitless in two at-bats before leaving the contest in the sixth inning.

DICK WILLIAMS

Of the All-Star managers meeting the usual criterion of having managed a major league pennant-winner the previous season, the only one to represent a club other than the team he led to a league championship a year earlier. Williams, who managed the Oakland A's to the American League pennant and World Series title in 1973 and then resigned, was named California manager three weeks before the 1974 All-Star Game and was in an Angels uniform when he directed the A.L. All-Stars in the '74 classic.

MAURY WILLS

The winner of the first Arch Ward Trophy, presented to the All-Star Game's Most Valuable Player. The award was initially given in 1962, a year in which Wills stood out in the first All-Star contest of the season. Wills, shortstop for the Los Angeles Dodgers, entered the game in the sixth inning as a pinch-runner for Stan Musial of the St. Louis Cardinals. After stealing second base, he scored the game's first run on a single by Dick Groat of the Pittsburgh Pirates. In the eighth, Wills led off with a single and raced to third on a single to left field by San Francisco's Jim Davenport. When the Giants' Felipe Alou followed with a foul fly to short right field, Wills tagged up after the catch and slid home with the National League's final run in a 3-1 triumph.

WILBUR WOOD

The pitcher with the highest victory total, 18, at the time of the first or only All-Star Game of a season—but he wasn't selected to his league's All-Star squad that year, 1973. Wood, a knuckleball specialist for the Chicago White Sox, boasted an 18-14 record when the '73 All-Star Game was played on July 24. His heavy loss total no doubt contributing to the lack of an All-Star invitation, Wood went on to compile a 24-20 mark for the White Sox in '73.

Whitey Ford of the New York Yankees and Don Drysdale of the Los An-

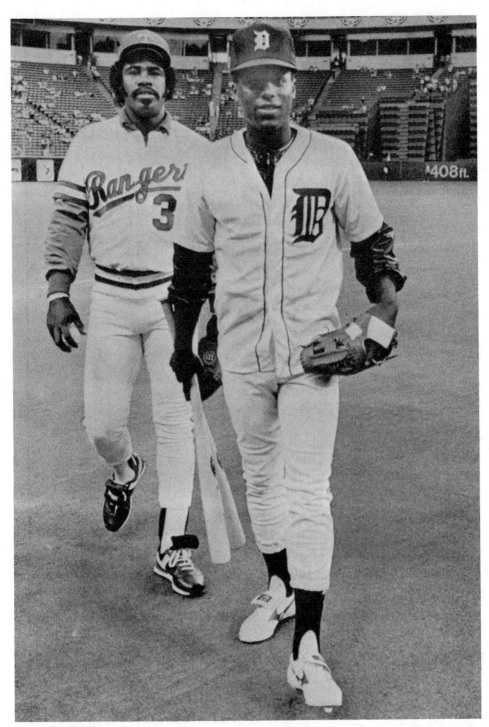

**When Detroit Tigers second baseman Lou Whitaker forgot to take his uni-
form to the 1985 All-Star Game in Minneapolis, he was forced to put together
a makeshift outfit purchased from a souvenir vendor.**

Chicago lefthander Wilbur Wood, shown comparing knuckleball grips with teammate Hoyt Wilhelm in 1967, was an All-Star snub in 1973 when he led the American League at the break with 18 victories.

geles Dodgers share the All-Star-break record for victories, having attained 19 triumphs at the time of the *second* All-Star Game of 1961 and the *second* classic of 1962, respectively. Ford's Yankees had played 101 games by the second-game break and Drysdale's Dodgers had played 106; Wood's White Sox had played 98 games by the All-Star break of '73.

Ford finished with a 25-4 record in '61; Drysdale went 25-9 in '62.

YANKEE STADIUM

The first and last ball park to play host to an All-Star Game and a World Series in the same year, doing so in 1939 and in 1977. Yankee Stadium also was an All-Star site (second game of the season) and World Series host in 1960.

Six other ball parks have served as hosts for baseball's two prime attractions in the same year: Fenway Park, Boston, 1946; Ebbets Field, Brooklyn, 1949; Cleveland Stadium, Cleveland, 1954; Memorial Coliseum, Los Angeles, 1959 (second All-Star Game of the season); Metropolitan Stadium, Bloomington, Minn., 1965; Riverfront Stadium, Cincinnati, 1970.

While teams hosting the All-Star Game have reached the World Series nine times overall, only three All-Star hosts—the '39 New York Yankees, the '59 Los Angeles Dodgers and the '77 Yanks—have won the Series.

GROVER CLEVELAND ALEXANDER

The highest-ranking pitcher on the big leagues' career-victory list never to have thrown a nine-inning no-hitter in the majors. While Alexander, whose 373 victories place him in a third-place tie with Christy Mathewson among the majors' all-time winningest pitchers, never threw a no-hit game, Charles (Bumpus) Jones (two lifetime victories) and Bobo Holloman (three) did toss no-hitters. Following are charts showing 300-game winners who failed to pitch no-hitters and pitchers with fewer than 20 career victories who did achieve no-hit fame:

Did Not Pitch No-Hitter

Grover C. Alexander	373-208
Charles (Kid) Nichols	361-208
Tim Keefe	342-224
Steve Carlton	323-229
Don Sutton	310-239
Mickey Welch	307-209
Eddie Plank	305-181
Lefty Grove	300-141
Early Wynn	300-244

Pitched No-Hitter

Charles (Bumpus) Jones	2-4
Bobo Holloman	3-7
George Davis	7-11
Mike Warren	9-13
Bill McCahan	16-14

St. Louis Browns pitcher Bobo Holloman, who won only three major league games, celebrated one of those victories, a no-hitter against the Philadelphia Athletics, with his wife and son in 1953.

Jones pitched his no-hitter for Cincinnati in 1892, Holloman for the St. Louis Browns in 1953, Davis for the Boston Braves in 1914, Warren for the Oakland A's in 1983 and McCahan for the Philadelphia A's in 1947.

Alexander narrowly missed a no-hitter for the Philadelphia Phillies on June 5, 1915, going 8⅔ innings against St. Louis before allowing the Cardinals' only hit of the game.

LEON (RED) AMES

New York Giants pitcher who threw a five-inning no-hitter in his major league debut. Ames' first appearance in the big leagues came in the second game of a doubleheader at St. Louis on September 14, 1903, and the 21-year-old righthander struck out seven batters and walked two while holding the Cardinals hitless in a 5-0 triumph. The game was halted after five innings because of darkness.

AL ATKISSON

The only man to pitch no-hitters in each of his first two years in the big leagues. Atkisson hurled his no-hit games for Philadelphia of the American Association (a major league at the time), the gems coming in a 10-1 victory over Pittsburgh in 1884 and a 3-2 triumph against New York in 1886. He did not pitch in the majors in 1885.

The only other pitcher to record two no-hitters by the end of his first two years in the big leagues was Johnny Vander Meer of the Cincinnati Reds. Both of Vander Meer's no-hit performances came in 1938, his second season in the majors.

Steve Busby fired no-hitters for the Kansas City Royals in his first two *full* seasons in the majors, 1973 and 1974. He had pitched in five games for Kansas City in 1972, however.

JIMMY AUSTIN

Third baseman who played in eight major league no-hitters—three of them on August 30 (1910, 1912 and 1916). On August 30, 1910, Austin played third for the New York Highlanders in the second game of a doubleheader when teammate Tom Hughes held Cleveland hitless through nine innings. Hughes then yielded seven hits in the next two innings and wound up a 5-0 loser. Two years to the day later, Austin was playing third for the Browns when St. Louis' Earl Hamilton tossed a 5-1 no-hitter against the Detroit Tigers. And, exactly four years after Hamilton's masterpiece, Austin again was stationed at third base for the Browns in a no-hit game; this time, though, Austin and his teammates were the victims, falling to Hubert (Dutch) Leonard of the Boston Red Sox in a 4-0 contest.

No other major leaguer has appeared in three no-hitters that occurred on the same date.

JOHN BALAZ

One of five players (all members of the 1974 and 1975 California Angels) to appear in no-hit games exactly one year apart—and he played in only 59 games in his two-year major league career. Balaz played left field for the Angels in teammate Nolan Ryan's no-hitter against the Minnesota Twins on September 28, 1974, and he was in right field for California in Oakland's four-man (Vida Blue, Glenn Abbott, Paul Lindblad and Rollie Fingers) no-hitter against the Angels on September 28, 1975. Bruce Bochte, Dave Chalk, Morris Nettles and Lee Stanton also played for the Angels in both games, a 4-0 California victory and a 5-0 A's triumph.

GEORGE BRADLEY

The first pitcher in major league history to throw a no-hitter, accomplishing the feat for St. Louis' National League club in a 2-0 triumph over Hartford on July 15, 1876. The N.L., baseball's first "big league," had begun its first season of operation the previous April.

TED BREITENSTEIN

The first of five pitchers to notch no-hitters in two major leagues. Breitenstein pitched his first no-hitter for the St. Louis Browns of the American

Association in 1891, then recorded his second for the National League's Cincinnati Reds in 1898.

Others pitching no-hitters in two major leagues: Cy Young, Cleveland, N.L., 1897, and Boston, A.L., 1904, 1908; Tom Hughes, New York, A.L., 1910, and Boston, N.L., 1916; Jim Bunning, Detroit, A.L., 1958, and Philadelphia, N.L., 1964; Nolan Ryan, California, A.L., 1973 (2), 1974, 1975, and Houston, N.L., 1981.

TED BREITENSTEIN, JIM HUGHES

The only pitchers in major league history to throw nine-inning no-hitters in different games on the same day. In National League contests played April 22, 1898, Cincinnati's Breitenstein pitched an 11-0 no-hit game against Pittsburgh and Baltimore's Hughes stopped Boston without a hit in an 8-0 triumph.

On May 2, 1917, Cincinnati's Fred Toney and Chicago's Jim (Hippo) Vaughn tossed nine-inning no-hitters against each other in an N.L. game that was scoreless entering the 10th inning. The Reds broke through for two hits and a run in the 10th against Vaughn and wound up 1-0 winners, with Toney holding the Cubs hitless throughout.

Charles (Bumpus) Jones of Cincinnati recorded a 7-1 no-hitter against Pittsburgh in an N.L. contest played October 15, 1892, the same day that Boston's Jack Stivetts held Washington hitless in an N.L. game that was called after five innings to enable the Boston club to catch a train for Cleveland (so N.L. split-season champions Boston and Cleveland could battle in a pennant-playoff).

SMOKY BURGESS

He caught two no-hit games in his big-league career—and his club lost both contests. Playing for the Cincinnati Reds on May 26, 1956, in Milwaukee, Burgess caught a combined nine-inning no-hitter by Johnny Klippstein, Hershell Freeman and Joe Black; the Braves got a 10th-inning hit, though, and two more in the next inning and scored a 2-1 victory in 11 innings. Three years later, in another May 26 game also played in Milwaukee, Burgess was behind the plate for Pittsburgh when the Pirates' Harvey Haddix pitched 12 perfect innings against the Braves. Milwaukee won that 1959 contest, 1-0, getting one hit in a 13-inning triumph.

JEFF BURROUGHS

The only player in major league history to slug a bases-loaded home run in a no-hit game of nine or more innings. Texas' left fielder hit a first-inning grand slam off Oakland's Vida Blue on July 30, 1973, in a game in which the Rangers' Jim Bibby pitched a 6-0 no-hitter against the A's.

Ed Cartwright of the St. Louis Browns hit a bases-full smash and a three-run shot—both homers coming in an 11-run third inning—in support of George

Don Cardwell, traded by Philadelphia to Chicago two days earlier, was literally surrounded by Cubs fans after pitching a no-hitter against the St. Louis Cardinals in the second game of a 1960 doubleheader at Wrigley Field.

Nicol's no-hit pitching on September 23, 1890, in a 21-2 mauling of Philadelphia. The Browns-Athletics American Association game was shortened to seven innings because of darkness.

BERT CAMPANERIS

The player who has appeared in the most no-hit games in the major leagues, 11. He was a member of the winning team five times. The no-hitters in which Campaneris played (with capitalization indicating participation with the victorious club):

Date	Club	No-Hit Pitcher
MAY 8, 1968	OAKLAND	JIM (CATFISH) HUNTER VS. MINNESOTA
Aug. 13, 1969	Oakland	Jim Palmer, Baltimore
July 3, 1970	Oakland	Clyde Wright, California
SEPT. 21, 1970	OAKLAND	VIDA BLUE VS. MINNESOTA
July 30, 1973	Oakland	Jim Bibby, Texas
July 19, 1974	Oakland	Dick Bosman, Cleveland
SEPT. 28, 1975	OAKLAND	BLUE-ABBOTT-LINDBLAD-FINGERS VS. CALIFORNIA
July 28, 1976	Oakland	Odom-Barrios, Chicago
SEPT. 22, 1977	TEXAS	BERT BLYLEVEN VS. CALIFORNIA
May 14, 1977	Texas	Jim Colborn, Kansas City
JULY 4, 1983	N.Y., A.L.	DAVE RIGHETTI VS. BOSTON

Campaneris played shortstop in the first 10 games and was at third base for the New York Yankees in Righetti's no-hitter.

DON CARDWELL

Two days after being traded from the Philadelphia Phillies to the Chicago Cubs in May 1960, he tossed a no-hitter for the Cubs in the second game of a doubleheader at Wrigley Field. Facing the St. Louis Cardinals, Cardwell allowed only one baserunner. After walking the Cards' Alex Grammas with one out in the first inning, he proceeded to retire the next 26 batters—the final out coming when Cubs left fielder Walt Moryn made a shoetop catch of Joe Cunningham's liner. Chicago won, 4-0, in the May 15 game.

JAMES (DOC) CASEY

The first of four major leaguers to appear in no-hit games in five consecutive years. Third baseman Casey played in no-hitters while with the Chicago Cubs in 1903, 1904 and 1905 and in no-hit performances while a member of the Brooklyn Dodgers in 1906 (three times) and 1907.

Others appearing in no-hit contests in five straight seasons: Deron Johnson, Philadelphia Phillies, 1969 through 1972, and Oakland A's, 1973; Bill North, Cubs, 1972, and A's, 1973 through 1976; Bert Campaneris, A's, 1973 through 1976, and Texas Rangers, 1977 (two games).

JOE CHRISTOPHER

The first player to make his major league debut in a perfect game. Christopher, playing for Pittsburgh, took over in right field for Roman Mejias in the 10th inning of Pirate lefthander Harvey Haddix's 12-inning perfect game against the Milwaukee Braves on May 26, 1959. Mejias had left the game for a pinch-hitter.

Only two other players have broken into the majors under perfect-game circumstances—and they did it in the same contest. Byron Browne and Don Young made their first big-league appearances on September 9, 1965— Browne played left field and Young was in center field for the Chicago Cubs—when Sandy Koufax of the Los Angeles Dodgers fired a 1-0 perfect game against Chicago.

Outfielder Joe Rudi made his Oakland A's debut on May 8, 1968, in the game in which A's pitcher Jim (Catfish) Hunter recorded a perfect game against the Minnesota Twins, 4-0. Rudi, though, had entered the majors in 1967 with the Kansas City A's and played 19 games for the Kansas City club.

LARRY CORCORAN

The first man to pitch two no-hitters in the majors—and the first to toss three as well. Corcoran, who pitched all three of his gems for the Chicago club of the National League, notched his first no-hitter on August 19, 1880, against Boston, his second on September 20, 1882, against Worcester and his third on June 27, 1884, against Providence. He won by 6-0, 5-0 and 6-0 scores.

JOSE CRUZ

The player who has appeared in the most major league no-hitters pitched indoors, having played in four such games. Cruz played in the outfield for the Astros when Houston's Larry Dierker (1976), Ken Forsch (1979), Nolan Ryan (1981) and Mike Scott (1986) pitched no-hit games at the Astrodome against the Montreal Expos, Atlanta Braves, Los Angeles Dodgers and San Francisco Giants, respectively. Dierker and Forsch were winners in 6-0 games, Ryan was victorious by a 5-0 score and Scott triumphed, 2-0.

Cruz went 8 for 14 at the plate in the four no-hitters, driving in three runs.

Only one other big-league no-hitter has been pitched in a domed stadium—and that also was achieved at the Astrodome. The Astros' Don Wilson accounted for that no-hit game, the first ever thrown indoors, when he beat the Braves, 2-0, at Houston in 1967.

HUGH DAILY

One-armed pitcher who on September 13, 1883, pitched a no-hitter for Cleveland in a 1-0 National League triumph over Philadelphia. Daily, who had part of his left arm amputated as a youngster, spent six seasons in the major leagues. He struck out 19 batters in an 1884 Union Association game and established a big-league season record for righthanders in '84 by striking out 483 batters.

BILL DAVIS

The last player in American League history to make his big-league debut in a no-hit game. Davis, a first baseman, broke into the majors as a pinch-hitter for the Cleveland Indians against Dave Morehead of the Boston Red Sox in a September 16, 1965, game. Morehead, en route to a 2-0 no-hitter, retired Davis—who was batting for Indians second baseman Pedro Gonzalez—on an eighth-inning fly ball.

DETROIT TIGERS

Club that played an American League-record 39 consecutive seasons without getting a no-hit pitching performance. In the second game of a July 4, 1912, doubleheader, against St. Louis, the Tigers' George Mullin threw a 7-0 no-hitter against the Browns. However, from 1913 through 1951, no Detroit pitcher turned in a no-hitter. Virgil Trucks tried to make up for lost time in 1952, fashioning two no-hitters for the Tigers in a little more than three months. His gems were 1-0 victories over the Washington Senators and New York Yankees on May 15 and August 25, respectively.

BILL DINNEEN

The last umpire in a big-league no-hit game to have pitched a no-hitter himself in the majors. Dinneen, who umpired in Bill Dietrich's 8-0 no-hitter for the Chicago White Sox against the St. Louis Browns on June 1, 1937, pitched a 2-0 no-hit game for the Boston Red Sox against the White Sox in the first game of a September 27, 1905, doubleheader.

GEORGE ESTOCK

Boston Braves pitcher who in his only major league start (he made 36 relief appearances) and lone decision was victimized by a no-hitter. Matched against Pittsburgh's Cliff Chambers in the second game of a May 6, 1951, doubleheader in Boston, Estock yielded eight hits and three runs in eight innings. Chambers walked eight Braves batters in his complete-game performance, but held Boston hitless in a 3-0 victory.

The no-hitter was the last triumph in a Pirates uniform for Chambers, who had led Pittsburgh in victories in 1949 (13) and 1950 (12). The gem against Boston gave Chambers a 3-2 record three weeks into the 1951 season, but on June 15—having dropped to a 3-6 mark—he was traded to the St. Louis Cardinals.

FORBES FIELD

A major league ball park for 61 years (mid-1909 until mid-1970), but never the site of a no-hitter. Jeff Tesreau of the New York Giants was on the brink of no-hit fame at Pittsburgh's Forbes Field, though, while pitching against the Pirates on May 16, 1914. Tesreau held the Bucs hitless for 8⅔ innings before yielding a single to Joe Kelly, Pittsburgh's center fielder and leadoff-hitter. Tesreau retired the next batter, finishing with a one-hit, 2-0 triumph.

KEN FORSCH, JACK MORRIS

Pitchers who tossed the earliest calendar-date no-hitters in major league history, recording their masterpieces in April 7 games. Forsch, pitching for the Astros, threw his no-hit game against the Atlanta Braves in 1979, posting a 6-0 victory at Houston; Morris, a member of the Detroit Tigers, stopped the White Sox without a hit in 1984, collecting a 4-0 triumph at Chicago. Forsch's no-hitter came in the Astros' second game of the '79 season, while Morris' gem came in the Tiger pitcher's second contest of '84 and Detroit's fourth game overall.

FOUR

The number of players who have ended their big-league careers in perfect games. John Anderson and Ossee Schreckengost of the Chicago White Sox saw their final major league action on October 2, 1908, in Cleveland—the day on which Addie Joss pitched a perfect game against the Sox. Schreckengost caught for Chicago that afternoon and Anderson pinch-hit for the Sox in Cleveland's 1-0 victory. And while Chicago played four more games that season, neither player got into another contest. Seventy-six years later, on the final day of the regular season, Texas' Marv Foley and Mickey Rivers bowed out of the majors in California pitcher Mike Witt's perfect game. Foley pinch-hit and Rivers saw duty as the designated hitter for the Rang-

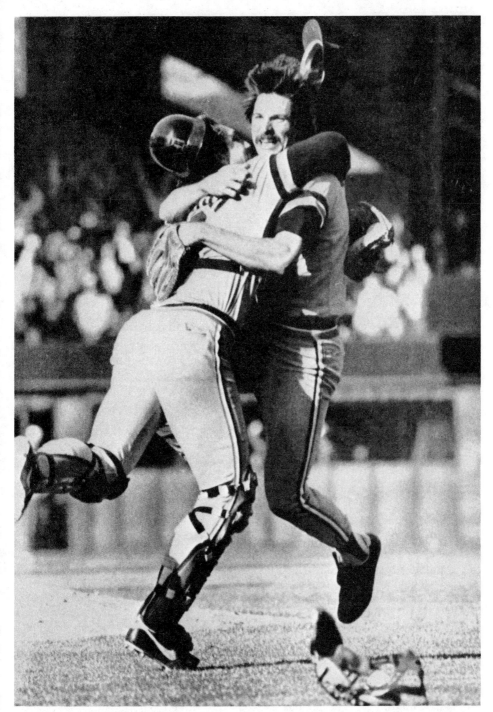

Detroit's Jack Morris received a well-deserved hug from catcher Lance Parrish after his April 7, 1984, no-hit performance against the Chicago White Sox. Morris matched the record for the earliest calendar-date no-hitter in big-league history.

ers in the September 30, 1984, game in Arlington, Tex., in which Witt retired all 27 Texas batters in a 1-0 Angels triumph.

One other player has finished his big-league career on the day in which his club was involved in a perfect game. Pitcher Tom Sturdivant of the New York Mets worked in both games of a June 21, 1964, doubleheader against Philadelphia, the relief roles marking his final appearances in the majors. In the first game of the twin bill, the Phillies' Jim Bunning pitched a 6-0 perfect game against the Mets in New York.

JAMES (PUD) GALVIN

The last big-leaguer to throw a no-hitter from 45 feet, which was baseball's prescribed pitching distance from the National League's inception in 1876 through 1880. Galvin, a member of the N.L.'s Buffalo club, held Worcester hitless on August 20, 1880, and was a 1-0 winner.

The pitching distance was moved to 50 feet from the plate in 1881.

JAMES (PUD) GALVIN

Winner of the most lopsided nine-inning no-hit game in major league history. Clearly, August 4, 1884, was a long day for the Detroit club of the National League; not only did Buffalo's Galvin pitch a no-hit, no-run game against Detroit, he received offensive support galore. Final score: Buffalo 18, Detroit 0.

The modern record for the most one-sided outcome in a nine-inning no-hitter is 15-0, the score by which Frank Smith of the Chicago White Sox beat Detroit in the second game of a September 6, 1905, doubleheader.

BILL HAWKE

Baltimore pitcher who threw the first big-league no-hitter from 60 feet, 6 inches, which became the majors' required pitching distance in 1893 (and remains the measurement in use today). Pitching against Washington on August 16, 1893, Hawke hurled no-hit ball while posting a 5-0 victory. Hawke pitched his gem from a rubber slab; previously, pitchers threw from a boxed-in area—a "pitcher's box"—that was 50 feet from home plate.

KEN HOLTZMAN

The last major leaguer to notch a no-hitter without recording a strikeout, achieving that oddity on August 19, 1969, when he pitched the Chicago Cubs to a 3-0 triumph over Atlanta. Holtzman walked three Braves.

Holtzman fired a second no-hitter on June 3, 1971, leading the Cubs past Cincinnati, 1-0. He struck out six Reds and walked four.

WILLIAM (DUMMY) HOY

The only man to play in no-hitters in three major leagues. In the American

Association, outfielder Hoy played for St. Louis in 1891 when the Browns' Ted Breitenstein pitched a no-hitter against Louisville. In the National League, Hoy and his Washington teammates were held hitless in 1893 by Baltimore's Bill Hawke and his Cincinnati club was victimized in 1897 by Cleveland's Cy Young; in 1899, he played behind Deacon Phillippe when the Louisville pitcher tossed a no-hitter against New York. And Hoy played for the American League's Chicago White Sox in 1901 when the Sox went nine innings without a hit against Cleveland's Earl Moore (before Chicago broke through for two hits and two runs in the 10th and beat Moore, 4-2).

TOM HUGHES

Of pitchers who wound up losing no-hit games, the one who suffered the worst defeat. Hughes, of the New York Highlanders, held Cleveland hitless for $9\frac{1}{3}$ innings in the second game of an August 30, 1910, American League doubleheader before yielding a single to Harry Niles. Cleveland collected six more hits off Hughes and won, 5-0, in 11 innings.

TIM HULETT

Infielder who had appeared in two no-hitters after his first eight major league games. Hulett, playing his fourth big-league contest, was at second base for the Chicago White Sox on September 29, 1983, when Mike Warren of the Oakland A's held the Sox hitless in a 3-0 triumph. On April 7, 1984, Hulett saw action at third base (but didn't start) for the Sox—it was his eighth game in the majors—as Jack Morris of the Detroit Tigers pitched a 4-0 no-hitter against Chicago.

REGGIE JACKSON

The last of eight players to appear in two major league perfect games. Jackson played right field for Oakland when A's pitcher Jim (Catfish) Hunter threw a 4-0 perfect game against the Minnesota Twins on May 8, 1968, and he was California's designated hitter when the Angels' Mike Witt retired all 27 Texas batters in a September 30, 1984, game. Jackson went 0 for 4 at the plate in each contest, although his fielder's-choice grounder against the Rangers drove in the only run of the game.

Others appearing in two perfect games in the majors: Patsy Dougherty, Fred Parent, Ossee Schreckengost, Harry Hooper, Joe Christopher, Wes Covington and Jim Gilliam.

CHARLES (BUMPUS) JONES

Pitcher who broke into the majors by hurling what proved to be the last big-league no-hitter from a distance of 50 feet—and this man won only one other game in the majors. Jones made his major league debut on the final day of the 1892 season, achieving a 7-1 no-hitter for Cincinnati against Pittsburgh. In 1893, a season in which Jones posted a 1-4 record before bowing out of the big leagues, the pitching distance was moved to its present length of 60 feet, 6 inches.

Jones' 1892 masterpiece, accomplished on October 15, ranks as the latest calendar-date no-hitter of nine innings or longer in major league history.

ADDIE JOSS

The only major leaguer to toss two nine-inning no-hitters against the same club. Joss, who spent all nine of his big-league seasons with Cleveland, pitched a perfect game against the Chicago White Sox on October 2, 1908, and came back with a second no-hitter against the White Sox on April 20, 1910. Cleveland was a 1-0 winner in each game.

JOE KERRIGAN

The last player to make his big-league debut in a no-hit game. Kerrigan, pitching in relief for Montreal against Houston, broke into the majors on July 9, 1976—the night Astros pitcher Larry Dierker spun a 6-0 no-hitter against the Expos. Kerrigan worked one inning of the National League game, allowing no runs, hits or walks and striking out one batter.

SAM KIMBER

The only man to pitch a major league no-hitter that ended in a tie game. Kimber, a member of the Brooklyn club of the American Association, shut out Toledo for 10 innings on October 4, 1884, not allowing a hit. However, Toledo's Tony Mullane matched Kimber's scoreless pitching—he allowed four hits—in a game that was halted after 10 innings because of darkness.

Kimber's effort in the 0-0 game marked the majors' first no-hitter exceeding nine innings.

ED KONETCHY

Boston Braves first baseman who in consecutive games against the New York Giants in 1916 spoiled no-hit bids—and wound up with the Braves' only hit in each contest. In the second game of a September 28, 1916, doubleheader, the Giants' Ferdie Schupp had a no-hitter until Konetchy singled in the seventh inning. After Schupp nailed down a one-hit, 6-0 victory, rain postponed the next day's Braves-Giants game. In the opening game of the September 30 twin bill between the same clubs, New York's Rube Benton carried a no-hitter into the eighth inning before Konetchy delivered another single. Benton went on to win his one-hitter by a 4-0 score.

Benton's September 30 triumph was the Giants' 26th consecutive victory, a major league record. Boston won the second game of that day's doubleheader, though, ending New York's winning streak.

SANDY KOUFAX

The first pitcher to toss a no-hitter in a Cy Young Award-winning season— and he accomplished the no-hitter/Cy Young feat twice. The Los Angeles Dodgers' lefthander pitched an 8-0 no-hit game against San Francisco on

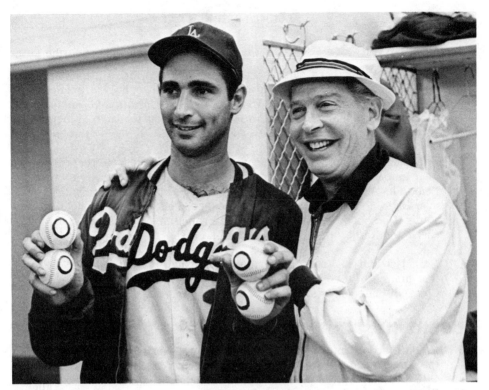

Dodgers ace Sandy Koufax posed with comedian Milton Berle on September 9, 1965, after pitching a perfect game against the Chicago Cubs en route to a 26-8 record and the National League Cy Young Award.

May 11, 1963, and went on to win the National League's '63 Cy Young honor with a 25-5 record, 306 strikeouts and a 1.88 earned-run average. In 1965, he hurled a 1-0 perfect game against the Cubs on September 9 en route to a 26-8 mark, 382 strikeouts, a 2.04 ERA and another Cy Young Award.

Houston's Mike Scott is the only other pitcher to throw a no-hitter and win the Cy Young Award in the same year. Scott held San Francisco hitless and struck out 13 Giants batters while winning, 2-0, on September 25, 1986. The Astros' righthander later was named the N.L.'s Cy Young winner for '86 after compiling a season record of 18-10, an N.L.-leading 2.22 earned-run average and a league-high 306 strikeouts.

JOE LAFATA

New York Giants first baseman-outfielder who appeared in one big-league game in 1948—Rex Barney's 2-0 no-hitter for Brooklyn. Brought up from Minneapolis of the American Association, Lafata was called upon as a pinch-hitter in the ninth inning of the Giants' September 9 game against the Dodgers and struck out against Barney.

Lafata appeared in 127 big-league games overall, playing 62 games for the Giants in 1947 and 64 for the National League club in 1949.

CHARLIE LEA

The only pitcher born outside the United States to throw a major league no-hitter outside the U.S. Lea, born in Orleans, France, in 1956, pitched a 4-0 no-hit victory for the Montreal Expos over the San Francisco Giants in the second game of a May 10, 1981, National League doubleheader at Montreal's Olympic Stadium.

Only four other pitchers born outside the United States have recorded complete-game no-hitters in the majors: Tony Mullane (Cork, Ireland, 1859), Louisville, American Association, 1882; Dick Fowler (Toronto, Ontario, Canada, 1921), Philadelphia, American League, 1945; Juan Marichal (Laguna Verde, Dominican Republic, 1938), San Francisco, N.L., 1963; Bert Blyleven (Zeist, the Netherlands, 1951), Texas, A.L., 1977.

Francisco Barrios, born in Hermosillo, Mexico, in 1953, pitched the final four innings of a combined no-hitter with John (Blue Moon) Odom for the Chicago White Sox in a 1976 A.L. game against the Oakland A's.

HUBERT (DUTCH) LEONARD

Boston Red Sox pitcher who fired a no-hitter against St. Louis the day after the Browns drove him from the mound in the first inning. On August 29, 1916, Leonard started the first game of a doubleheader but retired only one Browns batter. He allowed two hits, two runs and a walk, hit a batter and uncorked a wild pitch. The next day, Leonard allowed only two baserunners —both on walks—and held St. Louis hitless in a 4-0 triumph.

When Leonard was knocked out of the August 29 game, he was relieved by 21-year-old Babe Ruth (who was on the way to a 23-victory season for the Red Sox).

SAL MAGLIE

The losing pitcher in Don Larsen's perfect game in the 1956 World Series, but the last man to pitch a no-hitter in the majors prior to Larsen. Larsen pitched his 2-0 Series gem for the New York Yankees against the Brooklyn Dodgers on October 8, 1956. Thirteen days earlier, in the final week of the National League season, Maglie had fashioned a no-hit game against Philadelphia as the Dodgers downed the Phillies, 5-0.

Three other pitchers have tossed big-league no-hitters and then absorbed the loss in the majors' next no-hit game. Jim Tobin of the Boston Braves held the Brooklyn Dodgers hitless on April 27, 1944; in the big leagues' next no-hitter, Tobin was the loser when the Cincinnati Reds' Clyde Shoun baffled the Braves in a May 15, 1944, game. Cleveland's Bob Feller threw a no-hit game against the Detroit Tigers on July 1, 1951; 11 days later, the New York Yankees' Allie Reynolds pitched a no-hitter against Feller and the Indians. And Bo Belinsky of the Los Angeles Angels stopped the Baltimore Orioles without a hit on May 5, 1962; in the major leagues' next no-hit game, Belinsky and the Angels lost to Earl Wilson of the Boston Red Sox on June 26, 1962.

BILL McCAHAN

The losing pitcher when Don Black of the Cleveland Indians pitched a no-hitter against the Philadelphia A's on July 10, 1947, he proceeded to throw the major leagues' next no-hit game eight weeks later. Working against Washington on September 3, McCahan faced only 28 batters in his gem—the Senators' lone baserunner was the result of an error—and pitched the A's to a 3-0 American League victory.

Hugh (One Arm) Daily and Mal Eason are the only other major leaguers to be a losing pitcher in an opponent's no-hit game and then hurl the big leagues' next no-hitter. On September 13, 1883, Cleveland's Daily held Philadelphia hitless in a National League game after he had lost the majors' previous no-hit game (pitched by Hoss Radbourn of Providence seven weeks earlier). And on July 20, 1906, Brooklyn's Eason pitched an N.L. no-hitter against the St. Louis Cardinals 2½ months after he had been the losing pitcher in the big leagues' last hitless game (turned in by John Lush of the Phillies).

MIKE McCORMICK

San Francisco pitcher who allowed a hit during his June 12, 1959, outing against Philadelphia, but was still credited with a no-hit game against the Phillies—a five-inning no-hitter. Entering the bottom of the sixth inning, the Phils not only trailed the Giants, 3-0, they had failed to collect a hit off McCormick. The Phillies loaded the bases in the sixth, though, with McCormick walking two batters and yielding a single to Richie Ashburn. However, rain prevented the inning from being finished and, under the rules, records reverted to the last completed inning, the fifth. And McCormick had an abbreviated no-hitter.

MILWAUKEE BRAVES

National League club that was involved in six no-hitters (all played in Milwaukee) during its 13-season history and won all six games—despite being no-hit victims in two of the contests. Three Milwaukee pitchers accounted for four of the no-hitters, with Jim Wilson (1954), Lew Burdette (1960) and Warren Spahn (1960, 1961) tossing hitless games. In 1956, Cincinnati's Johnny Klippstein, Hershell Freeman and Joe Black held the Braves without a hit for nine innings, but Milwaukee collected a hit in the 10th and went on to win in 11 innings. In 1959, Pittsburgh's Harvey Haddix pitched 12 perfect innings against Milwaukee, only to lose on one hit in 13 innings.

TONY MULLANE

Pitching for Louisville of the American Association in an 1882 game, he hurled the major leagues' first no-hitter from a 50-foot distance. The length from the pitcher's box to home plate had been increased from 45 to 50 feet effective with the beginning of the 1881 season, but it wasn't until late in the 1882 season—September 11—that a no-hit game was pitched from the new distance, with Mullane achieving the feat in a 2-0 triumph over Cincinnati.

GEORGE MULLIN

The only man in major league history to toss a no-hitter on his birthday. Mullin, of the Detroit Tigers, turned 32 years old on July 4, 1912, the day he held the St. Louis Browns hitless in the second game of a doubleheader. Mullin's 7-0 gem was the first no-hit game thrown by a Tigers pitcher.

GRAIG NETTLES

The player who has appeared in the most major league games without participating in a no-hit game. From 1967 through 1986, Nettles had played in a total of 2,508 games for the Minnesota Twins, Cleveland Indians, New York Yankees and San Diego Padres, but his name had yet to appear in a no-hit box score.

The only other major leaguers to play in 2,300 or more games without appearing in a no-hitter are Charlie Gehringer (2,323) and Jimmie Foxx (2,317).

NEW YORK METS

The major league team that currently has gone the longest time without holding another club hitless in a game. The Mets, who entered the National League in 1962, have allowed at least one hit in every game in their 25-year history.

Four other existing big-league clubs—the San Diego Padres (born in 1969), Milwaukee Brewers (1970), Seattle Mariners (1977) and Toronto Blue Jays (1977)—have never held another team hitless.

Among teams with at least one no-hitter in their history, the Boston Red Sox currently have gone the longest time without holding an opponent hitless. Dave Morehead tossed Boston's last no-hit game on September 16, 1965, against the Cleveland Indians.

NEW YORK YANKEES

The big-league club that currently has gone the longest time without being victimized by a no-hitter. The last time the Yankees were held hitless was on September 20, 1958, by Hoyt Wilhelm of the Baltimore Orioles.

The Seattle Mariners are the only existing major league team never to have gone hitless in a game. The Mariners entered the American League in 1977.

MILT PAPPAS

Having retired the first 26 San Diego batters in a September 2, 1972, game, this Chicago Cubs pitcher had a one-ball, two-strike count on Padres pinch-hitter Larry Stahl as he attempted to nail down a perfect game. But Pappas proceeded to throw three straight balls in the two-out, ninth-inning situation. After walking Stahl, Pappas induced another pinch-hitter, Garry Jestadt, to pop out. While denied a perfect game, Pappas had completed an 8-0 no-hitter.

GEORGE (KEWPIE) PENNINGTON

Pitcher who made his only big-league appearance in the April 14, 1917, game in which Eddie Cicotte of the Chicago White Sox pitched a no-hitter. Working in relief for St. Louis, Pennington hurled a scoreless ninth inning as the Browns suffered an 11-0 trouncing.

Shortly after his stint in Cicotte's no-hit game, the 20-year-old Pennington was released to Newark of the International League.

PHILADELPHIA PHILLIES

National League club that went 57 consecutive seasons (1907 through 1963) without getting a no-hit performance from a member of its staff—a record span of no-hit futility in the major leagues. Actually, the Phils' no-hit failure lasted for more than 58 years in terms of the calendar date—from John Lush's no-hitter against Brooklyn on May 1, 1906, until Jim Bunning's perfect game against the New York Mets on June 21, 1964.

LEE RICHMOND

Retiring all 27 Cleveland batters he faced in a June 12, 1880, National League game, Worcester's Richmond hurled the big leagues' first perfect game and accounted for the majors' first no-hitter by a lefthanded pitcher. Worcester defeated Cleveland, 1-0.

PETE ROSE

The most recent of four players to appear in a National League-leading eight no-hitters. Rose, who played in all eight no-hit games while a member of the Cincinnati Reds, appeared in no-hitters pitched by the Reds' Jim Maloney (1965, two; 1969), George Culver (1968) and Tom Seaver (1978), and in hitless games hurled against Cincinnati by Ken Johnson of the Houston Colts (1964), Don Wilson of the Houston Astros (1969) and Rick Wise of the Philadelphia Phillies (1971).

Pee Wee Reese, Johnny Callison and Hank Aaron also participated in eight N.L. no-hit games.

AMOS RUSIE

The youngest pitcher in major league history to throw a no-hitter of nine or more innings. Rusie was just two months past his 20th birthday when, pitching for the New York Giants in a July 31, 1891, National League game, he beat Brooklyn, 6-0, without allowing a hit.

The youngest no-hit pitcher in modern big-league history was the Philadelphia Phillies' John Lush, who was about seven months past his 20th birthday when he hurled his gem on May 1, 1906. He also defeated Brooklyn, 6-0, in an N.L. contest.

Only four other major leaguers pitched no-hitters before reaching age 21: John Montgomery Ward, Providence, N.L., 1880 (perfect game); Richard Burns, Cincinnati, Union Association, 1884; Matt Kilroy, Baltimore, American Association, 1886, and Nick Maddox, Pittsburgh, N.L., 1907.

NOLAN RYAN

Holds the strikeout record for a nine-inning no-hit game in the majors. Pitching for the California Angels on July 15, 1973, Ryan held Detroit hitless and struck out 17 Tiger batters en route to a 6-0 triumph.

After nine innings of a June 14, 1965, Reds-Mets game, Cincinnati's Jim Maloney had 15 strikeouts while holding New York hitless in a 0-0 deadlock. Maloney struck out two more Mets in the 10th inning before New York's Johnny Lewis dashed the righthander's no-hit hopes in the top of the 11th by blasting a leadoff, game-winning home run. Maloney then recorded his 18th and final strikeout of the game (prior to yielding his second and last hit of the contest). Mets reliever Larry Bearnarth kept Cincinnati in check in the bottom of the 11th as New York hung on for a 1-0 victory.

ST. LOUIS BROWNS

The only major league team to hold an opposing club hitless on consecutive days. On May 5, 1917, Browns pitcher Ernie Koob hurled a 1-0 no-hitter against the Chicago White Sox. The next day, in the second game of a doubleheader, St. Louis' Bob Groom stopped the Sox without a hit in a 3-0 decision.

The no-hitters were the second and third involving the Browns and White Sox in a little more than three weeks. On April 14, Chicago's Eddie Cicotte had pitched an 11-0 no-hit game against the Browns at St. Louis' Sportsman's Park, also site of the no-hitters thrown by Koob and Groom.

ST. LOUIS CARDINALS

Club that was victimized by Cincinnati Reds pitcher Hod Eller's no-hitter on May 11, 1919—and then didn't suffer no-hit ignominy again for 40 consecutive seasons, 1920 through 1959, a record span. In fact, in calendar-date terms, it was 41 years and four days after Eller's gem that the Cardinals next went hitless, with Don Cardwell of the Chicago Cubs tossing a no-hitter against the Cards in the second game of a May 15, 1960, doubleheader.

When New York's Johnny Lewis (above, circling the bases) hit a leadoff home run in the 11th inning of a June 14, 1965, game against Cincinnati, he ruined the day for Reds righthander Jim Maloney (left), who had not allowed a hit up to that point in a 0-0 nail-biter.

Houston Astros righthander Mike Scott had two reasons to celebrate in 1986 after becoming the first pitcher in major league history to pitch a title-clinching no-hitter.

RAY SCHALK

He caught the most no-hitters in big-league history, four. Schalk was on the receiving end of no-hit games pitched by Jim Scott and Joe Benz (both in 1914), Eddie Cicotte (1917) and Charley Robertson (1922, a perfect game), all of the Chicago White Sox.

MIKE SCOTT

The only pitcher in major league history to toss a title-clinching no-hitter. Entering the 1986 season, a no-hit game had not been pitched in a contest that decided a divisional race, league championship or World Series crown. But on September 25, 1986, Scott, pitching for Houston on a day when the

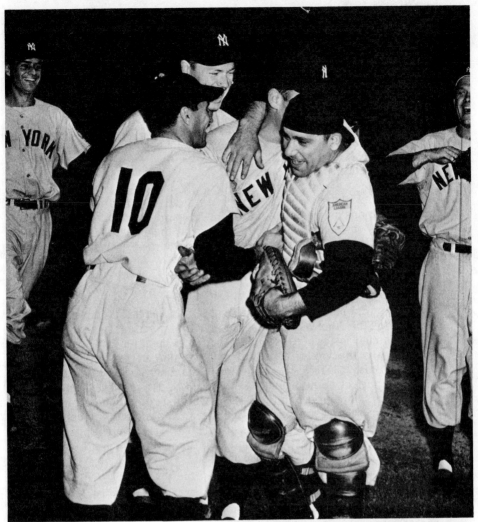

New York righthander Allie Reynolds was the center of attention in 1951 when he pitched no-hitters against Cleveland (above) and Boston, the latter assuring the Yankees of at least a tie in the American League pennant race.

Astros' "magic number" for clinching the National League West title was at "1," held San Francisco hitless and struck out 13 Giants. The drama-packed 2-0 triumph at Houston's Astrodome eliminated the Cincinnati Reds—the Astros' last mathematical threat—from West Division title contention.

Allie Reynolds of the New York Yankees is the only other big-league pitcher to hurl a no-hitter on the day his team clinched a championship. Reynolds' 8-0 no-hit game at Yankee Stadium on September 28, 1951, did not sew up a title, though; instead, the gem against the Boston Red Sox in the first game of a doubleheader assured the Yankees of at least a tie for first place in the American League pennant race. In the nightcap, the Yanks clinched the A.L. flag with an 11-3 triumph.

SEPTEMBER 20

The date on which the most no-hit games of nine or more innings have occurred in the major leagues. Six no-hitters have been thrown on September 20, the first achieved by Larry Corcoran of Chicago's National League club in 1882 and the last accomplished by Bob Moose of the Pittsburgh Pirates in a 1969 N.L. game. Other pitchers hurling no-hit games on September 20: James Callahan, Chicago, American League, 1902; Nick Maddox, Pittsburgh, N.L., 1907; Frank Smith, Chicago, A.L., 1908, and Hoyt Wilhelm, Baltimore, A.L., 1958.

Five no-hitters have been pitched on April 30, May 15 and September 18. Some historians may contend that six no-hit games have been thrown in the big leagues on May 15—the sixth coming in the Federal League in 1915. However, The Sporting News does not recognize the Federal League, which operated in 1914 and 1915, as a major league.

BOB SKINNER

Outfielder who played in two no-hit games, one as a teammate of a no-hit pitcher and the other as a member of the victimized team—and, startlingly, Skinner's club lost when its pitcher hurled a no-hitter and his team won when it was the victim of no-hit pitching. Skinner was Pittsburgh's left fielder on May 26, 1959, when Pirates lefthander Harvey Haddix hurled a 12-inning perfect game against the Milwaukee Braves. The Pirates ended up 1-0 losers, though, when the Braves scored a run on one hit in the 13th inning. On April 23, 1964, Skinner was Cincinnati's left fielder when the Reds were held hitless by Houston Colts pitcher Ken Johnson. Despite Johnson's performance, Cincinnati prevailed, 1-0, thanks to two ninth-inning Colt errors (one of which was made by Johnson).

WARREN SPAHN

The first big-league pitcher to throw no-hitters in consecutive years. Spahn was 39 years old and in his 16th season with the Braves when he spun his first no-hit game in the majors on September 16, 1960, against the Philadelphia Phillies. Then, five days past his 40th birthday, Milwaukee's Spahn hurled hitless ball against the San Francisco Giants on April 28, 1961.

Sandy Koufax of the Los Angeles Dodgers matched Spahn's feat by pitching no-hitters in 1962 and 1963, surpassed the accomplishment by fashioning another no-hitter in 1964 and then ran his consecutive-year streak of no-hitters to four in 1965 with a perfect game. Steve Busby threw no-hitters in 1973 and 1974 for the Kansas City Royals, while Nolan Ryan, the only other major leaguer to hurl no-hit games in consecutive seasons, pitched two no-hitters for California in 1973 and unfurled no-hit games for the Angels in 1974 and 1975.

BILL STONEMAN

Pitcher who fired the majors' first complete-game no-hitter hurled outside the United States, a 7-0 triumph for the Montreal Expos over the New York Mets in the first game of an October 2, 1972, doubleheader at Montreal's Jarry Park. The no-hit game was the second in the big leagues for Stoneman, who had held the Philadelphia Phillies hitless in a 7-0 victory on April 17, 1969, at Philadelphia's Connie Mack Stadium.

Besides Stoneman's gem in 1972, one other major league no-hitter has been thrown outside the U.S. That occurred on May 10, 1981, at Montreal's Olympic Stadium as the Expos' Charlie Lea baffled the San Francisco Giants by a 4-0 score in the second game of a doubleheader.

JOHNNY VANDER MEER

The first man to pitch two no-hitters in the big leagues in one season—and he accomplished the feat with a flair, hurling *consecutive* no-hit games. Vander Meer, of the Cincinnati Reds, held the Boston Bees hitless in a June 11, 1938, game and then notched a no-hitter on June 15 against the Brooklyn Dodgers. He finished the '38 season with a 15-10 record.

Also throwing two no-hitters in the majors in one season were Allie Reynolds, Virgil Trucks, Jim Maloney and Nolan Ryan. Reynolds turned the trick in 1951 for the New York Yankees (his second no-hitter coming in his final start of the regular season and giving him a 17-8 season mark), Trucks achieved the feat in 1952 for the Detroit Tigers (his second no-hit game proving his final victory of the year in a 5-19 season), Maloney did it in 1965 for the Cincinnati Reds (en route to a 20-9 mark) and Ryan accomplished his no-hit "double" in 1973 for the California Angels (on the way to a 21-16 record).

Maloney's 1965 no-hitters came in a 10-inning complete-game effort (which he won) and in an 11-inning contest (which he lost) wherein he hurled hitless ball through 10 innings before allowing two hits in the 11th.

VETERANS STADIUM

The Philadelphia Phillies' home ball park and the only current National League stadium in which a no-hitter has never been thrown. Veterans Stadium opened in 1971.

Three American League parks in current use have yet to be no-hit sites. They are the Metrodome in Minneapolis (the Minnesota Twins' home opened in 1982), the Seattle Mariners' Kingdome (1977) and the Toronto Blue Jays' Exhibition Stadium (1977).

MIKE WARREN

The last rookie to hurl a no-hitter in the major leagues. Working for Oakland in a September 29, 1983, game, the 22-year-old Warren pitched no-hit ball against the Chicago White Sox as the A's posted a 3-0 victory.

WASHINGTON SENATORS

Club that went an American League-record 29 consecutive seasons, 1918 through 1946, without being victimized by a no-hitter. Boston's Ernie Shore, replacing Red Sox starting pitcher Babe Ruth when Ruth was ejected after issuing a game-opening base on balls, pitched perfect ball the rest of the way in a June 23, 1917, contest against Washington. It wasn't until September 3, 1947, that the Senators were again held hitless, this time by Bill McCahan of the Philadelphia A's. Shore's victory, coming in the first game of a doubleheader, was by a 4-0 score; McCahan won, 3-0.

VIC WERTZ

Detroit outfielder whose two-out home run in the bottom of the ninth inning on May 15, 1952, enabled Tiger teammate Virgil Trucks to post a 1-0 no-hit victory over the Washington Senators. Wertz's dramatic smash came against Bob Porterfield.

Seven other players have slugged home runs in 1-0 no-hit games:

Date	No-Hit Pitcher, Club	Home Run Hitter	Inn.
May 15, 1944	Clyde Shoun, Cin.	Chuck Aleno	5
April 30, 1946	Bob Feller, Cleve.	Frankie Hayes	9
July 12, 1951	Allie Reynolds, N.Y., A.L.	Gene Woodling	7
Sept. 20, 1958	Hoyt Wilhelm, Balt.	Gus Triandos	7
June 14, 1965	Jim Maloney, Cin.	*Johnny Lewis	11
Aug. 19, 1965	Jim Maloney, Cin.	Leo Cardenas	10
Sept. 17, 1968	Gaylord Perry, S.F.	Ron Hunt	1

*Of the eight players whose homers have provided the only runs in 1-0 no-hit games, only Lewis connected for the team victimized by the no-hitter. Playing for the New York Mets, Lewis socked an 11th-inning homer off Cincinnati's Maloney after the Reds' pitcher had hurled hitless ball through 10 innings (thereby gaining credit for a no-hitter).

The late-inning homers by the Indians' Hayes, the Mets' Lewis and the Reds' Cardenas all came in the top half of the innings indicated.

Cincinnati's Aleno hit only one other homer in his major league career.

EARL WILSON

The last American League pitcher to hurl a no-hitter and hit a home run in the same game. Wilson, of the Boston Red Sox, stopped the Los Angeles Angels without a hit on June 26, 1962, and socked a bases-empty home run off Bo Belinsky in a 2-0 decision.

RICK WISE

The last major league pitcher to slug a home run during his no-hit performance—and the only pitcher to hit two homers while recording a no-hitter. The Philadelphia Phillies' Wise held the Cincinnati Reds hitless in a 4-0 National League triumph on June 23, 1971, and drilled a two-run homer off Ross Grimsley and a bases-empty shot off Clay Carroll.

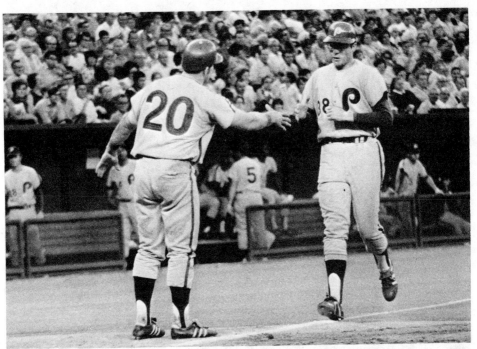

Philadelphia's Rick Wise, not one to take chances, embellished his 1971 no-hitter against Cincinnati with a pair of home runs and three RBIs in a 4-0 victory.

MIKE WITT

The only pitcher in major league history to hurl a perfect game of nine or more innings in his club's last game of the season. Witt, of the California Angels, did not allow a Texas Rangers batter to reach base on the final day of the 1984 regular season.

Harry Vickers of the Philadelphia A's pitched perfect ball against the Washington Senators in a five-inning game played on the last day of the 1907 season. However, many historians do not recognize no-hitters of fewer than nine innings.

A complete list of major league no-hit performances—including those of fewer than nine innings—that have occurred on the last day of a team's season:

*Oct. 4, 1891, Ted Breitenstein, St. Louis, vs. Louisville, A.A., 8-0
Oct. 15, 1892, Charles (Bumpus) Jones, Cincinnati, vs. Pittsburgh, N.L., 7-1
**Oct. 15, 1892, Jack Stivetts, Boston, vs. Washington, N.L., 6-0
**Oct. 5, 1907, H. Vickers, Phil., vs. Washington, A.L., 4-0 (perfect game)
Sept. 28, 1975, Vida Blue (5 inn.), Glenn Abbott (1 inn.), Paul Lindblad
        (1 inn.), Rollie Fingers (2 inn.), Oakland, vs. Calif., A.L., 5-0
Sept. 30, 1984, Mike Witt, California, vs. Texas, A.L., 1-0 (perfect game)

*First game of a doubleheader
**Five-inning second game of a doubleheader

California righthander Mike Witt saved his best for last in 1984, becoming the first pitcher in big-league history to throw a perfect game of nine or more innings on the final day of the regular season.

CY YOUNG

The oldest pitcher to toss a major league no-hitter of nine innings or more. Young was three months past his 41st birthday when he hurled an 8-0 no-hit game for the Boston Red Sox against the New York Highlanders on June 30, 1908.

The only other 40-year-old pitcher to record a no-hitter in the majors was the Milwaukee Braves' Warren Spahn, who had just turned 40 when he stopped the San Francisco Giants without a hit in a 1961 game.

ZERO

The number of times triple plays have been made in no-hit-game history.

138

WILLIE AIKENS

The only player to hit two home runs in one game *twice* in the same World Series. Playing for the Kansas City Royals against the Philadelphia Phillies in the 1980 Series, first baseman Aikens rifled two homers off Bob Walk in Game 1 (the Royals lost, 7-6) and connected off Larry Christenson and Dickie Noles in Game 4 (Kansas City won, 5-3).

MIKE ANDREWS

Oakland player whose fielding lapses prompted his "firing" by A's Owner Charlie Finley during the 1973 World Series. Andrews, signed by the A's in August of '73 after his release by the Chicago White Sox, made two costly errors against the New York Mets in the 12th inning of Game 2 of the '73 fall classic, and Finley announced the next day that he was deactivating him.

Supporting Cast:
● **Willie Mays.** His 12th-inning single in Game 2 at Oakland broke a 6-6 tie

and ignited a four-run Mets outburst. The hit was the last for Mays in his major league career.

● **John Milner.** With the bases loaded later in the Mets' 12th, Milner hit a ground ball to Andrews at second base. Andrews, who had entered the game in the eighth inning as a pinch-hitter, let the ball get through his legs and two runs scored. Mets 9, A's 6.

● **Jerry Grote.** Batting after Milner, he also grounded to Andrews. The A's infielder made a poor throw to first baseman Gene Tenace, pulling him off the bag, and another run scored. While the A's mounted a rally in the bottom of the 12th—they scored once and had the bases loaded with only one out—the Mets hung on for a 10-7 triumph.

Finley tried to place Andrews on the disabled list, citing a shoulder injury, and even got the veteran player to sign a statement saying he was hurting physically. The day after Finley instructed Andrews to pack his bags, Finley himself received a directive. Commissioner Bowie Kuhn ordered Finley to reinstate the 30-year-old Andrews, much to the delight of Andrews' teammates, who had reacted angrily to Finley's move. And, later, the commissioner fined the A's boss.

Andrews, who had batted .308 and fielded flawlessly in part-time duty for the Boston Red Sox in the 1967 World Series, was back in uniform for Game 4 of the '73 Series. Called upon as a pinch-hitter in that contest, he received a rousing greeting from New York fans before grounding out. The at-bat proved his last in the big leagues.

A's Manager Dick Williams, who was in the process of guiding the A's to their second straight Series championship, told his players before Game 3 that he would not be back in 1974. While Williams reportedly had tired of Finley's interference long before the Andrews affair and may have intended to resign anyway, the "firing" of Andrews seemingly ensured the manager's departure.

JIMMY ARCHER

The first man to play for both American League and National League teams in World Series competition. Archer caught one game for the Detroit Tigers in the 1907 Series against the Chicago Cubs; in 1910, he played three games for the Cubs (one at first base, two behind the plate) against the Philadelphia A's in the fall classic.

HANK BAUER, GEORGE STALLINGS

The only World Series managers who never lost a game in the fall classic. Each managed in only one Series, with Bauer guiding the Baltimore Orioles to a four games-to-none rout of the Los Angeles Dodgers in 1966 and Stallings directing the Boston Braves to a four-game sweep of the Philadelphia A's in 1914.

The 1914 Braves were the first team to win a World Series in four games.

Oakland second baseman Mike Andrews made two costly 12th-inning errors in Game 2 of the 1973 World Series that resulted in embarrassment on the field and face-covering dejection in the A's dugout.

(The 1907 Chicago Cubs were the first club to go unbeaten in a Series, though, winning four games and tying one against the Detroit Tigers.)

JOHNNY BENCH

Victim of an Oakland A's ruse in the 1972 World Series. With Cincinnati ahead, 1-0, in the eighth inning of Game 3 and Reds runners on third and second base with one out, A's reliever Rollie Fingers had a 3-2 count on Reds cleanup hitter Bench. At this juncture, Oakland Manager Dick Williams went to the mound. With first base open, the forthcoming strategy was obvious—or so it seemed. Bench, who had led the National League in 1972 with 40 home runs and 125 runs batted in (and won N.L. Most Valuable Player honors), would not be given a hittable pitch in this situation. Instead, the A's would pitch to first baseman Tony Perez. After Williams gestured toward first base and headed toward the dugout, A's catcher Gene Tenace dutifully extended his mitt for an intentional fourth ball. One problem, though: As Fingers let go of what virtually everyone assumed was "ball four," Tenace stepped back behind the plate and the ball dipped into the strike zone. Bench was transfixed—and an embarrassed strikeout victim.

Following the trickster antics against Bench that resulted in the called third strike, the A's did issue an intentional walk—to Perez. Denis Menke then fouled out, ending the inning, but the Reds held on for a 1-0 triumph at Oakland.

BOSTON, PHILADELPHIA

Cities represented in the 1914 and 1915 World Series—but the matchups for the two fall classics were entirely different. In 1914, the National League's Boston Braves downed the American League's Philadelphia A's in the Series. A year later, the Braves dropped to second place in the N.L. and the A's plummeted to last place in the A.L.—but the Philadelphia Phillies succeeded the Braves as N.L. champions and the Boston Red Sox supplanted the A's as A.L. titlists. In the continuation of the Boston-Philadelphia rivalry, the Red Sox prevailed over the Phils in the 1915 Series.

Oddly, in neither 1914 nor 1915 did the Boston club play its World Series home games in its own ball park. In the '14 Series, the Braves played their home contests at the Red Sox's Fenway Park, citing it as a more attractive facility than their South End Grounds. In '15, the Red Sox opted to play their Series home games at the Braves' new park (Braves Field) because its seating capacity was superior to Fenway's.

LOU BOUDREAU

The last player-manager to appear in—and win—a World Series. Boudreau played the entire 1948 Series at shortstop for Cleveland and guided the Indians to a four games-to-two triumph over the Boston Braves.

Managers who won World Series in which they made at least one playing appearance:

Year—Player, Manager, Club	Pos.	G	AB-H	B.A.
1903—Jimmy Collins, Boston, A.L.	3B	8	36-9	.250
1906—Fielder Jones, Chicago, A.L.	CF	6	21-2	.095
1907—Frank Chance, Chicago, N.L.	1B	4	14-3	.214
1908—Frank Chance, Chicago, N.L.	1B	5	19-8	.421
1909—Fred Clarke, Pittsburgh, N.L.	LF	7	19-4	.211
1912—Jake Stahl, Boston, A.L.	1B	8	32-9	.281
1915—Bill Carrigan, Boston, A.L.	C	1	2-0	.000
1916—Bill Carrigan, Boston, A.L.	C	1	3-2	.667
1920—Tris Speaker, Cleveland, A.L.	CF	7	25-8	.320
1924—Bucky Harris, Washington, A.L.	2B	7	33-11	.333
1926—Rogers Hornsby, St. Louis, N.L.	2B	7	28-7	.250
1933—Bill Terry, New York, N.L.	1B	5	22-6	.273
1934—Frank Frisch, St. Louis, N.L.	2B	7	31-6	.194
1948—Lou Boudreau, Cleveland, A.L.	SS	6	22-6	.273

GEORGE BRETT

The only player in big-league history to slug three home runs in a postseason game that his club lost. Brett hit bases-empty homers for the Kansas City Royals against the Yankees' Jim (Catfish) Hunter in the first, third and fifth innings of Game 3 of the 1978 American League Championship Series. New York overcame Brett's performance, though, and notched a 6-5 victory.

Only three other major leaguers have hit three homers in a postseason game—the Yankees' Babe Ruth (who accomplished the feat in Game 4 of the 1926 World Series and again in Game 4 of the 1928 classic), the Yanks' Reggie Jackson (Game 6 of the 1977 World Series) and the Pittsburgh Pirates' Bob Robertson (Game 2 of the 1971 National League Championship Series).

MARK BROUHARD

Outfielder who played in only one postseason game in his major league career—an American League Championship Series game in which he went 3 for 4, drove in three runs and scored four times (the latter feat tying the Championship Series record). Playing left field for Milwaukee against California in Game 4 of the 1982 A.L. title series, Brouhard singled, doubled and homered as the Brewers won, 9-5, and tied the best-of-five playoff at two games apiece.

Brouhard, who had not seen action for the Brewers in almost a month, was penciled into the lineup only because of an injury to outfielder Ben Oglivie.

Milwaukee, which had lost the first two games of the series, beat the Angels, 4-3, in Game 5 and reigned as the A.L. champion.

BUSCH STADIUM TARPAULIN

An unlikely central figure in the 1985 National League Championship Series —and nearly a tragic interloper. As the St. Louis Cardinals worked out in their home ball park before Game 4 of the '85 N.L. pennant playoff, a light rain began to fall. The batting cage was removed and the Cardinals' Vince Coleman, coming off a season in which he established a big-league rookie record with 110 stolen bases, started walking toward the dugout when he paused and turned to flip his glove—just as the tarpaulin-spreading device was activated. A mechanized, 150-foot-long aluminum cylinder began rolling across the infield to position the tarpaulin, and the tube ran across Coleman's left foot and up his leg. The 24-year-old left fielder fell to the ground, crying out in pain. Once Coleman was extricated and examined, observers' worst fears were *not* realized: As potentially career-threatening as the accident appeared, Coleman had suffered no lasting injuries, only contusions and a bone chip on the knee. But the suddenly hobbled Coleman, the catalyst in St. Louis' speed-oriented offense, was through for postseason play in '85.

Tito Landrum took over for Coleman in left field that night and, by game's end, was himself in the spotlight. Landrum went 4 for 5 and drove in three runs in Game 4 as the Cardinals pummeled the Dodgers, 12-2, and deadlocked the Championship Series. The Cards advanced to the '85 World Series, and Landrum continued to fill in admirably—he batted .360 in seven games against the Kansas City Royals.

DONIE BUSH, GABBY HARTNETT, EDDIE SAWYER

The only men to have lost all World Series games in which they managed. Each manager was at the helm in only one Series—and was victimized by a sweep. Bush's Pittsburgh Pirates fell to the New York Yankees in four games in 1927, Hartnett's Chicago Cubs dropped four straight to the Yankees in 1938 and Sawyer's Philadelphia Phillies were vanquished by the Yanks in four consecutive games in 1950.

CINCINNATI REDS

The last team whose World Series participants were all first-time performers in the fall classic. No Reds player who appeared in the 1961 World Series had seen Series action (for *any* club) previously, and the experience-shy Cincinnati team lost to the New York Yankees, four games to one, in the '61 Series.

Other teams whose World Series players were all first-time participants in the classic: Boston Red Sox and Pittsburgh Pirates, 1903 (first-time status was automatic since the Series was introduced that year); Philadelphia A's and New York Giants, 1905 (the year that the second Series was played); Chicago Cubs, 1906; Detroit Tigers, 1907; Red Sox, 1912, and St. Louis Browns, 1944.

CINCINNATI REDS

Club that compiled the best cumulative won-lost record in the major leagues in 1981—but didn't qualify for postseason play. A 50-day players strike inter-

When St. Louis rookie sensation Vince Coleman was attacked by a Busch Stadium tarpaulin before Game 4 of the 1985 N.L. Championship Series, he had to be removed from the field on a stretcher and limped through the remainder of the postseason on crutches.

rupted the '81 season and resulted in the adoption of a split-season format, with first-half divisional winners (those teams leading their divisions at the time of the June 12 walkout) to face the champions of the second-half race (which began with the post-strike resumption of play on August 10) in a best-of-five divisional title series. The extra tier of playoffs proved disastrous for the Reds, who finished the first half with a 35-21 record, one-half game behind Los Angeles, and ended the second half with a 31-21 record, 1½ games behind Houston. While the Dodgers (63-47 overall) and Astros (61-49) wound up battling for the West Division crown and a berth in the National League Championship Series, the Reds sat at home—despite compiling the majors' top overall mark in '81, 66-42.

CLARK'S DRAMATIC SHOT

With his team ahead in the best-of-seven 1985 National League Championship Series, three games to two, but trailing Los Angeles by a 5-4 score in the ninth inning of Game 6, St. Louis' Jack Clark approached the plate. There were two out and Cardinals perched on second and third base. While first base was open, Dodgers Manager Tom Lasorda elected to take his chances with cleanup hitter Clark, who had hit 22 home runs and driven in 87 runs during the regular season. Clark jumped on the first pitch, belting the ball into the left-field bleachers. The three-run, pennant-deciding blow in the October 16 game sent shock waves through the Dodger Stadium crowd. Cardinals 7, Dodgers 5.

Supporting Cast:

• **Ken Dayley.** Relief pitcher who retired the Dodgers in order in the ninth inning, nailing down the N.L. pennant for St. Louis.

• **Mike Marshall.** Los Angeles outfielder whose eighth-inning homer off Cardinals reliever Todd Worrell had broken a 4-4 tie. Worrell turned out to be the winning pitcher.

• **Willie McGee.** St. Louis outfielder who, with the Dodgers ahead, 4-1, in the seventh inning, rifled a two-run single off Dodgers starter Orel Hershiser (and subsequently scored the tying run). In the ninth inning, he kept St. Louis' hopes alive with a one-out single and a steal of second base. Ozzie Smith's walk and Tommy Herr's groundout put runners on second and third with two men out and Clark coming up.

• **Tom Niedenfuer.** While he had struck out Clark when working out of a seventh-inning jam, Niedenfuer yielded Clark's momentous homer in the ninth. Charged with the defeat, Niedenfuer also was the Dodgers' loser in the previous game of the N.L. playoffs.

• **Ozzie Smith.** His seventh-inning triple off Niedenfuer, who had just come in to pitch, scored McGee and tied the game, 4-4. Two days earlier, the Cardinal shortstop's ninth-inning homer off Niedenfuer had given St. Louis a 3-2 victory in Game 5.

• **Andy Van Slyke.** When Lasorda decided to have righthanded reliever Niedenfuer pitch to righthanded batter Clark in the ninth inning, it was the lefthanded-hitting Van Slyke (13 homers, 55 RBIs in the regular season) who was on deck.

Jack Clark's dramatic ninth-inning home run in Game 6 of the 1985 National League Championship Series brought the Cardinals to their feet and sent the Los Angeles Dodgers packing for a long winter.

JACK COOMBS

The first man to pitch for both American League and National League teams in World Series play. Coombs hurled for the A.L.'s Philadelphia A's in the 1910 and 1911 Series and he pitched for the N.L.'s Brooklyn Dodgers in the 1916 classic.

STEVE CRAWFORD

Boston Red Sox relief pitcher who failed to win a game during the 1986 American League season, finishing with a 0-2 record while making 40 appearances, but was credited with the victory in Game 5 of the '86 A.L. Championship Series against the California Angels and then was the winning pitcher in Game 2 of the '86 World Series against the New York Mets.

MIKE CUELLAR, TOM SEAVER

Pitchers who started against each other in a World Series game in a year in which both won the Cy Young Award. Baltimore's Cuellar, who shared the 1969 American League pitching honor with Denny McLain of the Detroit Tigers, and '69 N.L. honoree Seaver of the New York Mets were the starting pitchers in Games 1 and 4 of the 1969 Series. Cuellar tossed a six-hitter in the opener and defeated Seaver and the Mets, 4-1; Seaver copped Game 4, a 2-1,

147

10-inning decision in which he allowed six hits and beat Dick Hall (one of three Orioles who worked in relief of Cuellar).

The only other World Series in which the season's Cy Young honorees started against each other was the 1968 classic, in which N.L. winner Bob Gibson of the St. Louis Cardinals and Detroit's McLain (an outright winner this time in the A.L.) dueled in Games 1 and 4. Gibson downed McLain and the Tigers in both contests, striking out a Series-record 17 batters in a 4-0 victory in Game 1 and coasting to a 10-1 triumph in Game 4.

Jim (Catfish) Hunter of the Oakland A's and Mike Marshall of the Los Angeles Dodgers are the only other men to pitch in the same World Series game in a year in which each was a Cy Young recipient. In Game 1 of the 1974 Series, both made ninth-inning relief appearances; in Game 3 of that classic, A.L. Cy Young winner Hunter started and worked 7⅓ innings (and got credit for a 3-2 victory), while N.L. award winner Marshall pitched two innings of relief.

MIKE CUELLAR, ROSS GRIMSLEY

Baltimore pitchers who combined on a one-hitter in Game 4 of the 1974 American League Championship Series—a contest that the Orioles lost, 2-1, to the Oakland A's. Cuellar didn't allow a hit in 4⅔ innings, but permitted nine bases on balls (including four straight, one of which was an intentional walk, in the fifth inning that boosted the A's into a 1-0 lead). Reggie Jackson collected Oakland's only hit, a seventh-inning double that scored Sal Bando and extended the A's edge to 2-0 in a game that nailed down the third consecutive A.L. pennant for Oakland, a three games-to-one victor in the playoff.

No other team has been held to fewer than two hits in a Championship Series game.

BILL DINNEEN

The first of six major leaguers to have played and umpired in World Series competition. Dinneen notched three pitching victories for the Boston Red Sox in the 1903 Series, then umpired in seven fall classics from 1911 through 1932.

Also playing and umpiring in World Series were George Moriarty, George Pipgras, Ed Rommel, Frank Secory and Lon Warneke.

Ken Burkhart and Bill Kunkel were World Series eligibles (Burkhart for the St. Louis Cardinals in 1946, Kunkel for the New York Yankees in 1963) who didn't see playing action in the classic, but later umpired in the Series.

TIM FLANNERY

San Diego pinch-hitter who hit the crucial ground ball that first baseman Leon Durham of the Chicago Cubs muffed in the seventh inning of the fifth and decisive game of the 1984 National League Championship Series. Trying to clinch their first pennant since 1945, the Cubs—13-0 and 4-2 winners in the first two games of the best-of-five playoff but 7-1 and 7-5 losers in Games 3 and 4—held a 3-0 lead midway through Game 5 in San Diego. Pitcher Rick Sutcliffe, 16-1 in the regular season for Chicago after his mid-June acquisition from the Cleveland Indians, then yielded sixth-inning sacrifice flies to Graig Nettles and Terry Kennedy (following Alan Wiggins' bunt single, Tony Gwynn's single and a walk to Steve Garvey)...and that elusive N.L. flag was slipping away from the Cubs.

Supporting Cast:

● **Jody Davis.** After Durham had rapped a two-run home run in the first inning off the Padres' Eric Show, catcher Davis staked the Cubs to a 3-0 lead with a second-inning homer off Show. Sutcliffe maintained that three-run edge through five innings, allowing only two infield hits.

● **Carmelo Martinez.** With the Cubs ahead, 3-2, San Diego's left fielder drew a leadoff walk against Sutcliffe in the seventh inning.

● **Garry Templeton.** Padres shortstop who sacrificed Martinez to second, bringing Flannery to the plate to bat for reliever Craig Lefferts. Flannery, a utility infielder, grounded to Durham, and the ball squirted through his legs. Martinez dashed home on the miscue, tying the score at 3-3.

● **Ryne Sandberg.** After Wiggins followed Durham's error with a check-swing single, Cubs second baseman Sandberg saw Gwynn's smash—a potential double-play ball—take a bad hop over his shoulder and rocket into right-center for a two-run double. Padres 5, Cubs 3. Gwynn, who took third on a throw to the plate, then scored on a single by Garvey, whose five-RBI performance (capped by a game-winning, two-run homer in the ninth inning) had jolted the Cubs in Game 4.

The Padres went on to win by the 6-3 score, copping the club's first N.L. pennant in the franchise's 16th year of operation.

BUD HARRELSON

The only man to be in uniform for the New York Mets in all 19 of the National League club's World Series games. Harrelson played shortstop for the N.L. champions in all five games of the 1969 fall classic against the Baltimore Orioles and in all seven games of the 1973 Series against the Oakland A's, and he also served as third-base coach for the Mets in the club's seven-game battle against the Boston Red Sox in 1986.

BUCKY HARRIS

He guided Washington to the 1924 World Series title in his first season as the Senators' manager (at age 27, he also was the club's second baseman) and directed the New York Yankees to the 1947 Series crown in his first year as the Yanks' pilot—a first-season championship "double" that is unequaled in Series managerial history. Harris' 1924 Senators and 1947 Yankees were four games-to-three Series victors over the New York Giants and Brooklyn Dodgers, respectively.

The only other manager to win pennants in his first year at the helm of two teams is Pat Moran, who led the Philadelphia Phillies to the National League title in 1915 and managed the Cincinnati Reds to the N.L. pennant in 1919. Moran's 1915 Phils lost the World Series in five games to the Boston Red Sox, while his 1919 Reds won the Series in eight games against the Chicago White Sox.

LUMAN HARRIS, BILL RIGNEY, JOE TORRE

The only Championship Series managers never to have won a game in the league postseason playoffs. All three managed in only one Championship Series—and their clubs were swept in three games (when a best-of-five format was in effect). Harris' Atlanta Braves lost to the New York Mets in the 1969 National League title series, Rigney's Minnesota Twins fell to the Baltimore Orioles in the 1970 American League playoffs and Torre's Atlanta club succumbed to the St. Louis Cardinals in the 1982 N.L. Championship Series.

BILLY HATCHER

Houston center fielder who supplied perhaps the most dramatic moment in the drama-filled sixth game of the 1986 National League Championship Series, hitting a one-out home run in the bottom of the 14th inning that enabled the Astros—down three games to two in the playoff—to tie the New York Mets, 4-4. As it turned out, though, Hatcher's homer—a shot to left field that was barely fair—merely gave the Astros a stay of execution. Two innings later, the Mets wrapped up the best-of-seven title series.

Supporting Cast:

• **Bob Knepper.** Houston pitcher who took a two-hit shutout—and a 3-0 lead—into the ninth inning of Game 6. But the Mets broke through against Knepper in the ninth as pinch-hitter Lenny Dykstra tripled, Mookie Wilson singled and, following a groundout, Keith Hernandez doubled. With the score now 3-2, Dave Smith relieved Knepper and allowed two walks and Ray Knight's game-tying sacrifice fly.

• **Wally Backman.** After the clubs battled through the 13th inning in a 3-3 deadlock, the Mets seized the lead in the 14th when Backman stroked a run-scoring single following Gary Carter's single, Darryl Strawberry's walk and a forceout.

• **Jesse Orosco.** Reliever who, with New York ahead, 4-3, came on to pitch in the bottom of the 14th in hopes of wrapping up the N.L. pennant for the Mets. But, after Bill Doran, struck out, Hatcher belted his clutch home run. (Hatcher had hit only six homers during the 1986 season.)

• **Aurelio Lopez.** Having allowed New York's run in the 14th, the Astros' reliever was victimized again in the 16th as the Mets scored three times (Lopez was charged with two of the runs, Jeff Calhoun with one). Strawberry opened the inning with a double (Hatcher got a slow start on the fly ball) and Knight singled him home. Calhoun later wild-pitched a run home, while Dykstra contributed an RBI single in the inning as the Mets built a 7-4 advantage.

Dave Henderson's valiant leap in Game 5 of the American League Championship Series against the California Angels turned Bobby Grich's long fly ball into a home run and almost spelled doom for the Boston Red Sox.

● **Kevin Bass.** After Hatcher and Glenn Davis delivered RBI singles in the Astros' half of the 16th, Bass strode to the plate with two on and two out and struck out against Orosco. The final score, in the majors' longest postseason game in history (in terms of time, 4 hours and 42 minutes, as well as innings): Mets 7, Astros 6. New York had won its first N.L. pennant in 13 years.

DAVE HENDERSON

Boston outfielder who, three innings after deflecting a California Angels smash over the wall for a crucial home run and with the Red Sox one strike

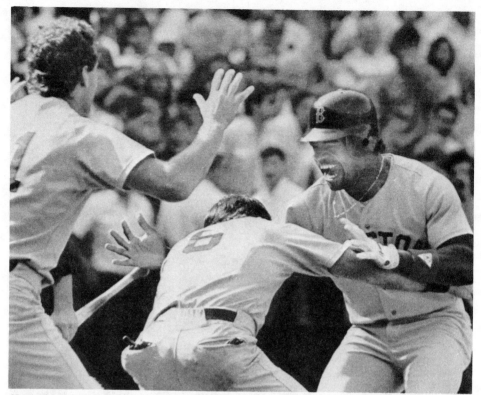

Henderson turned his misery into ecstasy with a dramatic two-run, ninth-inning home run that kept the Red Sox alive and vaulted them toward the A.L. pennant.

away from postseason elimination, smashed a two-run homer in the top of the ninth that gave the Sox a 6-5 lead in Game 5 of the 1986 American League Championship Series. Boston squandered the edge in the bottom of the ninth, but came back to win, 7-6, in 11 innings at Anaheim Stadium on a sacrifice fly by . . . Henderson.

Supporting Cast:

● **Bob Boone.** Angels catcher who drilled a bases-empty homer in the third inning, cutting Boston's lead to 2-1.

● **Rich Gedman.** Boston catcher who, with his team trailing three games to one in the best-of-seven series, smacked a two-run homer in the second inning.

● **Bobby Grich.** California first baseman who hit the sixth-inning drive that glanced off Henderson's glove and dropped over the center-field fence. Doug DeCinces' double had preceded the homer, a blast that thrust the Angels into a 3-2 lead.

● **Mike Witt.** Angels starting pitcher who took a 5-2 lead into the ninth—California had scored seventh-inning runs on Rob Wilfong's pinch double and Brian Downing's sacrifice fly—before faltering. Bill Buckner led off Boston's ninth with a single and, after Dave Stapleton ran for Buckner and Jim Rice struck out, Don Baylor homered. His lead now cut to 5-4, Witt got Dwight

Evans to pop out, but then gave way to reliever Gary Lucas as Gedman (3 for 3 at the plate at that point) came up to bat.

● **Donnie Moore.** After Lucas hit Gedman with a pitch, Moore came on in relief and, after battling Henderson to a two-ball, two-strike count, yielded the go-ahead homer to Henderson, who had entered the game in the fifth inning as a replacement for injured Red Sox center fielder Tony Armas.

● **Ruppert Jones.** Pinch-running in the Angels' ninth for Boone (who led off the inning with a single), Jones advanced to second on Gary Pettis' sacrifice and scored on Wilfong's single off Joe Sambito, his slide around Gedman making the score 6-6.

● **Calvin Schiraldi.** The loser in relief the night before in a game that the Red Sox had led, 3-0, entering the bottom of the ninth but wound up losing, 4-3, in 11 innings, he was Boston's fifth and last pitcher of the day. Entering Game 5 after the Red Sox had seized a 7-6 lead in the top of the 11th on Henderson's sacrifice fly (which followed Moore's hitting of Baylor with a pitch, Evans' single and Gedman's bunt single), he retired the Angels in order and nailed down the victory for fellow reliever Steve Crawford. Boston's Crawford had wriggled out of a one-out, bases-loaded jam in the ninth when the score was tied.

Boston's victory in the dramatic game—which also featured Red Sox left fielder Rice's leaping catch against the wall of a Pettis drive in the 10th inning and Angels left fielder Downing's wall-banging catch of Ed Romero's smash in the 11th (after Boston had regained the lead)—sent the teams back to Boston for Game 6 and, if necessary, Game 7. The Red Sox, given new life, coasted to a 10-4 triumph and an A.L. pennant-winning 8-1 decision at Fenway Park.

TOMMY HERR

St. Louis Cardinals second baseman who drove in two runs with one sacrifice fly in the 1982 World Series. Batting against Milwaukee pitcher Moose Haas with Willie McGee on third base and Ozzie Smith on second in the second inning of Game 4, Herr belted a one-out drive to center field. The Brewers' Gorman Thomas tracked down the long smash and, after Thomas made the catch, McGee tagged up and headed for the plate. Herr's "conventional" sacrifice fly turned into a one-for-the-book occurrence, though, when Thomas subsequently slipped on the warning track. Smith not only sped on to third base, but raced home behind McGee. Despite Herr's two-RBI sacrifice fly, which sent the Cardinals ahead, 3-0, Milwaukee rebounded for a 7-5 triumph.

TOMMY JOHN

The last of three pitchers to start and win a World Series game for both a National League club and an American League team. John started and won a game for the N.L.'s Los Angeles Dodgers against the New York Yankees in the 1978 Series and was a starter and winner for the A.L.'s Yankees against the Dodgers in the 1981 fall classic.

Jack Coombs posted four Series victories as a starting pitcher for the A.L.'s Philadelphia A's (winning three times in 1910 and once in 1911) and won one game as a starter for the N.L.'s Brooklyn Dodgers in 1916. And Hank Borowy was a Series starter and winner for the N.L.'s Chicago Cubs in 1945, two years after a victorious starting assignment for the Yankees in the fall classic. (Borowy also won in relief for the Cubs in the '45 Series.)

DARRELL JOHNSON, CHUCK TANNER

The only Championship Series managers never to lose a game in the league playoff competition. Both won with three-game sweeps in their only Championship Series managerial experience, Johnson's Boston Red Sox downing the Oakland A's in the 1975 American League playoffs and Tanner's Pittsburgh Pirates stopping the Cincinnati Reds in the 1979 National League title series.

Championship Series competition was a best-of-five battle from the playoffs' inception in 1969 through 1984. In 1985, a best-of-seven format was adopted.

KANSAS CITY ROYALS, NEW YORK METS

The only teams to lose the first two games of a World Series in their home ball park and then rebound to win the Series crown—and they accomplished the feat in successive years. Kansas City lost the first two games of the 1985 Series at Royals Stadium, falling to St. Louis by 3-1 and 4-2 scores, but then won two of three games at the Cardinals' Busch Stadium before copping the Series title with two victories in Kansas City. The Mets dropped the opening two games of the 1986 Series at Shea Stadium, losing 1-0 and 9-3 decisions to Boston, but then won two of three games at the Red Sox's Fenway Park before seizing the Series championship with two victories in New York.

JIM KONSTANTY

The relief ace (74 appearances, all out of the bullpen) of the 1950 National League champion Philadelphia Phillies—but, astonishingly, the Phils' starting pitcher in Game 1 of the 1950 World Series. Konstanty, who won N.L. Most Valuable Player honors in '50 with a 16-7 record and 2.66 earned-run average, was Phils Manager Eddie Sawyer's first-game pitching choice after staff leader Robin Roberts (20 victories) was forced to pitch three times in the last five days of the season. The late-season loss of pitcher Curt Simmons (17 triumphs) to the Army and nagging injuries to Bob Miller and Bubba Church also took their toll on the Phils' staff and contributed to Sawyer's surprise selection of Konstanty to open the Series. The 33-year-old Konstanty was up to the challenge, though, allowing only one run and four hits against the New York Yankees in eight innings. However, the Yanks won as Vic Raschi tossed a two-hit, 1-0 shutout.

Konstanty, who had pitched exclusively in relief (133 appearances overall) for the Phillies since joinng the club in 1948 (he had made a total of 13 starts for the Cincinnati Reds and Boston Braves earlier in his career), returned to bullpen duty in Games 3 and 4 of the 1950 Series, which the Yankees won in a sweep.

TITO LANDRUM

Acquired by the Baltimore Orioles from the St. Louis Cardinals' organization on August 31, 1983, the cutoff date for postseason eligibility, Landrum entered the '83 American League Championship Series with only three home runs in 227 regular-season major league games—but he broke a 0-0 tie against the Chicago White Sox in Game 4 of the playoffs by lining a one-out, 10th-inning home run off Britt Burns. The Orioles scored two more runs after the blast by Landrum (who spent most of the season in the minor leagues), and the 3-0 triumph at Comiskey Park clinched the best-of-five playoff for Baltimore, three games to one.

LOS ANGELES DODGERS

The last of only three teams to win a World Series in four games against an opponent that had a better winning percentage during the regular season. The 1963 Dodgers won the National League pennant with a 99-63 record (.611 winning percentage), compared with the New York Yankees' American League championship mark of 104-57 (.646); Los Angeles then swept the Yanks in four games in the '63 Series, winning by scores of 5-2, 4-1, 1-0 and 2-1.

Also pulling off World Series sweeps despite posting lesser records than their fall-classic opponents were the 1954 New York Giants and the 1914 Boston Braves. The Giants, N.L. titlists with a 97-57 record (.630), won the '54 Series in four straight games over the Cleveland Indians, who had notched an A.L.-record 111 victories (against 43 losses, while playing .721 ball). The N.L. champion Braves went 94-59 (.614), then dispatched the Philadelphia A's in four consecutive contests in the '14 Series. The A's had captured the A.L. flag with a 99-53 mark (.651).

The 1922 Giants couldn't quite match the season record of their Series rivals, the Yankees—the National Leaguers were 93-61, .604, and the American Leaguers finished 94-60, .610—but the Giants were unbeatable in the fall classic. The N.L. champions won the '22 Series, four victories to none, although the Yankees avoided some embarrassment by playing the Giants to a 10-inning, darkness-called tie and thus extending the postseason clash to five games.

Teams with the higher regular-season winning percentage had won 46 of the 83 World Series played through 1986. (Two Series, the 1949 and 1958 classics, were contested between clubs with identical records.)

JON MATLACK

The last of four pitchers to start the opening game of a World Series despite compiling a losing record in the regular season. Matlack started Game 1 of the 1973 Series for the New York Mets after compiling a season mark of 14-16. Despite yielding only two runs and three hits in six innings, he was a 2-1 loser to the Oakland A's.

Alvin Crowder, 9-11 overall in 1934 (4-10 for Washington, 5-1 for Detroit), started and lost for the Tigers, 8-3, in Game 1 of the 1934 World Series against the St. Louis Cardinals. After turning in a 9-10 season record in 1944, Denny Galehouse of the St. Louis Browns pitched a complete-game 2-1 victory over the St. Louis Cardinals in the first game of the '44 Series. And Don Drysdale put together a 13-16 season for the Los Angeles Dodgers in 1966 before starting—and suffering a 5-2 loss—in the opening game of the '66 Series against the Baltimore Orioles.

STUFFY McINNIS

The first man to play for World Series championship teams from both major leagues. First baseman McInnis saw action for Series-winning clubs from the American League in 1911 (Philadelphia A's), 1913 (A's) and 1918 (Boston Red Sox) and from the National League in 1925 (Pittsburgh Pirates).

McInnis also played on one World Series loser, the 1914 A's.

BOB MOOSE

With defending World Series champion Pittsburgh and Cincinnati tied, 3-3, with two out in the bottom of the ninth inning of the fifth and deciding game of the 1972 National League Championship Series, Pirates reliever Moose fired a wild pitch that gave the Reds the N.L. pennant.

Supporting Cast:

• **Johnny Bench.** With his team trailing, 3-2, entering the bottom of the ninth, the majors' leader in home runs (40 in '72) sent the Cincinnati crowd into a frenzy with a game-tying shot over the right-field fence off Pittsburgh's Dave Giusti, who had just entered the game.

• **George Foster.** A future two-time N.L. home run champion, this 23-year-old reserve outfielder went in to run for Tony Perez after Perez followed Bench's homer with a single.

• **Denis Menke.** His single advanced Foster to second base.

• **Cesar Geronimo, Darrel Chaney.** The Reds' seventh- and eight-place hitters, they were up next. When the count reached 2-0 on Geronimo, Moose replace Giusti. Geronimo and Chaney were retired on a fly ball and a popup, respectively, but Geronimo's drive advanced Foster to third base.

• **Hal McRae.** Sent up as a pinch-hitter for Reds relief pitcher Clay Carroll, he was at the plate in the ninth when Moose let fly with a wild pitch that skipped past catcher Manny Sanguillen and scored Foster, giving Cincinnati a 4-3 triumph and a berth in the World Series.

• **Roberto Clemente.** Pirates' Hall of Fame-bound right fielder who went 1 for 3 in the game and received an intentional walk in what proved his last career at-bat, an eighth-inning appearance against Cincinnati's Tom Hall. Clemente was killed in a plane crash about 2½ months later.

Cincinnati Manager Sparky Anderson couldn't contain his enthusiasm after George Foster had scored the winning run on a wild pitch by Pittsburgh's Bob Moose to give the Reds the 1972 National League pennant.

NINE GAMES

While 79 of the 83 World Series played through 1986 were contested under a best-of-seven format, four Series—including the first one in 1903—were best-of-nine confrontations. While none of the best-of-nine Series was played to the limit, three of those fall classics did require eight games. The best-of-nine World Series:

Year—Winner, Games Won	Loser, Games Won
1903—Boston Red Sox, A.L., 5	Pittsburgh Pirates, N.L., 3
1919—Cincinnati Reds, N.L., 5	Chicago White Sox, A.L., 3
1920—Cleveland Indians, A.L., 5	Brooklyn Dodgers, N.L., 2
1921—New York Giants, N.L., 5	New York Yankees, A.L., 3

1954

The last year in which the season's major league batting champions met in the World Series. Willie Mays of the National League pennant-winning New York Giants won the '54 N.L. hitting title with a .345 average, while Bobby Avila of the American League champion Cleveland Indians captured the A.L. batting crown with a .341 mark. In the '54 World Series, which the Giants won in four straight games, Mays batted .286 and Avila hit .133.

The only other World Series matchups of batting-title winners occurred in 1909 and 1931. In 1909, Detroit's Ty Cobb won the A.L. batting title with a .377 mark as the Tigers advanced to the Series against Pittsburgh, led by the N.L.'s top hitter, Honus Wagner, who fashioned a .339 mark. The Pirates won the Series in seven games, with Wagner hitting .333 and Cobb finishing at .231. The St. Louis Cardinals won the '31 Series against the Philadelphia A's, but got little help from N.L. batting champion Chick Hafey in another seven-game battle. Hafey, a .349 hitter during the season, managed only a .167 mark in the Series. Philadelphia's Al Simmons, the A.L. batting titlist with a .390 figure, hit .333 against the Cardinals.

1976

The last year in which no pitcher started more than one game for either side in the World Series. In the '76 Series, which National League titlist Cincinnati won in four games, the Reds called upon Don Gullett, Fred Norman, Pat Zachry and Gary Nolan as starters; the American League champion New York Yankees used Doyle Alexander, Jim (Catfish) Hunter, Dock Ellis and Ed Figueroa.

The Yankees' four-game Series sweeps of 1927 (over the Pittsburgh Pirates) and 1950 (against the Philadelphia Phillies) also featured different starting pitchers throughout for both clubs.

JORGE ORTA

Pinch-hitting for Kansas City with the Royals trailing the St. Louis Cardinals, 1-0, in the ninth inning of Game 6 of the 1985 World Series, he hit a ground ball on which first-base umpire Don Denkinger made a hotly disputed call—a call that helped the American League champions, down three games to two in the Series, to a game-winning, two-run rally.

Supporting Cast:

● **Brian Harper.** Pinch-hitting for Cardinals starting pitcher Danny Cox, who had shut out the Royals over seven innings, he delivered a run-scoring bloop single in the eighth inning that gave St. Louis a 1-0 lead at Royals Stadium.

● **Pat Sheridan.** Kansas City's lefthanded-hitting right fielder and the first man scheduled to bat in the bottom of the ninth. With Cardinals lefthander Ken Dayley ready to begin his second inning of relief, righthanded hitter Darryl Motley was announced as a pinch-hitter for Sheridan. St. Louis Manager Whitey Herzog then summoned hard-throwing righthander Todd Wor-

Kansas City catcher Jim Sundberg was understandably ecstatic after scoring the winning run in the ninth inning of Game 6 of the 1985 World Series against the St. Louis Cardinals.

rell, and Royals Manager Dick Howser countered with Orta, a lefthanded batter, to hit for Motley.

● **Jack Clark.** St. Louis first baseman who fielded Orta's ensuing grounder and threw to Worrell, who was covering first. Television replays indicated Orta was out on the play, but Denkinger called him safe. Herzog argued vehemently, but to no avail. Kansas City's Steve Balboni then lifted a catchable popup near the first-base dugout, but Clark inexplicably failed to make the play and the ball fell untouched. Balboni then singled, with Orta stopping at second base.

● **Jim Sundberg.** After Onix Concepcion ran for Balboni, Sundberg bunted into a forceout at third base.

● **Hal McRae.** Pinch-hitting for Buddy Biancalana, he was at the plate when Cardinals catcher Darrell Porter committed a passed ball. With runners now at second and third, McRae was walked intentionally (and replaced by pinch-runner John Wathan).

● **Dane Iorg.** Batting for Royals reliever Dan Quisenberry, he poked a single to right field that scored Concepcion and Sundberg and gave Kansas City a Series-squaring 2-1 triumph over St. Louis.

The Royals won their first World Series crown the next night. The Cardinals, two outs away from nailing down the Series title in Game 6 and clearly showing the effects of the game that got away (because of an umpire's apparent mistake and their own faulty play), unraveled in Game 7 and dropped the Series finale, 11-0.

ROGER PECKINPAUGH

Washington shortstop who made errors in six of the seven games of the 1925 World Series—including two misplays in both Game 2 and Game 7. His eight errors established a Series record for one player (regardless of position) that still stands and helped the Pittsburgh Pirates to a four games-to-three triumph in the fall classic.

The Senators' Peckinpaugh had been voted the A.L.'s "most valuable player to a club" (the terminology in those days) in '25.

DEACON PHILLIPPE

The only pitcher to win three games in a World Series for the losing club. Pitching for the Pittsburgh Pirates in the 1903 Series against the Boston Red Sox, Phillippe was a winner in Games 1, 3 and 4 (and a loser in Games 7 and 8) as the Pirates fell to the Red Sox, five games to three.

Phillippe pitched five complete games and 44 innings (both records) in the Series, which ran for 13 days.

ALLIE REYNOLDS

The only pitcher to win at least one World Series game in five consecutive years. Reynolds, of the New York Yankees, beat the Brooklyn Dodgers in

The New York Yankees lost the 1960 World Series to the Pittsburgh Pirates, but they weren't lacking for offense. The biggest producer was little second baseman Bobby Richardson, who received a warm welcome after hitting his third-game grand slam.

Game 1 of the 1949 Series (on a two-hit shutout), defeated the Philadelphia Phillies in Game 2 of the 1950 classic (allowing one run in 10 innings), stopped the New York Giants in Game 4 of the 1951 Series (yielding two runs), downed the Dodgers twice in 1952 (via a shutout in Game 4 and a relief stint in Game 7) and won over Brooklyn in Game 6 of the 1953 Series (while working two innings of relief).

Reynolds was a two-time World Series loser in the 1949-1953 streak and fashioned a 7-2 Series record overall (having posted a victory against Brooklyn in 1947).

Only four other pitchers have even *appeared* in five consecutive Series—the Yankees' Eddie Lopat, Vic Raschi, Whitey Ford and Ralph Terry. Lopat and Raschi, like Reynolds, were Series pitchers from '49 through '53; Ford and Terry appeared in the Series from 1960 through 1964.

JIM RICE

Boston Red Sox left fielder who collected only five hits and batted .161 in the seven-game 1986 American League Championship Series against the California Angels—but set a Championship Series record by scoring eight runs. Rice, who had two singles, a double and two home runs, scored in every

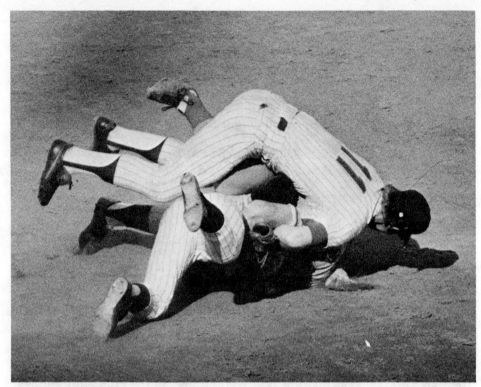

Push came to shove in the 1973 N.L. Championship Series when Mets short-stop Bud Harrelson and Cincinnati's Pete Rose exchanged unpleasantries. Mets third baseman Wayne Garrett (11) arrived on the scene in short order.

inning in which he collected a hit or a base on balls (he drew one walk). He also scored after reaching base on a fielder's choice and after getting aboard on an error.

BOBBY RICHARDSON

After driving in only seven runs (in 194 at-bats) for the New York Yankees in the final 75 games of the 1960 season and finishing the year with 26 runs batted in, he established a World Series record with 12 RBIs (in 30 at-bats) in the Yanks' seven-game classic against the Pittsburgh Pirates in '60. Richardson set a one-game Series mark with six RBIs in Game 3, a contest in which he slugged a bases-full home run off Pirates reliever Clem Labine in the first inning. He drilled two triples and knocked in three runs in Game 6.

Richardson, who became a front-line Yankee player in 1957 and retired after the 1966 season, never had more than 59 RBIs in one major league season.

PETE ROSE, BUD HARRELSON

Combatants in a 1973 National League Championship Series fight that led to a stoppage of play when New York Mets fans rained debris on Cincinnati

162

left fielder Rose. With the playoff deadlocked at a game apiece and the Mets ahead, 9-2, in the fifth inning of Game 3 at New York's Shea Stadium, Rose collected a one-out single off Jerry Koosman. Joe Morgan then grounded into a first base-to-shortstop-to-first double play—John Milner was the Mets' first baseman and Harrelson the shortstop—but not before Rose made a hard slide into Harrelson in an attempt to break up the play. Harrelson and Rose began pushing and shoving and soon fell to the ground, flailing away at each other. Players from both benches and bullpens raced onto the field. After order was restored, Rose took his position in left field—and was soon the target of garbage-throwing fans. Cincinnati Manager Sparky Anderson pulled his club off the field and the Reds didn't return until a Mets contingent—headed by Manager Yogi Berra and outfielder Willie Mays—made a trip to left field and pleaded with the fans to settle down. The unruliness ended, and New York went on to win by the 9-2 score.

Rose got "revenge" the next day at Shea when he belted a game-winning, 12th-inning home run off Harry Parker—he circled the bases with a fist raised high—as the Reds edged the Mets, 2-1, and squared the Championship Series at two games each. New York won the best-of-five title playoff, though, with a subsequent 7-2 triumph.

CLARENCE (PANTS) ROWLAND

The first of eight World Series managers with no playing experience in the major leagues. Rowland, in his only Series managerial role, piloted the Chicago White Sox to a four games-to-two triumph over the New York Giants in 1917.

Other World Series managers who never played in the big leagues: Ed Barrow, who guided the Boston Red Sox into the Series in 1918; Joe McCarthy, Chicago Cubs, 1929, and New York Yankees, 1932, 1936 through 1939 and 1941 through 1943; Eddie Sawyer, Philadelphia Phillies, 1950; Johnny Keane, St. Louis Cardinals, 1964; Earl Weaver, Baltimore Orioles, 1969 through 1971, 1979; Jim Frey, Kansas City Royals, 1980, and Paul Owens, Phillies, 1983. Barrow was a Series winner in 1918, McCarthy won seven times (missing only in 1929 and 1942), Keane was triumphant in 1964 and Weaver prevailed in 1970. Teams managed by Sawyer, Frey and Owens failed to win the Series.

VERN RUHLE

Houston Astros pitcher who was at the center of a major controversy that flared in Game 4 of the 1980 National League Championship Series. Houston, leading the best-of-five playoff, two games to one, was locked in a 0-0 battle with Philadelphia when the Phillies came to bat in the top of the fourth inning.

Supporting Cast:
● **Bake McBride, Manny Trillo.** The Phils' first two batters in the fourth, they collected singles off Ruhle.
● **Garry Maddox.** He followed Trillo to the plate and hit a low, soft liner to

163

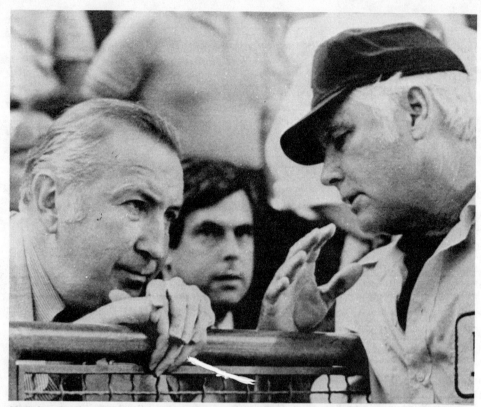

Umpire Doug Harvey was forced to the sideline during Game 4 of the 1980 Championship Series for a chat with N.L. President Chub Feeney. Both the Houston Astros and Philadelphia Phillies were vehemently protesting a call that, after considerable confusion and deliberation, became a double play.

Ruhle, who wheeled and threw to Houston first baseman Art Howe in an apparent attempt to double up the baserunner, who was off the bag. The Phillies mounted a strenuous protest, insisting that Ruhle had trapped the ball. (Television replays were inconclusive.) And as the Phils voiced their grievance, Howe ambled down to second base, touched the bag and thereby put in a claim for a triple play.

● **Doug Harvey.** Home-plate umpire who first indicated the play was a "trap," then asked for help after acknowledging that he didn't have a clear view of the action because Maddox had stepped into his line of vision. Harvey conferred with his fellow umpires and with N.L. President Chub Feeney (seated nearby) and, accepting their collective judgment, ruled the play a catch—and a double play. Since time had been called after Ruhle's throw to Howe, the subsequent triple-play attempt by Howe was not allowed (and McBride returned to second base). The next batter, Larry Bowa, ended the inning by grounding out.

The Phillies went on to win Game 4, prevailing by a 5-3 score in 10 innings, and then won a 10-inning, 8-7 stem-winder that gave them their first N.L. pennant in 30 years.

164

77

The number of postseason games—divisional-playoff, Championship Series and World Series contests—in which Reggie Jackson has appeared, a major league record. Jackson has played in five divisional-playoff games (the extra tier of playoff competition that was part of the 1981 split season), 45 Championship Series games and 27 World Series games. Jackson, whose divisional-playoff action came with the New York Yankees, has played in 20 Championship Series games with Oakland, 14 as a member of the Yankees and 11 while a California Angels player. And he participated in 12 World Series games for the A's and 15 with the Yanks. (Jackson also played for the Yankees against the Red Sox in the one-game playoff that broke a 1978 American League East title tie. However, a championship-season tiebreaking game isn't considered part of postseason play because the contest applies directly to the regular season and all records from the game are included in regular-season statistics.)

The all-time leader in World Series games played is Yogi Berra, who appeared in 75 contests for the Yankees from 1947 through 1963, while the No. 1 man in Championship Series games played is Jackson, whose 45 appearances have come from 1971 through 1986. (Berra played in 74 percent of all World Series games contested from '47 through '63; Jackson participated in 64 percent of all A.L. Championship Series games played from '71 through '86.)

LONNIE SMITH

The first man to bat in big-league postseason play in Canada in both the National League and the American League. Smith was Philadelphia's center fielder and leadoff batter on October 7, 1981, at Montreal's Olympic Stadium when the Phillies and Expos met in Canada's first postseason game —the opening game of the N.L. East divisional playoffs. (The divisional playoff competition, which would determine Championship Series entrants, was an extra round in the majors' postseason structure and part of the split-season format adopted during the strike-torn season of '81.) Four years later, on October 8, 1985, at Toronto's Exhibition Stadium, Smith became the first player to bat in an A.L. postseason game when, as Kansas City's left fielder, he led off for the Royals in Game 1 of the Championship Series against the Blue Jays.

LONNIE SMITH

The last of four players to see World Series duty in at least one game for three different Series-winning franchises, having played for the Philadelphia Phillies in 1980, the St. Louis Cardinals in 1982 and the Kansas City Royals in 1985. Smith, an outfielder/designated hitter, played in all 20 games of the '80, '82 and '85 Series.

Bullet Joe Bush and Wally Schang were teammates on the 1913 Philadelphia A's, 1918 Boston Red Sox and 1923 New York Yankees, all of whom won

World Series crowns. And Stuffy McInnis played for the Series-winning A's of 1911 and 1913, Red Sox of 1918 and Pittsburgh Pirates of 1925.

OZZIE SMITH

Switch-hitting shortstop who, when he went to the plate as a lefthanded batter for St. Louis against Los Angeles in the ninth inning of Game 5 of the 1985 National League Championship Series, had not slugged a home run as a lefthanded hitter in his eight-year major league career (a span that included 2,967 regular-season at-bats as a lefthanded batter). However, with the score tied, 2-2, and one out, Smith picked on a 1-2 pitch from Dodgers reliever Tom Niedenfuer and slammed the ball off the cement facing above the right-field wall at Busch Stadium. The homer not only gave the Cardinals a 3-2 victory, it enabled St. Louis to take a three-games-to-two lead in the playoffs. The Cards won the N.L. pennant-deciding series in six games.

BILL TERRY

The last player-manager to hit a home run in a World Series. Terry, first baseman and manager of the New York Giants, slugged a bases-empty homer off Washington's Monte Weaver in the fourth inning of Game 4 of the 1933 Series. The Giants won that contest, 2-1, in 11 innings and wrapped up the Series title over the Senators in five games.

The only other player-managers to rap Series home runs were Fred Clarke of the Pittsburgh Pirates and Bucky Harris of the Senators. Clarke, an out-fielder, hit two homers against the Detroit Tigers in the 1909 classic, and second baseman Harris slammed two homers against the Giants in 1924.

JIM THORPE

Famed Olympic Games athlete and college and pro football star who "appeared" in one World Series game—but, in fact, never got onto the playing field in that contest. Listed as the New York Giants' starting right fielder for Game 5 of the 1917 Series in Chicago, the righthanded-hitting Thorpe was sixth in the batting order as the Giants faced White Sox lefthander Reb Russell. After yielding a walk and two hits to New York's first three batters of the game, Russell gave way to righthander Eddie Cicotte. By the time Thorpe was due to hit in the first inning, the Giants already had scored one run and had two men on base. At this juncture, Giants Manager John McGraw sent up lefthanded-hitting Dave Robertson, New York's starting right fielder in the first four games, to bat for Thorpe. Robertson delivered a run-scoring single, then took over in right field in a game that the Giants wound up losing, 8-5.

Robertson, who went 3 for 5 in Game 5, hit safely in all six Series games—the White Sox prevailed, four games to two—and was the top hitter in the classic with a .500 average (11 hits in 22 at-bats).

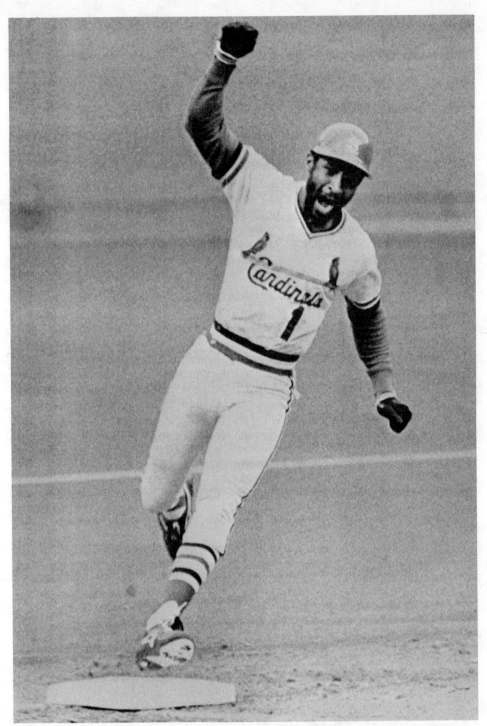

Ozzie Smith's first major league home run as a lefthanded hitter resulted in a jubilant trot around the bases and a Game 5 victory for St. Louis over Los Angeles in the 1985 N.L. Championship Series.

MOOKIE WILSON

New York Mets outfielder who was at bat with two out in the 10th inning of Game 6 of the 1986 World Series when the game-tying run was wild-pitched home. Wilson then proceeded to hit a grounder to Boston first baseman Bill Buckner, who misplayed the ball into a game-deciding error. The two runs that scored during Wilson's at-bat capped a three-run rally and enabled the Mets—on the brink of elimination—to beat the Red Sox, 6-5, in New York and deadlock the Series at three games apiece.

Supporting Cast:

● **Dave Henderson.** Boston outfielder who snapped a 3-3 tie in the top of the 10th with a leadoff homer against Rick Aguilera. The Red Sox expanded their lead to 5-3 later in the inning when Wade Boggs doubled and Marty Barrett singled him home.

● **Wally Backman, Keith Hernandez.** The Mets' first two batters in the bottom of the 10th, they flied out against Red Sox reliever Calvin Schiraldi.

● **Gary Carter.** He kept the Mets' faint hopes alive by lining a single on a 2-1 pitch.

● **Kevin Mitchell.** Batting for Aguilera, he rifled a one-strike pitch for a base hit.

● **Ray Knight.** With Carter on second base and Mitchell on first, the Mets were down to their last strike when Knight swung at a no-ball, two-strike offering and looped a single to center field. Carter scored on the play, cutting New York's deficit to 5-4, and Mitchell advanced to third.

● **Bob Stanley.** Boston reliever who entered the game at this juncture and battled Wilson to a 2-2 count, bringing the Red Sox within one strike of the Series championship for the second time. Wilson fouled off the next two pitches before Stanley uncorked a wild pitch that scored Mitchell, tied the game at 5-5 and sent Knight to second base. Wilson hit two more foul balls and then slapped another 3-2 offering to Buckner, who let the grounder get through his legs. Knight raced home on the error, and the Mets had a storybook 6-5 victory.

The Mets went on to win the '86 World Series, scoring an 8-5 comeback triumph over the Red Sox in Game 7 (a contest that was delayed one night because of rain).

GEORGE WRIGHT

A pennant winner in his only season as a big-league manager—a distinction unequaled in major league history. Wright, a middle infielder on brother Harry Wright's Boston clubs in the National League's first three seasons of existence (1876 through 1878), took the managerial reins of Providence's N.L. club in 1879 and guided the team to a first-place finish. Harry Wright, whose teams had won N.L. flags in 1877 and 1878, saw his Boston club finish second to Providence in '79.

George Wright played briefly for Boston again in 1880 and 1881 before rounding out his big-league playing career with Providence in 1882.

CHAPTER 6
THE TRADING SEASON

FELIPE ALOU, MATTY ALOU

Brothers who were sold by the same major league team on the same day. On September 6, 1973, the New York Yankees sent first baseman-outfielder Felipe Alou to the Montreal Expos and dispatched outfielder Matty Alou to the St. Louis Cardinals. Felipe had joined the Yankees in the first week of the 1971 season, while Matty had been a member of the Yanks since November 1972.

JAY BELL, BERT BLYLEVEN

Involved in a 1985 trade between the Minnesota Twins and the Cleveland Indians, they had a noteworthy introduction to each other in the major leagues in 1986. Bell, who as a Twins' minor-league infielder had been part of a three-for-one deal with the Indians that sent veteran pitcher Blyleven to Minnesota on August 1, 1985, appeared in his first big-league game on September 29, 1986, and homered for Cleveland on the first pitch he saw in the majors—a pitch thrown by Minnesota's Blyleven. Not only did Bell enter the record books with a homer on his first at-bat, he took Blyleven with him. The home run was the 47th allowed by Blyleven in '86, establishing a big-league record for the most homers yielded by one pitcher in one year. (By season's end, Blyleven had given up 50 homers.)

VIDA BLUE, JOE RUDI, ROLLIE FINGERS

Three standout Oakland players whom A's Owner Charlie Finley attempted to sell in June 1976. Faced with the prospect of losing some of his top, unsigned players to free agency at the end of the '76 season, Finley readied plans to sell pitcher Blue to the New York Yankees for a reported $1.5 million and outfielder Rudi and reliever Fingers to the Boston Red Sox for $1 million apiece. "I'm disappointed with the necessity of having to make these sales," Finley said after announcing completion of the transactions on June 15. "But I just refused to let these players drive me into bankruptcy with their astronomical salary demands." On the night of the sales, the Red Sox were in Oakland to play the A's and Rudi and Fingers changed club-houses and uniforms. However, Boston Manager Darrell Johnson did not use either player that evening. The next day, Commissioner Bowie Kuhn ordered the Red Sox and Yankees to refrain from using their new players until he finished an investigation into the deals. On June 18, Kuhn voided the sales, saying they were not in "the best interests of the game."

Rudi and Fingers played out their options with the A's in 1976 and, achieving free-agent status, signed with the California Angels and San Diego Padres, respectively. Blue, who agreed to contract terms with Finley just before the June 15 sale (the Yankees did not want to acquire an unsigned player in fear of losing him to free agency), pitched for the A's again in 1977 before being traded.

BOSTON RED SOX, CHICAGO CUBS

Teams that made the first deal in major league baseball's initial interleague trading period, which came after the 1959 season. Previously, transactions between teams of the American League and clubs in the National League could be made only after a player had cleared waivers in his league. Starting on November 21, 1959, and continuing for $3\frac{1}{2}$ weeks, clubs could make waiver-free interleague trades—and the Red Sox and Cubs went right to work. On November 21, Boston dealt first baseman Dick Gernert to the Cubs for pitcher Dave Hillman and first baseman-outfielder Jim Marshall.

By the first interleague trading deadline of December 15, 1959, 30 players had changed leagues.

DAN BROUTHERS

Hall of Fame-bound first baseman who, in an era of disbanding franchises and short-lived leagues, played for Boston of the National League in 1889, Boston of the Players League in 1890 and Boston of the American Association (a major league at the time) in 1891.

Though it does not appear in the playing records of either Rollie Fingers (left) or Joe Rudi (above with Manager Darrell Johnson), both were brief members of the Boston Red Sox in 1976. After being sold to Boston by Oakland Owner Charlie Finley on June 15, both donned their new uniforms for one game (neither played) before the deal was voided.

BILL CAMPBELL

Of the players available in major league baseball's initial free-agent re-entry draft (held November 4, 1976), the first to sign a contract. Campbell, The Sporting News' Fireman of the Year in the American League in '76 when he fashioned a 17-5 record for the Minnesota Twins, signed a long-term contract with the Boston Red Sox two days after the draft.

OWNIE CARROLL

The only player in major league history to be traded three times in deals for future Hall of Fame members. A righthanded pitcher who compiled a 65-89 record for four clubs in a big-league career that began in 1925 and ended in 1934, Carroll was first traded in May 1930 when he, George Wuestling and Harry Rice were sent from the Detroit Tigers to the New York Yankees for Mark Koenig and future Hall of Famer Waite Hoyt. Sold to Cincinnati later in 1930, Carroll and Reds teammate Estel Crabtree were dealt to the St. Louis Cardinals in December 1932 for Cooperstown-bound Jim Bottomley. And in February 1933, the Cards dispatched Carroll and Jake Flowers to the Brooklyn Dodgers for Gordon Slade and future Hall of Fame inductee Dazzy Vance.

Only one other player, Curt Davis, was involved in three trades involving future Hall of Famers. Davis was swapped in separate deals *for* Chuck Klein and Dizzy Dean and in a trade *with* Joe Medwick.

While Carroll and Davis rate special niches for their three-time roles in trades of future Hall of Famers, players involved in two trades for and/or with future Cooperstown inductees merit recognition, too:

Player	Hall of Famer in First Trade	Hall of Famer in Second Trade
Vic Aldridge	For Rabbit Maranville	For Burleigh Grimes
Lloyd Brown	For Goose Goslin	With Rick Ferrell
Tony Cuccinello	For Ernie Lombardi	With Al Lopez
Fred Hatfield	For George Kell	For Early Wynn
Harvey Hendrick	For Chick Hafey	For Chuck Klein
Babe Herman	With Ernie Lombardi	For Fred Lindstrom
Percy Jones	For Rogers Hornsby	For Burleigh Grimes
Mark Koenig	With Waite Hoyt	For Chuck Klein
Grover Lowdermilk	With Joe Tinker	For Mordecai Brown
*Christy Mathewson	For Amos Rusie	With Roush, McKechnie
Dave Nicholson	With Wilhelm for Aparicio	For Eddie Mathews
Del Pratt	With Eddie Plank	For Waite Hoyt
Carl Reynolds	For Goose Goslin	For Heinie Manush
Jimmy Ring	For Eppa Rixey	With Frisch for Hornsby
*Edd Roush	With Mathewson, McKechnie	For George Kelly
Al Smith	With Early Wynn	With Aparicio for Wilhelm
Billy Southworth	For Rabbit Maranville	For Stengel, Bancroft
*Casey Stengel	For Burleigh Grimes	With Dave Bancroft

*Also elected to Hall of Fame

CEPEDA, SADECKI, TORRE

Players who went round-robin for each other in a series of major league trades. First baseman Orlando Cepeda was dealt from the San Francisco Giants to the St. Louis Cardinals for pitcher Ray Sadecki on May 8, 1966. Cepeda then was swapped from St. Louis to the Atlanta Braves for catcher-first baseman Joe Torre on March 17, 1969. And on October 13, 1974, Sadecki and pitcher Tommy Moore were traded from the Mets to the Cardinals for Torre.

LU CLINTON

American Leaguer who played one game for Kansas City in 1965—a game that he apparently wasn't supposed to play. When the California Angels placed Clinton on waivers in early September of '65—marking the third time that waivers had been asked that year on the 27-year-old outfielder— the A.L. office failed to designate the waivers as irrevocable (as befits a three-time waiver situation). Believing that Clinton could still be recalled from the waiver wire, all A.L. clubs except one—Cleveland—passed on him. When A.L. officials discovered that the waivers should have been listed as irrevocable, they informed all teams of the oversight and gave clubs with a lower standing than the fourth-place Indians a chance to enter a claim. And the last-place A's did just that. With California playing in Kansas City on the night of the waiver wildness (September 8), Clinton donned an A's uniform and went hitless in one at-bat against his former team. The following day, the A.L. office notified the A's that the Clinton case was being reopened and that Kansas City should not use Clinton pending a ruling. After Commission-er Ford Frick's entry into the matter and following a disclosure that Cleve-land had claimed Clinton earlier in year, too, it was decided on September 10 that—procedurally amiss or not—the first-come Indians would be first-served. Clinton was awarded to the Tribe.

Clinton's one appearance with Kansas City happened to come in one of the most memorable games in the Athletics' 13 seasons in the Missouri city. It was the contest in which Bert Campaneris of the A's became the first player in major league history to play all nine positions in one game.

COFFMAN-FISCHER, DAVIS-NORDHAGEN

These major league players were traded even up for each other—*twice*. On June 9, 1932, the St. Louis Browns dealt righthanded pitcher Dick Coffman to the Senators for lefthander Carl Fischer. The following December, the Sen-ators swapped Coffman back to the Browns for Fischer. Fifty years later, in a June 15, 1982, transaction, the Philadelphia Phillies sent outfielder Dick Davis to the Toronto Blue Jays for outfielder Wayne Nordhagen. The same day, the Phils traded Nordhagen to Pittsburgh for outfielder Bill Robinson. Then, just a week later, the Pirates and Blue Jays hooked up in a one-for-one deal—Nordhagen going to Toronto in exchange for Davis.

Other players have been swapped twice for each other, but in most cases the transactions involved additional players and/or cash. Among players

Jim (Catfish) Hunter, the American League's reigning Cy Young Award winner, was the center of considerable attention on December 31, 1974, when he ended a bidding war by agreeing to a contract with the New York Yankees after being declared a free agent because of Oakland's breach of contract.

traded for each other twice in multi-player deals were: Larry Benton and Hugh McQuillan, Spud Davis and Jimmie Wilson, Kiddo Davis and Chick Fullis, Ron Northey and Harry Walker, Fred Sanford and Dick Starr, Smoky Burgess and Andy Seminick, Hoot Evers and Bill Wight, Ray Katt and Dick Littlefield, Larry Doby and Tito Francona, Tim Cullen and Ron Hansen and Jim Essian and Dick Allen.

NATE COLBERT

Of the 24 players available in the majors' first free-agent re-entry draft (conducted in November 1976), the only one who didn't hook on with a big-league club. While 22 of the pool's players were drafted (13 were picked the maximum 13 times), Colbert and Willie McCovey, both of whom finished the '76 season with brief stints for the Oakland A's, went unclaimed. McCovey eventually signed with the San Francisco Giants (the team for whom he had played from 1959 through 1973), but former San Diego star Colbert did not catch on with another major league team (although he was invited to the Toronto Blue Jays' 1977 spring-training camp).

DECEMBER 31, 1974

The date on which pitcher Jim (Catfish) Hunter, declared a free agent a little more than two weeks earlier because the deferred-compensation portion of his contract had been breached by the Oakland A's, ended the frenzied auction for his services by agreeing to a five-year contract with the New York Yankees. The deal reportedly was worth more than $3 million. Major league club officials, caught up in baseball's first free-agent bidding war, had flocked to Hunter's home state of North Carolina to make pitches for the 28-year-old righthander, who had just won the American League's Cy Young Award after a 25-victory season for the A's (which marked his fourth straight year of winning 20 games).

BRUCE ELLINGSEN

The player Cleveland received from Los Angeles in the April 4, 1974, one-for-one deal that sent Pedro Guerrero to the Dodgers' organization. Ellingsen, nearing his 25th birthday, was a lefthanded pitcher who in 1973 had posted a 5-10 record (with a 6.71 earned-run average) for Class AAA Albuquerque. Third baseman Guerrero, just 17 years old, had played only 44 games of professional ball at that juncture, all in a rookie league. Ellingsen went on to appear in 16 major league games, all for the 1974 Indians, and compiled a 1-1 record with a 3.21 ERA. On the other hand, Guerrero, who saw his first extensive duty for Los Angeles in 1981, developed into one of the majors' top hitters—both for average and power. Through 1986, Guerrero had hit .304 for the Dodgers in 825 games, twice had driven in 100 or more runs and three times had topped the 30-homer mark.

RICK FERRELL, WES FERRELL

A major league brother battery, the Ferrells were traded together by the Boston Red Sox to the Washington Senators on June 10, 1937. Rick, a catcher, had batted .301 for Boston in 1935 and .312 in 1936, while pitcher Wes had won 25 games for the Red Sox in '35 and 20 in '36. Accompanying the Ferrells to Washington was outfielder Mel Almada. In return, the Red Sox received outfielder Ben Chapman and pitcher Bobo Newsom from the Senators.

The Ferrell brothers, Rick (left) and Wes (right), greet Washington Manager Bucky Harris after their June 1937 trade from the Red Sox to the Senators.

Outfielder Gus Zernial (left), one of 57 players to perform with the Philadelphia A's and not play under Manager Connie Mack, looks over an Official Baseball Guide with Jimmie Dykes, the A's manager from 1951 through 1953. Zernial played 528 games in the four years that the A's remained in Philadelphia after Mack's retirement.

57

In the 54-year history of the Philadelphia A's, the number of players to perform for that team who did not play for Connie Mack. Of the 57, outfielder Gus Zernial appeared in the most games (528) for the Philadelphia club without ever playing under Mack and he was the only non-pitcher to play for the Philadelphia A's all four years (1951 through 1954) that Mack didn't manage the team.

Of the Philadelphia A's pitchers who never played for Mack (there were 25, compared with 32 non-pitchers), Morrie Martin appeared in the most games for the Philadelphia club (111) and was the only hurler to pitch for the team in all four of the non-Mack years.

VERN GEISHERT, FRANK DUFFY

The players the San Francisco Giants received when they sent George Foster to the Cincinnati Reds in a May 29, 1971, swap. Geishert, a pitcher, never saw action for the Giants and appeared in only 11 big-league games in his entire career, all for the 1969 California Angels. In fact, Geishert, after being shifted from Cincinnati's Class AAA farm club to San Francisco's top affiliate in the wake of the deal, left baseball. Duffy, an infielder, batted .179

176

DECEMBER 1913—BUCK HERZOG. Infielder Herzog became playing manager of the Cincinnati Reds after he and catcher Grover Hartley were traded from the New York Giants to Cincinnati for outfielder Bob Bescher.

JULY 1916—CHRISTY MATHEWSON. Pitcher Mathewson became manager of the Reds (he pitched in one game for Cincinnati in '16) after he, infielder Bill McKechnie and outfielder Edd Roush were traded from the Giants to Cincinnati for infielder Buck Herzog and outfielder Red Killefer.

NOVEMBER 1923—DAVE BANCROFT. Infielder Bancroft became playing manager of the Boston Braves after he and outfielders Casey Stengel and Bill Cunningham were traded from the Giants to Boston for outfielder Billy Southworth and pitcher Joe Oeschger.

OCTOBER 1928—BUCKY HARRIS. Harris, playing manager of the Washington Senators, became manager of the Detroit Tigers (he appeared in seven games for Detroit in 1929) after a trade in which the Tigers sent infielder Jack Warner to Washington.

NOVEMBER 1933—JIMMIE WILSON. Catcher Wilson became playing manager of the Philadelphia Phillies after he was traded from the St. Louis Cardinals to Philadelphia for catcher Spud Davis and infielder Eddie Delker.

JANUARY 1934—BOB O'FARRELL. Catcher O'Farrell became playing manager of the Reds after he and pitcher Syl Johnson were traded from the Cardinals to Cincinnati for pitcher Glenn Spencer and cash.

DECEMBER 1951—EDDIE STANKY. Infielder Stanky became playing manager of the Cardinals after he was traded from the Giants to St. Louis for pitcher Max Lanier and outfielder Chuck Diering.

SEPTEMBER 1958—SOLLY HEMUS. Infielder Hemus became playing manager of the Cardinals after he was traded from the Phillies to St. Louis for third baseman Gene Freese.

MAY 1963—GIL HODGES. First baseman Hodges became manager of the Senators after being released as a player by the New York Mets. The day after Hodges was given his freedom to take the managerial position, the Washington club sold outfielder Jim Piersall to the Mets as an apparent "consideration."

OCTOBER 1967—GIL HODGES. Hodges, manager of the Senators, became manager of the Mets in a transaction that involved his release as Washington's pilot, a cash payment from New York to Washington and the November dispatch of pitcher Bill Denehy from the Mets to the Senators.

NOVEMBER 1976—CHUCK TANNER. Tanner, manager of the Oakland A's, became manager of the Pittsburgh Pirates after the Pirates sent catcher Manny Sanguillen and cash to Oakland in exchange for Tanner's services.

MATHEWSON, McKECHNIE, ROUSH

Principals in the only major league trade involving three future Hall-of-Famers. Amazingly, the swap did not involve a mix of the three; instead, the Cincinnati Reds acquired all three of the Cooperstown-bound figures—Christy Mathewson, Bill McKechnie and Edd Roush—in the five-man swap with the New York Giants that was made on July 20, 1916. While a deal netting one team three eventual Hall-of-Famers would appear decidedly one-sided (if not a case of highway robbery), all was not as it now seems.

The 35-year-old Mathewson, after all, was going to Cincinnati to manage, not pitch (the Giants' 372-game winner would pitch only once—it was a winning effort—for the Reds). And McKechnie was an infielder of marginal ability, a .234 lifetime hitter who won his way to the Hall of Fame via his managerial skill (which he exhibited by directing three National League franchises to pennants and managing four N.L. championship teams overall). The acquisition of Roush, though, clearly was a coup for Cincinnati in terms of bolstering its playing talent. Only 23 years old at the time of the deal, outfielder Roush went on to win two batting crowns while a member of the Reds and attained a .325 career average in the majors.

In return for Mathewson, McKechnie and Roush, New York received infielder Buck Herzog (who had played for the Giants in the 1911, 1912 and 1913 World Series) and outfielder Red Killefer from Cincinnati. Herzog didn't distinguish himself in his third stint with the New York club and, after appearing in the 1917 Series with the Giants and then being traded two more times, bowed out of the big leagues in 1920 with a .259 career batting mark. Killefer appeared in only two games for the Giants, then left the majors for good as a .248 hitter.

KEVIN McREYNOLDS

Outfielder who on December 11, 1986, was traded from San Diego to the New York Mets in an eight-man deal that netted the Padres five players— including outfielder-infielder Kevin Mitchell and pitchers Kevin Brown and Kevin Armstrong. While tripling their pleasure in the "Kevin" department, the Padres also acquired promising outfielders Shawn Abner and Stanley Jefferson in the swap and sent pitcher Gene Walter and infielder Adam Ging to the Mets.

OAKLAND A'S

American League team for whom Felipe Alou played in 1971, Matty Alou played in 1972 and Jesus Alou played in 1973. Felipe, an A's regular in 1970, played only two games for Oakland in '71 before being traded to the New York Yankees. Matty appeared in 32 games for the A's in '72 following his late-August acquisition from the St. Louis Cardinals. And Jesus played 36 games for Oakland in '73 after being obtained in a July 31 transaction with the Houston Astros. (Matty moved on to the Yankees in November 1972, while Jesus played for Oakland again in 1974 before drawing his release from the A's organization in March 1975.)

OCTOBER 7, 1969

Date of the seven-man St. Louis Cardinals-Philadelphia Phillies trade that involved Curt Flood and precipitated Flood's court fight against baseball's reserve system. The swap sent outfielder Flood (a Cardinal since 1958 and a lifetime .293 hitter in the majors), catcher Tim McCarver, outfielder Byron Browne and pitcher Joe Hoerner from St. Louis to Philadelphia for first baseman Dick Allen, second baseman Cookie Rojas and pitcher Jerry Johnson. Contending that he should be able to make a deal for himself and not be

Curt Flood, the man who instigated the fight against baseball's reserve system, sat out the 1970 season before becoming a member of the 1971 Washington Senators in a comeback that lasted only 13 games.

shipped around without his approval (he also had been swapped in 1957, from Cincinnati to St. Louis), Flood sat out the 1970 season and began a long assault on the reserve clause, which reserved a player's services to one team from one year to the next until the player was traded, sold or released, or until he retired. As compensation for Flood's failure to report, the Cards sent first baseman-outfielder Willie Montanez (in April 1970) and pitcher Bob Browning (in August 1970) to the Phillies.

Flood, assured that a return to action would not affect his court case, was induced back to the playing field in 1971 by Washington Senators Owner Bob Short. The Phillies, to whom Flood technically belonged, agreed to let Flood join the Senators in a November 3, 1970, deal that sent first baseman-catcher Greg Goossen, first baseman-outfielder Gene Martin and pitcher Jeff Terpko to the National League team. The 33-year-old Flood played only 13 games for Washington in '71—he batted .200—before leaving the club and major league baseball for good.

The U.S. Supreme Court upheld baseball's reserve system in 1972.

DAVE REVERING

Power-hitting prospect whom the Oakland A's were to receive—along with an estimated $1.75 million—as the result of a December 9, 1977, trade sending Vida Blue, a three-time 20-game winner for the A's, to the Cincinnati Reds. A's Owner Charlie Finley, defying Commissioner Bowie Kuhn's directive that the commissioner's office should be consulted before any transaction involving $400,000 or more was made, was foiled on January 30, 1978, when Kuhn voided the deal.

First baseman Revering, who had slugged 29 home runs and driven in 110 runs at Class AAA Indianapolis in 1977, wound up with the A's after all, going to Oakland along with an undisclosed amount of cash in a February 25, 1978, trade in which the Reds received relief pitcher Doug Bair. And Blue, the American League's Cy Young Award winner in 1971, wound up in the National League after all—but with the San Francisco Giants, not the Reds. In a March 15, 1978, deal, the A's sent the lefthanded pitcher to the Giants for seven players and an estimated $390,000.

JIMMY RING

A 118-149 pitcher in 12 National League seasons, he was the third man in two memorable trades—first, a swap involving a future Pro Football Hall of Fame inductee and a future member of baseball's Hall of Fame and, second, a stunning deal featuring the exchange of two of the major leagues' best and most colorful players (both of whom also won places at Cooperstown). In February 1921, the Cincinnati Reds traded outfielder Earle (Greasy) Neale, a veteran of five N.L. seasons at that juncture, and pitcher Ring to the Philadelphia Phillies for pitcher Eppa Rixey. After only 22 games with the Phillies, Neale was sold back to the Reds, for whom he wound up his big-league career in 1924. Neale, a lifetime .259 hitter in 768 games in the majors, later became coach of the National Football League's Philadelphia Eagles (he had coached Washington and Jefferson to an appearance in the 1922 Rose Bowl) and directed the Eagles to NFL championships in 1948 and 1949. In 1969, Neale was elected to the Pro Football Hall of Fame. Rixey, an eight-year major leaguer at the time of the 1921 Phils-Reds trade, went on to pitch 13 years for Cincinnati and finished his big-league career with a 266-251 record. In 1963, Rixey was named to baseball's Hall of Fame. Ring, who was traded to the New York Giants in December 1925, accompanied Giants second baseman Frankie Frisch (a homegrown New Yorker and crowd favorite) to St. Louis in the momentous December 1926 swap that sent second baseman Rogers Hornsby, playing manager of the Cardinals' '26 World Series champions, to New York's N.L. club.

BROOKS ROBINSON, CARL YASTRZEMSKI

Of players who spent their entire major league careers with one club, the ones who performed for the most years—23. Robinson broke into the big leagues with Baltimore in 1955 and played for the Orioles through 1977, while Yastrzemski made his debut in the majors with Boston in 1961 and was a member of the Red Sox through 1983. Players who spent 20 or more seasons in the majors, all with one team:

Years	Player, Club, League	Career Span
23	Brooks Robinson, Baltimore, A.L.	1955-1977
23	Carl Yastrzemski, Boston, A.L.	1961-1983
22	Cap Anson, Chicago, N.L.	1876-1897
22	Al Kaline, Detroit, A.L.	1953-1974
22	Stan Musial, St. Louis, N.L.	1941-1963
22	Mel Ott, New York, N.L.	1926-1947
21	Walter Johnson, Washington, A.L.	1907-1927
21	Ted Lyons, Chicago, A.L.	1923-1946
21	Willie Stargell, Pittsburgh, N.L.	1962-1982
20	Luke Appling, Chicago, A.L.	1930-1950
20	Red Faber, Chicago, A.L.	1914-1933
20	Mel Harder, Cleveland, A.L.	1928-1947

BRAGGO ROTH, RED SHANNON

Major leaguers who twice were traded as a package, first for two players and then for three. On June 27, 1919, the Philadelphia A's swapped outfielder Roth and infielder Shannon to the Boston Red Sox for outfielder Amos Strunk and infielder Jack Barry (whose subsequent retirement did not nullify the deal). The following January, the Red Sox dealt Roth and Shannon to the Washington Senators for outfielder Mike Menosky, infielder Eddie Foster and pitcher Harry Harper.

While other big-league pairs have been traded together twice, additional players usually accompanied the two to their new teams. Among other players swapped together twice were Johnny Hodapp and Bob Seeds, Red Kress and Bobo Newsom, Billy Cox and Preacher Roe, Clint Courtney and Bob Chakales, Ryne Duren and Jim Pisoni, Tom Morgan and Mickey McDermott, Ken Brett and Jim Lonborg, Joe Ferguson and Bobby Detherage and Ed Farmer and Gary Holle. (After Cox and Roe were traded together for a second time—the circumstances being a December 1954 relocation from the Brooklyn Dodgers to the Baltimore Orioles—Roe retired. The deal then was completed in March 1955 with an additional exchange of players and cash.)

RON SANTO

The first major league player to exercise his right to refuse a trade under the Basic Agreement's "10 and five" rule. In February 1973, big-league owners and players agreed on a new contract containing a stipulation that a player who had 10 or more years of major league service and had spent the last five years with the same club had the right to veto a trade. On December 5, 1973, Santo, a Chicago Cub since entering the majors in 1960, vetoed a deal that would have sent him to California (reportedly for Angels pitching prospects Andy Hassler and Bruce Heinbechner). The power-hitting third baseman, wanting to stay in Chicago, consented a week later to a swap shipping him to the crosstown White Sox. In return, the Sox received catcher Steve Swisher and pitchers Steve Stone, Ken Frailing and Jim Kremmel.

The "10 and five" rule had received its first test in March 1973 when Minnesota made plans to deal pitcher Jim Perry, a big-leaguer since 1959 and a Twins pitcher since 1963, to Detroit. Perry agreed to go to the Tigers, thus becoming the majors' first player with "10 and five" veto privileges to consent to a trade. In return for Perry, the Twins received pitching prospect Danny Fife and cash from the Tigers in the March 27 swap.

ED SAUER, HANK SAUER

Brothers who were involved in separate National League deals on the same day in 1949—and Ed Sauer was peddled twice before the day was out. On June 15, the St. Louis Cardinals sent Ed, an outfielder, to the Pittsburgh Pirates for cash, and the Pirates turned around and shipped Ed to the Boston Braves for catcher Phil Masi. Also that day, the Cincinnati Reds traded outfielders Hank Sauer and Frankie Baumholtz to the Chicago Cubs for outfielders Harry Walker and Peanuts Lowrey.

SEVEN

The number of games that Ernie Broglio won for the Chicago Cubs in the remainder of his big-league career after the Cubs gave up outfielder Lou Brock to obtain Broglio from the St. Louis Cardinals in a June 15, 1964, trade. While the swap was, in fact, a six-player deal—pitcher Bobby Shantz and outfielder Doug Clemens accompanied Broglio to Chicago and pitchers Paul Toth and Jack Spring moved to St. Louis with Brock—the principals clearly were Broglio, a 21-game winner for St. Louis in 1960 and an 18-game winner for the Cards in 1963, and Brock, a fleet outfielder whose enormous potential had gone largely untapped since his arrival in the majors at the end of the 1961 season. Broglio, who had a 3-5 record for the Cards in '64, was 4-7 for the Cubs the rest of the year and, beset by arm problems, finished 1-6 and 2-6 for Chicago in 1965 and 1966, respectively. He never pitched again in the majors, his big-league career having ended before he turned 31. Brock, batting .251 for the Cubs at the time of the trade, hit .348 for St. Louis in 103 games and helped the '64 Cardinals to the National League pennant and World Series crown. Brock went on to collect 3,023 career hits in the majors, steal a record 938 bases (including 118 in 1974, still an N.L. mark) and win election to the Hall of Fame in 1985.

17, 64

The number of transactions made between the New York Yankees and the Kansas City Athletics from March 1955 through June 1961 and the number of players involved in those deals. The powerful Yankees seemed to trade quantity for quality when dealing with the also-ran A's, often obtaining future stars, solid players or stretch-run help for packages of steady-but-unspectacular performers. In the view of many, the Yankees had developed a "parent club-farm team" relationship with Kansas City, tapping the Midwest pipeline for just the right player when the situation demanded it. The irony was that until '55—when the Philadelphia A's moved to Kansas City— K.C., in fact, had been a New York farm club, serving as a longtime Class AAA affiliate of the Yankees. The heavy trading between the two clubs came to a halt when Charlie Finley took ownership of the A's in December 1960.

Nine players made "round-trips" between New York and Kansas City during the six-year trading binge. Traded from the Yankees to the A's and then back to the Yanks were Enos Slaughter, Ralph Terry, Bob Cerv, Bob Martyn, Jack Urban and Milt Graff (the last three of whom, though, never appeared in a regular-season game with the Yankees); going from the Athletics to the Yanks and then back to the A's were Harry (Suitcase) Simpson, Murry Dickson and Art Ditmar.

Typical of the Yankees' good fortune in their dealings with Kansas City was the pinstripe success enjoyed by Roger Maris, Ralph Terry and Enos Slaughter. Outfielder Maris, infielder Joe DeMaestri and first baseman Kent Hadley were obtained from the A's in a December 11, 1959, swap in which New York traded pitcher Don Larsen, outfielders Hank Bauer and Norm Siebern and first baseman Marv Throneberry to Kansas City. Maris won the American League's Most Valuable Player honor the next two seasons while smashing a total of 100 home runs for the Yankees (including a record 61 in 1961). Terry began his big-league career with the Yankees in 1956 before moving to Kansas City in a June 15, 1957, deal. After what critics of Yankees-A's bartering called a little "seasoning," pitcher Terry was reacquired by New York in a May 26, 1959, deal and posted a 16-3 record for the Yankees in 1961, won 23 games in 1962 and notched 17 victories in 1963. Slaughter, a Yankee reserve in 1954, was traded to Kansas City on May 11, 1955, but was reacquired by New York via an August 25, 1956, purchase. The 40-year-old outfielder hit .289 for the Yanks in the last month of the season, then starred in the '56 World Series (hitting a game-winning homer and batting .350).

Kansas City profited from the swap mart, too, most notably as a result of its October 15, 1956, purchase of outfielder Cerv from the Yankees. In 1958, Cerv blossomed into one of the top power hitters in the majors, walloping 38 homers, driving in 104 runs and batting .305 for the A's.

ROYLE STILLMAN

Having driven in one run and batted .091 in 20 games for the 1976 Baltimore Orioles, this outfielder-first baseman was one of the 24 players available in major league baseball's first free-agent re-entry draft, held November 4, 1976. Stillman, like the other 23 big-leaguers on the open market, was eligible for the draft after failing to sign a contract in '76 and playing out his option that year (part of which he spent in the minor leagues). Obviously, Stillman, who wound up signing with the Chicago White Sox on December 5, was not one of the plums of the draft. Others in the pool were: Reggie Jackson, Don Gullett, Sal Bando, Rollie Fingers, Joe Rudi, Don Baylor,

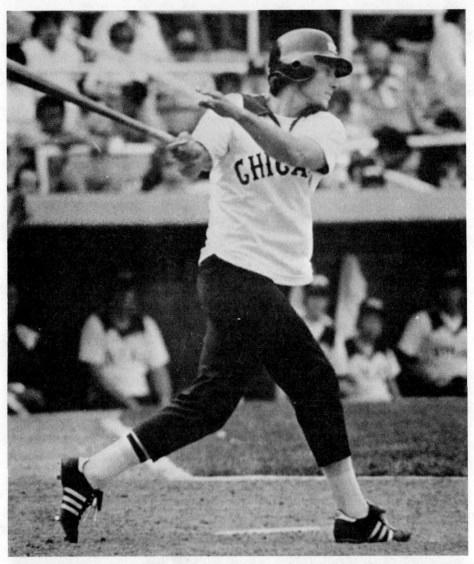

Royle Stillman, who had seen only limited service for the Orioles, was probably the least known player among the 24 who made up baseball's first free-agent re-entry list in 1976. Stillman was signed by the White Sox.

Bobby Grich, Doyle Alexander, Bert Campaneris, Bill Campbell, Dave Cash, Gene Tenace, Eric Soderholm, Nate Colbert, Paul Dade, Tito Fuentes, Wayne Garland, Willie McCovey, Richie Hebner, Gary Matthews, Steve Stone, Tim Nordbrook and Billy Smith.

The re-entry draft was formulated in an agreement between management and the Major League Players Association as an outgrowth of arbitrator Peter Seitz's decision in December 1975 to grant free-agent status to pitchers Andy Messersmith and Dave McNally, both of whom had played without contracts in '75 (Messersmith with the Los Angeles Dodgers and McNally

186

with the Montreal Expos until his retirement in June). Seitz's decision, upheld in subsequent court challenges, struck at the centerpiece of baseball's reserve system, the renewal clause, by which a team could renew the contract of a player into perpetuity. Seitz's ruling, in effect, no longer bound a player to one club until that player was released, traded or sold. (Messersmith moved on to Atlanta, signing a free-agent contract with the Braves in April 1976. McNally remained in retirement.)

PETE SUDER

One of eight men to play for all three managers in Philadelphia A's history. Infielder Suder played 1,014 games for Connie Mack (who guided the club from its inception in 1901 through 1950), 312 games for Jimmie Dykes (the American League team's pilot from 1951 through 1953) and 69 games for Eddie Joost (who directed the last Philadelphia A's entry, the 1954 club).

Also playing for all three Philadelphia A's pilots (with figures in parentheses indicating the number of games played under, in order, Mack, Dykes and Joost): Joe Astroth (108, 250, 77), Ed Burtschy (9, 7, 46), Joost (561, 337, 19), Alex Kellner (87, 92, 27), Carl Scheib (196, 127, 1), Bobby Shantz (69, 81, 7) and Elmer Valo (843, 302, 95).

12

The number of players winning major league Most Valuable Player awards in their first full season with a new team after being traded, sold or released by another club. The first player to win MVP honors under such conditions was the Boston Braves' Johnny Evers, recipient of the 1914 Chalmers Award (the MVP equivalent of the day) in the National League. Second baseman Evers, the Chicago Cubs' playing manager in 1913, had been released by the Cubs after the '13 season. The last player to attain MVP status the season after a change in scenery was Detroit's Willie Hernandez, the American League's MVP in 1984. The Tigers obtained Hernandez in a trade with the Philadelphia Phillies 10 days before the start of the '84 season.

Other players receiving MVP awards (or their equivalent) in their first full season with a new club after being traded, sold or released by another team: Bob O'Farrell, St. Louis, N.L., 1926 (acquired by the Cardinals from the Cubs in a May 1925 trade); Rogers Hornsby, Chicago, N.L., 1929 (from the Braves, after the 1928 season); Mickey Cochrane, Detroit, A.L., 1934 (from the Philadelphia A's, after the 1933 season); Bucky Walters, Cincinnati, N.L., 1939 (from the Phillies, during the 1938 season); Bob Elliott, Boston, N.L., 1947 (from Pittsburgh, after the 1946 season); Roger Maris, New York, A.L., 1960 (from Kansas City, after the 1959 season); Frank Robinson, Baltimore, A.L., 1966 (from Cincinnati, after the 1965 season); Orlando Cepeda, St. Louis, N.L., 1967 (from San Francisco, during the 1966 season); Dick Allen, Chicago, A.L., 1972 (from Los Angeles, after the 1971 season); Rollie Fingers, Milwaukee, A.L., 1981 (from St. Louis, in a 1980 postseason trade, after Fingers spent the '80 season with San Diego).

Maris was an MVP repeater in his second season (1961) with the Yankees.

St. Louis Cardinals fans well remember Ernie Broglio (left) and Bob Sykes, the pitchers who were traded in deals for outfielders Lou Brock (1964) and Willie McGee (1981), respectively. Broglio went on to win seven games for the Cubs and Sykes never appeared in a game for the Yankees.

ZERO

The number of games in which pitcher Bob Sykes appeared in the majors after the October 21, 1981, trade in which the New York Yankees dealt minor league outfielder Willie McGee to the St. Louis Cardinals in exchange for Sykes. Sykes, 26 years old, had a 23-26 career record in the majors at the time of the deal; McGee, two weeks from his 23rd birthday, had played five years in the minor leagues and was coming off a .322 season in Class AA ball. Sykes, a lefthander who had incurred various arm and shoulder ailments earlier in his career, was troubled again by injuries in 1982. After compiling a 1-2 record for Class AAA Columbus and a 2-1 mark for Class AA Nashville in '82, Sykes disappeared from baseball. McGee, meanwhile, helped the Cardinals to the 1982 World Series title and won the National League's Most Valuable Player honor in 1985 when he hit a league-leading .353 in the Cards' pennant-winning year.

A December 14, 1982, deal in which the Cardinals sent promising prospects Bobby Meacham (shortstop) and Stan Javier (outfielder) to the Yankees for three not-so-prime minor leaguers was viewed in many baseball circles as an apparent "pot sweetener" for the McGee deal.

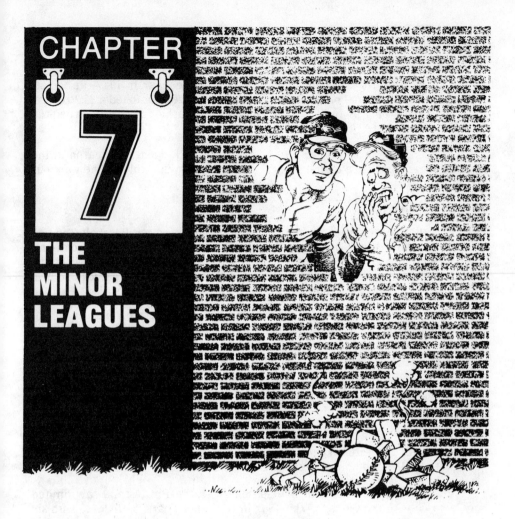

CHAPTER 7

THE MINOR LEAGUES

BUZZ ARLETT

He slugged four home runs in one game *twice* in a five-week span of the 1932 International League season. Playing for Baltimore in a June 1 game against Reading, outfielder Arlett belted four homers and drove in seven runs as the Orioles defeated the Keys, 14-13. Then, in the first game of a July 4 Baltimore-Reading doubleheader, he repeated the four-homer salvo and knocked in nine runs as the Orioles romped to a 21-10 victory. (For good measure, Arlett homered once in the nightcap of the Independence Day twin bill.)

The switch-hitting Arlett, who finished the '32 season with 54 home runs, hit 30 or more homers eight times in the minor leagues. His only big-league experience came in 1931 when, after 13 years with Oakland of the Pacific Coast League, he played a full season with the Philadelphia Phillies. After performing capably for the Phils (.313 batting average, 18 homers and 72 RBIs), Arlett was back in the minors the next season and excelling for Baltimore.

ORIE ARNTZEN

The Sporting News' Minor League Player of the Year in 1949—at age 39. Pitching for Albany of the Eastern League, Arntzen compiled a 25-2 record. He walked only 41 batters in 216 innings and fashioned a 2.79 earned-run average.

Arntzen, who broke into professional ball in 1931, spent one season in the major leagues. As a member of the 1943 Philadelphia Athletics, he won four of 17 decisions.

JOE BAUMAN

The all-time single-season homer champion in Organized Baseball (the umbrella under which both the major leagues and the National Association's minor leagues fall). Bauman slammed 72 home runs for Roswell of the Longhorn League in 1954, achieving his record total in 138 games and also driving in 224 runs and batting an even .400.

From 1952 through 1955, Bauman averaged 55 homers per season in the Longhorn League (compiling yearly totals of 50, 53, 72 and 46).

TED BEARD

Hollywood outfielder who in a 3½-week span of the 1953 Pacific Coast League season accomplished the feats of slugging four home runs in one game and reeling off 12 consecutive hits over four contests.

Beard, a 5-foot-8, 165-pounder, had attracted attention in 1950 when, in a stint with the Pittsburgh Pirates, he became the first player since Babe Ruth (in 1935) to homer over the right-field stands at Forbes Field.

Beard, who spent parts of five seasons with the Pirates and saw limited service with the Chicago White Sox in two other years, batted .198 with six homers in 474 career at-bats in the majors.

STEVE BILKO

One of the most feared hitters in the history of the high minors, as reflected by his successive 50-plus homer seasons for Los Angeles of the Pacific Coast League. Playing 162 games for the PCL's Angels in 1956, Bilko smashed 55 home runs, knocked in 164 runs and batted .360 (all league-leading figures). In 1957, Bilko slammed 56 homers for the Angels and drove in 140 runs— both league highs—while hitting .300 in 158 games.

Bilko also topped the PCL in homers in 1955, hitting 37 for Los Angeles in 168 games. He batted .328 that year and had 124 RBIs.

WADE BOGGS, CAL RIPKEN JR.

The opposing third basemen in the longest game in Organized Baseball history, a 33-inning International League contest between Pawtucket and Rochester that was played in 1981. Boggs collected four hits in 12 at-bats for

Steve Bilko, one of the most prodigious power hitters in minor league history for the Pacific Coast League's Los Angeles Angels, is pictured above (right) with another Bilko, Phil Silvers, who played Sergeant Ernie Bilko in the late 1950s on television's hit comedy series 'The Phil Silvers Show.'

Pawtucket, while Ripken was 2 for 13 for Rochester. Both played errorless ball in the field.

Two years later, Ripken won Most Valuable Player honors in the American League while playing shortstop for the Baltimore Orioles and Boggs, having settled into the third-base job for the Boston Red Sox, captured his first A.L. batting championship.

FRAN BONIAR

Dodger farmhand who enjoyed two of the best seasons in minor league history, batting .435 for Hornell of the Pony League in 1955 and .436 for Reno of the California League in 1957.

Outfielder Boniar, who embellished those seasons with home run/runs-batted-in totals of 18 and 100 and then 11 and 138, never made the major leagues and played as high as the Class AAA level only briefly.

IKE BOONE

The minors' Ty Cobb, having posted the best lifetime average, .370, in baseball's "bush leagues." Boone, a .319 career hitter in the majors in 356 games (he batted .333 and .330 for the Boston Red Sox in 1924 and 1925), played 1,857 games in the minor leagues and posted such full-season averages as .407, .402, .389 and .380. And, in an 83-game stint (310 at-bats) for the Pacific Coast League's Missions club in 1930, he batted .448.

Danny Boone, Ike's brother, also was a robust minor league hitter. A one-time pitcher (he went 8-13 for the Philadelphia A's, Detroit Tigers and Cleveland Indians in a big-league career that ended in 1923), Danny became an outfielder and batted .356 in 1,336 minor league games.

The Boones combined for 101 minor league home runs in 1929, Ike slugging 55 for the PCL Missions and Danny walloping 46 for High Point of the Piedmont League.

RAY BOYER

Pawtucket player who figured in the battle for the 1980 International League batting championship—despite the fact he hit .238 in '80. When Pawtucket came to bat in the bottom of the ninth inning of its season finale against Toledo, the Mud Hens' Dave Engle had a batting average of .30674 and Pawtucket's Wade Boggs had a league-leading mark of .30695. With little threat of extra innings (Toledo led, 6-1), Engle surely had made his last trip to the plate of the season. Boggs, though, would bat fourth in the Pawtucket ninth—if the Red Sox's top farm club got that far into the order. Toledo players, wanting Engle to win the batting title by whatever means, made *certain* Pawtucket got that far. After Pawtucket's first two batters were retired in the ninth, the light-hitting Boyer was walked intentionally. Boyer, thinking turnabout was fair play in this help-a-teammate-in-need scenario, set out for second base in hopes of being thrown out to end the game. No luck. He didn't even draw a throw. Boyer then trotted toward third base and, again, the Toledo catcher (Ray Smith) ignored him. What waukee Braves. A 7-2 pitcher for the National League club in 1961, Cloninger parlayed his improved control into 19- and 24-victory seasons for Milwaukee in 1964 and 1965 and a total of 113 major league victories.

BOB COLEMAN

A manager in the minors for 35 seasons, he first guided a team in 1919 (Mobile) and last piloted a minor league club in 1957 (Evansville). Coleman, second on the minors' managerial victory list with 2,496 games won, had four managerial stints—totaling 20 years—with Evansville's Three-I League franchise. He guided the Indiana team from 1928 through 1931, 1938 through 1942, 1946 through 1949 and 1951 through '57.

Coleman, a former reserve catcher in the majors, managed the Boston Braves in 1944 and for more than half of the 1945 season.

CORDELE

The Georgia-Florida League team that in 1952 didn't exactly rely on the long ball. The Cordele Athletics, fifth-place finishers in the league with a 66-73 record, hit *one* home run in the entire season. Third baseman Ralph Betcher connected for Cordele in the club's 73rd game of the year.

BOB CRUES

In 1948, while playing for Amarillo of the West Texas-New Mexico League, he put together what surely ranks—in terms of sheer numbers, regardless of the competition or playing conditions—as the greatest all-around single-season performance in professional baseball history. Competing in a Class C league little-known as a breeding ground for future major leaguers but well-known for its small ball parks, Crues hammered 69 home runs and drove in 254 runs (a record for Organized Baseball)—and he posted those figures in a 140-game schedule. Sure, but could he hit for average? Would you believe .404? That's the batting mark Crues fashioned, based on his 228 hits in 565 at-bats.

MATTHEW MARIO (MATT) CUOMO

An outfielder who appeared in 81 games for the Pittsburgh Pirates' Brunswick farm club of the Georgia-Florida League in 1952 and batted .244 with one home run and 26 runs batted in.

While Cuomo never realized most players' ambition of reaching the big leagues, Brunswick teammate Fred Green did. Lefthanded pitcher Green, a 20-game winner for Brunswick, made the majors in 1959 and was a member of the 1960 World Series-champion Pittsburgh Pirates. On the other hand, Mario Cuomo made the "big time" in another field—he was elected governor of New York in 1982 and re-elected to that post in 1986.

STEVE DALKOWSKI

Pitcher who could throw a ball through a brick wall—that, or 10 feet *over* it. Regarded as one of the prime prospects in baseball history, Dalkowski had

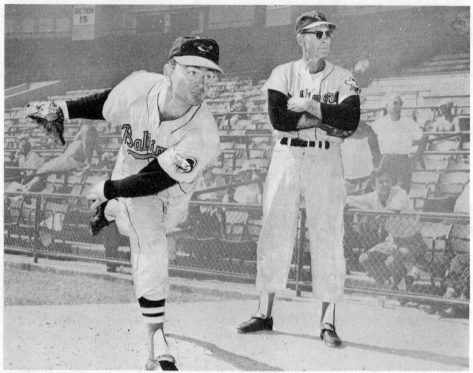

Lefthander Steve Dalkowski, shown warming up in 1963 under the watchful eye of Orioles pitching coach Harry Brecheen, might have been the fastest, and wildest, pitcher ever to play Organized Baseball.

blazing—perhaps even unprecedented—speed. But the lefthander also had monumental—perhaps even unprecedented—control problems. Signed by the Baltimore Orioles in 1957, Dalkowski averaged 17 walks and 15 strikeouts per nine innings in his first five seasons of pro ball (1,022 walks and 907 strikeouts in 537 innings) while compiling a 19-52 won-lost record. Dalkowski abruptly harnessed his skills in 1962, averaging nearly 11 strikeouts and not quite 6½ walks per nine innings for Elmira of the Eastern League. And he had a shot at making the Orioles' roster in the spring of 1963 until beset by arm problems. Never again the overpowering pitcher he once was (but, by the same token, never again the wild man of his earlier days), Dalkowski began to drift. Baltimore released him during the 1965 season and he caught on with a California Angels farm club. But Dalkowski never pitched again professionally after '65, winding up with a 46-80 career record in the minors. Through at age 26 without having thrown a pitch in the majors, Dalkowski stood out as a classic case of what-might-have-been.

JOE DiMAGGIO

Owner of the longest hitting streak (56 consecutive games) in major league history, he has the second longest batting streak in minor league history. Playing his first full season of professional ball in 1933, the 18-year-old DiMaggio hit safely in 61 straight games for San Francisco of the Pacific Coast League.

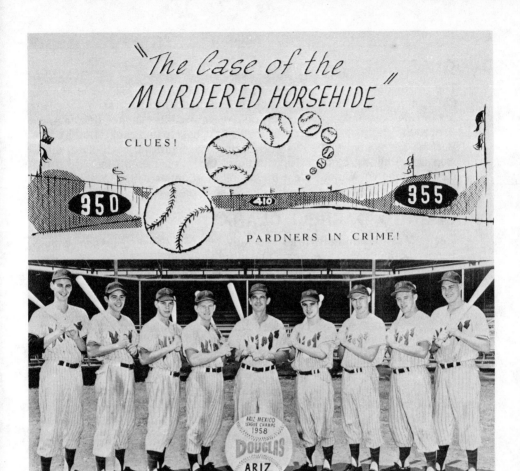

"The Case of the MURDERED HORSEHIDE"

CLUES!

350   410   355

PARDNERS IN CRIME!

RF · FILIPELLI — 2B · TORRES — 3B · McCALL — LF · WILKINS — P MGR. · CLEAR — CF · PREVEDELLO — SS · PULFORD — C · BINFORD — 1B · VAN BURKLEO

GUILTY!

SET NEW ALL TIME ORGANIZED BASEBALL RECORD
NEVER ACCOMPLISHED BEFORE — LIKELY NEVER AGAIN

DOUGLAS, ARIZONA, POPULATION 12,000. SMALLEST SPORTS MINDED CITY IN CLASS C BASEBALL. WINNERS OF 1958 ARIZONA-MEXICO LEAGUE PENNANT. ON AUGUST 19th AT CHIHUAHUA, MEXICO EACH OF THE ABOVE NINE DOUGLAS PLAYERS HIT AN "OUT OF THE PARK" HOME RUN. THE DISTANCES GREATER THAN SEVERAL MAJOR LEAGUE PARKS.

Douglas, Ariz., was rightfully proud of its nine players who went on a record-setting home run binge in a 1958 Arizona-Mexico League game.

197

DOUGLAS

The Arizona-Mexico League team that in an August 19, 1958, game against Chihuahua hit nine home runs—one by each player in the lineup. Connecting for the Copper Kings were left fielder Ron Wilkins, center fielder Andy Prevedello, right fielder Fred Filipelli, first baseman Frank (Dutch) Van Burkleo, second baseman Luis Torres, third baseman Darrell McCall, shortstop Don Pulford, catcher Rich Binford and pitcher Bob Clear (also the club's manager). Wilkins went 6 for 6 as the Copper Kings won, 22-8, in a contest stopped after eight innings because of darkness.

DICK DRAGO, DARRELL CLARK

Rocky Mount teammates who in a May 15, 1966, Carolina League double-header *both* pitched seven-inning no-hitters against Greensboro. Drago was a 5-0 victor in the opener and Clark was a 2-0 winner in the nightcap.

Drago went on to win 108 games in a 13-year big-league career that began in 1969 with the Kansas City Royals. While Clark never made the majors, his batterymate on May 15, 1966, was Jim Leyland, who 20 years later was managing the Pittsburgh Pirates.

HARRY DUNLOP

Bristol catcher whose error with two out in the ninth inning of a May 13, 1952, Appalachian League contest against Welch gave teammate Ron Necciai the opportunity to shoot for a game-total 27 strikeouts. Necciai had 25 strikeouts and was one out away from completing a no-hitter when he faced Welch center fielder Bobby Hammond. Having allowed three baserunners to that point (a hit batsman, a walk and an error), the 19-year-old Necciai proceeded to strike out Hammond—but the low pitch eluded Dunlop and Hammond reached first base. With his strikeout total at 26, Necciai then fanned left fielder Bob Kendrick to nail down a 7-0 no-hit triumph that featured, incredibly, 27 strikeouts.

Dunlop was Bill Bell's catcher when Bell hurled consecutive no-hitters for Bristol on May 22 and May 26—meaning that the Bristol receiver had caught three no-hitters in 14 days.

While Dunlop never made it to the big leagues as a player, he has served as a coach for the Kansas City Royals, Chicago Cubs, Cincinnati Reds and San Diego Padres.

VALLIE EAVES, JERRY EAVES

A father-son combination that pitched for the Hobbs club of the Southwestern League—in the *same* season. Jerry Eaves, 20, worked in 15 games and compiled a 2-4 record for Hobbs in 1957 and father Vallie, a 45-year-old former major leaguer who served the Hobbs club mainly in an advisory role, posted a 1-0 record in four appearances that year.

Vallie Eaves, who broke into the big leagues in 1935 with the Philadelphia A's and also pitched for the Chicago White Sox and Chicago Cubs, managed

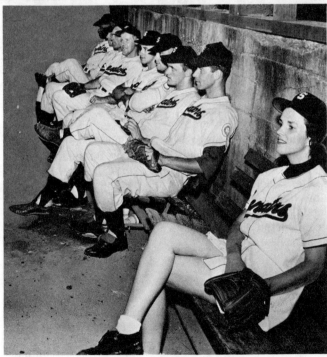

Rocky Mount
pitchers Dick Drago
(above left) and
Darrell Clark
(above right) posed
with Manager Al
Federoff after their
no-hitters in both
ends of a 1966
doubleheader.
Eleanor Engle
looked out of place
in the Harrisburg
Senators' dugout
(left) in her brief
1952 stay with the
Inter-State League
team.

a 4-8 record in the majors.

EL PASO, BEAUMONT

Texas League teams that scored a total of 89 runs in successive games in the 1983 season. On April 30, host El Paso scored in each of its at-bats—the Diablos had four six-run innings and one five-run outburst—and outslugged Beaumont, 35-21, in a wind-swept game that featured 56 hits (nine of which were home runs) and nine errors. El Paso's Mike Felder and Stan Levi each rapped two home runs, with Felder driving in nine runs and Levi knocking in seven (Levi also scored seven times). Any notion that the Texas League rivals had ended their scoring binge with the completion of the April 30 contest was disproved in their very next meeting when Beaumont struck for 11 runs in the top of the first inning on the way to a 13-0 lead. El Paso battled back, eventually coming within 15-13, but Beaumont wound up a 20-13 winner in a May 1 game that had "only" 36 hits (including five homers) and four errors.

ELEANOR ENGLE

A 24-year-old stenographer who in June 1952 signed to play with the Harrisburg Senators of the Inter-State League. After watching her work out at shortstop, one veteran scout cracked, "She threw like a girl." Whatever *that* meant, there were other opinions. One reporter said she "scooped up hard grounders and threw to first base like a pro," and a club director suggested that "she can hit the ball a lot better than some of the fellows on the club." Harrisburg Manager Buck Etchison vehemently opposed the presence of Mrs. Engle on his roster, and National Association President George Trautman, backed by Commissioner Ford Frick, quickly voided the signing and made it known that any future such attempts in Organized Baseball to sign female players would be subject to severe penalties.

Mrs. Engle, while having appeared in uniform for Harrisburg, never played for the Senators.

FRANK ETCHBERGER, JIM MITCHELL

Minor league pitchers who tossed no-hitters—in the same game. The hard-to-fathom double no-hitter unfolded on August 20, 1952, in Batavia, N.Y., as Bradford slipped past Batavia, 1-0, in a Pony League game. Bradford's Etchberger walked five batters and struck out six while holding Batavia hitless; Mitchell issued one base on balls, hit a batter and fanned seven Bradford hitters in his no-hit loss. The game's only run was scored in the eighth inning on a walk, a sacrifice, a wild pitch and an error by Batavia's player-manager, shortstop George Genovese.

59

The number of minor leagues in operation in 1949, a record one-season total.

LEW FLICK

Little Rock outfielder who banged out nine consecutive hits in a 19-inning

Southern Association game played on July 21, 1946. Playing against the Memphis Chicks in the first game of a doubleheader, Flick hit safely in his first nine at-bats before grounding out. He followed up his 9-for-10 plate performance by going 3 for 3 in the nightcap.

Flick teammate Kerby Farrell, who went on to manage the Cleveland Indians in 1957, had eight hits for Little Rock in the opener of the twin bill. Despite the heroics by Flick and Farrell and the fact Little Rock pulled off a triple play in the long contest, the Travelers wound up 8-6 losers.

.477

Willie Mays' batting average for the Minneapolis Millers when he left the American Association club to make his major league debut with the New York Giants in May 1951. Mays' 35-game statistics for the Millers included eight home runs and 30 runs batted in.

LOU FRIERSON, CECIL DUNN

Players who gave the minor leagues two five-homers-in-one-game performers in less than two calendar years. On May 30, 1934, Frierson smacked five home runs for Paris in a West Dixie League game (a contest that Paris lost), and on April 29, 1936, Dunn belted five homers for Alexandria in an Evangeline League game.

PETE GRAY

One-armed outfielder who had a scintillating minor league season before winning a spot on the St. Louis Browns' roster in 1945. Appearing in 129 games for Memphis of the Southern Association in 1944, Gray batted .333, stole a league-leading 68 bases and topped the league's outfielders in fielding percentage with a .983 figure. Additionally, he struck out only 12 times and, despite an obvious inability to hit for power, managed to rap five home runs for the Chicks.

BRUCE HAROLDSON

Lewiston relief pitcher who entered an August 6, 1961, Northwest League game against Tri-Cities in the sixth inning with the bases loaded and no one out and retired the side—with one pitch. Tri-Cities' Ray Youngdahl slapped Haroldson's first offering to third baseman Dick Green, who stepped on the bag for one out and threw on to Ossie Chavarria. After getting the forceout at second base, Chavarria rifled the ball to first baseman Ed Olsen to nail Youngdahl and complete a triple play.

Five years later, Green and Chavarria were teammates with the Kansas City A's.

JOE HAUSER

The only player in Organized Baseball history to have two 60-homer seasons. First baseman Hauser slugged 63 home runs for Baltimore of the International League in 1930 and belted 69 for Minneapolis of the American Association in 1933.

Hauser played six seasons in the big leagues—all of them *before* his 60-homer productions in the minors. His best year in the majors was 1924, when he hit 27 homers and drove in 115 runs for the Philadelphia A's. In 1929, as a member of the Cleveland Indians, Hauser wound up his big-league career at age 30.

LEE HEFFNER

Welch third baseman who started triple plays in consecutive innings for his Appalachian League team in a July 26, 1954, game against Johnson City. In the seventh inning, Heffner fielded a ground ball, stepped on third base for one out and threw on to second for out No. 2. The relay to first base completed the triple killing. In the eighth inning, Heffner snared a line drive and rifled a throw to second base to double up the runner. The relay to first caught another runner off base.

Lodi of the California League pulled off two triple plays in one game in 1978. In a July 25 contest, Lodi turned a first-inning line drive off the bat of Fresno's Jim Rothford into a triple play and then converted a fifth-inning grounder by Bill Young into an around-the-horn triple killing. (Bob Brenly, three years away from making his major league debut with the San Francisco Giants, was a Fresno baserunner when each triple play occurred.)

HOLLYWOOD

The Pacific Coast League club whose players trotted out for an April 1, 1950, game against Portland attired in T-shirt-style uniform tops and pin-striped shorts. "This isn't a gag (April Fools' Day or not), nor are we 'going Hollywood,'" Stars Manager Fred Haney said of the shorts. "It stands to reason that players should be faster wearing them—and that half step down to first wins or loses many games." And, of course, the outfits seemed a natural for yet-to-come steamy summer days. Fans greeted the scantily clad Hollywood players with catcalls and hoots, and Portland Manager Bill Sweeney joined in the kidding by wearing an apron and a purple hat (over a long, curly wig) when he appeared at home plate for the lineup exchange, at which he presented Haney with a bouquet of pansies.

While the shorts style subsequently was tried out elsewhere in the minors in 1950, the Hollywood club wound up wearing the "briefs" infrequently.

WALTER JUSTIS

Three years after seeing his only big-league service (two appearances with the Detroit Tigers), he pitched four no-hitters for Lancaster during the 1908 Ohio State League season.

BILL KENNEDY

Rocky Mount pitcher who in 1946 posted a 28-3 Coastal Plain League record, embellished by a 1.03 earned-run average and 456 strikeouts in 280 innings.

Kennedy reached the majors in 1948 and wound up pitching for five clubs (Cleveland Indians, St. Louis Browns, Chicago White Sox, Boston Red Sox

Hollywood Stars Manager Fred Haney (left) models the uniform that caught everybody by surprise on April 1, 1950. Hub Kittle (right), at age 63, became the oldest player in Organized Baseball history when he started and pitched one inning for Springfield, the Cardinals' Triple-A affiliate, in 1980.

and Cincinnati Reds) in a big-league career that ended in 1957.

HUB KITTLE

At age 63, the oldest man to play in an Organized Baseball game. While serving as a minor league pitching instructor for the St. Louis Cardinals, Kittle, six months past his 63rd birthday, started for Springfield against Iowa in an August 27, 1980, American Association game. He retired the side in order in the first inning—two fly balls and a groundout doing the trick—and, as planned, threw one pitch in the second inning before leaving the contest.

Kittle, a longtime minor league pitcher and manager, never played in the major leagues but did serve as a coach with the Houston Astros and the St. Louis Cardinals. He was, in fact, pitching coach for the 1982 World Series-champion Cards.

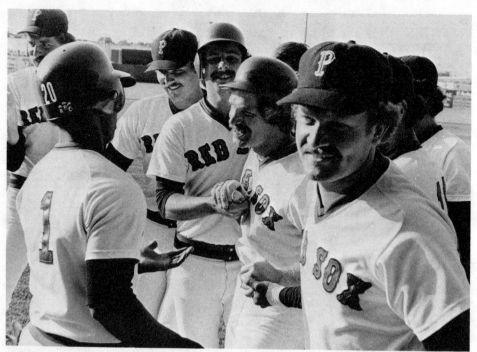

Pawtucket first baseman Dave Koza gets a warm reception after delivering a 33rd-inning single that beat Rochester and ended the longest game in baseball history.

DAVE KOZA

Pawtucket first baseman whose bases-loaded single ended the longest game in Organized Baseball history, a 33-inning International League contest between Pawtucket and Rochester that began on the night of April 18, 1981, in Pawtucket and was completed on June 23 in the Rhode Island city. Thirty-two innings of the game were played April 18-19—the contest was suspended at 4:07 a.m.—at which point the clubs were deadlocked, 2-2 (Rochester having seized a 1-0 lead in the seventh inning, Pawtucket tying the game in the ninth and each club scoring a run in the 21st). When play resumed more than nine weeks later on Rochester's next visit to Pawtucket, the home club broke through in its first at-bat. Marty Barrett was hit by a pitch, Chico Walker singled Barrett to third and, with no one out, Russ Laribee was walked intentionally. Rochester pitcher Cliff Speck then was summoned to replace reliever Steve Grilli, who had entered the game at the outset of the inning. Speck and Koza battled to a 2-2 count before Koza singled to left field. Pawtucket 3, Rochester 2.

After battling 8 hours and 7 minutes in the April portion of the marathon, the two clubs needed just 18 minutes in the June continuation to decide the issue. The total time of 8:25 also established a professional record.

DICK LANE

After hitting five home runs in 125 minor league games (123 in the Cotton

204

States League and two in the Southern Association) in 1947, he slammed five homers in *one* Central League game in 1948. Playing for Muskegon against Fort Wayne on July 3, Lane homered in the first, fourth (connecting twice), seventh and eighth innings and knocked in 10 runs. Three of Lane's homers were off Walter (Boom-Boom) Beck, Fort Wayne's player-manager and a former big-league pitcher.

Lane, who finished the '48 season with 12 home runs for Muskegon, saw his only major league service in 1949. Playing for the Chicago White Sox, outfielder Lane got into 12 games but managed only five hits (all singles) in 42 at-bats.

TONY LAZZERI

While Babe Ruth made major league history by cracking 60 home runs in 1927, it was Lazzeri—a teammate of Babe's on the '27 New York Yankees—who was the first man to smash 60 homers in an Organized Baseball season. Playing 197 games for Salt Lake City in 1925, Lazzeri drilled exactly 60 homers and knocked in 222 runs for the Pacific Coast League team.

JIM LEMON

He accomplished the feat of slugging four home runs in an all-star game—the 1955 Southern Association classic. Playing for the league's All-Stars against first-place Birmingham, Chattanooga's Lemon socked homers in the first, third, seventh and ninth innings and drove in seven runs in the July 19 game, which the All-Star squad won, 10-5.

Lemon had big seasons for the Washington Senators in 1959 and 1960, hitting 33 home runs in '59 and 38 in '60 and notching exactly 100 RBIs each year.

BOB LENNON

While the New York Giants marched toward a National League pennant and World Series championship in 1954, Giants farmhand Lennon buoyed the New Yorkers' hopes of future success by clouting 64 home runs for Nashville of the Southern Association in '54. Lennon never made the grade with the Giants, though; in fact, he appeared in only 29 games for New York (three in '54, 26 in 1956) and failed to hit a homer for the N.L. club.

While his banner season at Nashville (a noted home run haven because of its cozy Sulphur Dell home grounds) shot Lennon into the spotlight as a potential big-league slugger, the Brooklyn native finished his career with *one* home run in the majors (in 79 at-bats). Playing for the Chicago Cubs in an April 30, 1957, game at Brooklyn's Ebbets Field, Lennon hammered a three-run shot off the Dodgers' Sal Maglie.

D.C. MILLER

Wichita Falls outfielder who finished the 1947 Big State League season with 57 home runs and 196 runs batted in—and did not lead the league in either category. Sherman-Denison's Buck Frierson, who had played briefly with the Cleveland Indians in 1941, was the Big State's homer and RBI champion in '47, boasting totals of 58 and 197.

BRENT MUSBURGER

A noted television sports journalist of today and a former newspaper reporter in Chicago, he served as a Midwest League umpire in 1959 before pursuing other interests.

KENNY MYERS

Las Vegas slugger who bashed two bases-loaded home runs in the third inning of a 1947 Sunset League game—teammate Ned Klingensmith, a pitcher, also smacked a grand slam in the believe-it-or-not inning—as the Wranglers annihilated Ontario, 30-5. In addition to his exploits in Las Vegas' 16-run inning, Myers hit two other homers in the contest.

Myers later became a noted scout for the Brooklyn and Los Angeles Dodgers and the California Angels.

Armando Flores, playing for Laredo, hit two bases-full homers in the eighth inning of a June 25, 1952, Gulf Coast League game, and Redwood's Lance Junker walloped two grand slams in the ninth inning of a June 30, 1983, California League contest.

RON NECCIAI, BILL BELL

The pitching wunderkinds of the Pittsburgh Pirates' Bristol farm club of the Appalachian League in 1952. Necciai, a month from his 20th birthday, struck out 27 batters in a nine-inning no-hitter against Welch on May 13 and then fanned 24 Kingsport batters on May 21 before being promoted within the Pirates' organization. Bell, 18, pitched consecutive no-hit games against Kingsport (May 22) and Bluefield (May 26) and fired a third no-hitter, a seven-inning affair, against Bluefield (August 25).

One of Necciai's 27 strikeout victims on May 13 reached base when the catcher couldn't handle the third strike, meaning that one Welch batter (right fielder Bob Ganung, who grounded out) was *not* retired on strikes.

Necciai posted a 4-0 record for Bristol in 1952, notching 109 strikeouts and allowing only 10 hits in 43 innings. After going 7-9 with 172 strikeouts in 126 innings for Burlington of the Carolina League, Necciai finished the '52 season with the Pirates, for whom he was 1-6 with 31 strikeouts in 55 innings. Bell, who had started the 1952 season with Burlington as he fought control problems, went 11-3 for Bristol and also earned a call-up from Pittsburgh. In four appearances with the '52 Pirates, Bell was 0-1.

After 1952, the careers of Necciai and Bell plummeted. Wildness continued to haunt Bell (he had walked 11 batters in his first no-hitter of 1952), and arm problems and other physical ailments contributed to both pitchers' rapid decline. Only Bell, with one relief appearance for Pittsburgh in 1955, appeared in the majors after '52.

JOHN NEVES

A .240-hitting second baseman for Fargo-Moorhead of the Northern League

John Neves didn't hit much for Fargo-Moorhead of the Northern League in 1951, but he did raise some eyebrows with his backward '7' uniform number.

in 1951, he wore a backward "7" on his uniform—reflecting the fact that spelling out S-E-V-E-N in reverse fashion would produce his last name.

1956

The year in which three minor league players walloped 60 or more home runs. Leading the way was Dick Stuart, who poled 66 homers for Lincoln of the Western League. Ken Guettler hit 62 homers for Shreveport of the Texas League that season, while Forrest (Frosty) Kennedy rapped exactly 60 for the Southwestern League's Plainview club.

BOB OJEDA

The winning pitcher in the longest game in the history of professional baseball. Ojeda worked only one inning and threw just 13 pitches, but he was credited with the victory in Pawtucket's 3-2, 33-inning triumph over Rochester in a 1981 International League game. Ojeda replaced Bruce Hurst, who had allowed no runs and two hits over five innings, in the top of the 33rd of a 2-2 game. After Ojeda held Rochester at bay, Pawtucket scored a game-winning run in the bottom of the inning.

Ojeda was Pawtucket's eighth pitcher of the game. The loser was Steve Grilli, the fifth of Rochester's six hurlers. Grilli succeeded Jim Umbarger, who had pitched 10 innings of shutout relief (allowing only four hits, striking out nine and walking none).

ROGER OSENBAUGH

Sacramento hurler who, according to Manager Tommy Heath, needed a "stiff workout" against Los Angeles on June 22, 1957, to combat the effects of a recent illness and an accompanying lack of pitching time. "Stiff" hardly describes the kind of workout Osenbaugh got against the Angels. Los Angeles raked Osenbaugh for 22 runs and 18 hits—nine of them home runs—before Heath decided his pitcher had endured enough, a decision that came after 6⅔ innings. Hitting stars for the Angels included Bert Hamric, who rapped three home runs, and George (Sparky) Anderson, who walloped a bases-full homer (his first professional home run since 1953).

Despite the merciless pounding, Osenbaugh was effective enough overall for Sacramento in 1957 (9-14 record, 4.36 earned-run average for a team that finished 63-105) to be drafted by the Pittsburgh Pirates at the '57 winter meetings. Osenbaugh failed to make the Pirates' roster in 1958, though, and never appeared in the major leagues.

PAUL OWENS

Best known as manager of the 1983 National League champion Philadelphia Phillies (as the club's general manager, he fired Manager Pat Corrales at midseason and took over the managerial reins himself), he was a two-time .400 hitter in the low minors. In 1951, Owens broke into pro ball by batting a Pony League-leading .407 for Olean. Six years later, as Olean's player-manager, Owens again topped the league (renamed the New York-Pennsylvania League) in hitting and did so with a familiar figure—.407.

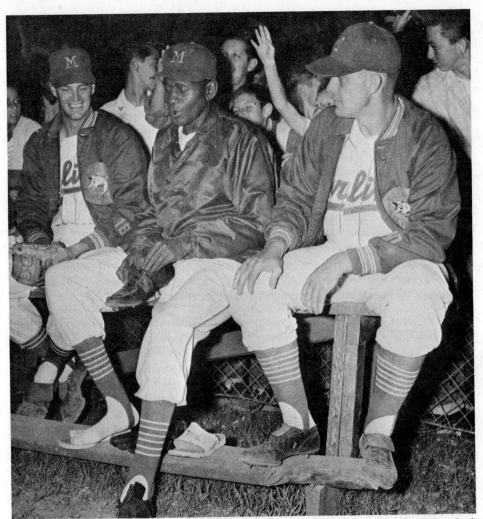

Former Negro League great Satchel Paige made 37 appearances for Miami of the International League in 1956 at age 50, finishing 11-4 with a 1.86 ERA.

SATCHEL PAIGE

At age 50, he made 37 pitching appearances for Miami of the International League in 1956—and compiled an earned-run average of 1.86. He won 11 games, lost four and walked only 28 batters while striking out 79 in 111 innings.

RANCE PLESS

Denver player who socked four bases-loaded home runs for the American Association club in a 34-day period of the 1957 season. Pless' spree began July 3 when, in his debut with the Bears after his acquisition from Omaha, he hit two home runs, one of them a grand slam. Pless hit another bases-full shot three nights later, connected again with the bases loaded on July 30 and cracked another grand slam on August 5.

PONCA CITY, GREENVILLE

Sooner State League clubs that executed triple plays in successive half innings of the first game of a June 28, 1957, doubleheader. Ponca City's Carl Reynolds lined into a triple play in the bottom of the first inning of the opener, and Greenville's Carlos Mobley followed with a triple-play liner in the top of the second.

CHARLEY PRIDE

He had a 0-1 pitching record for Fond du Lac of the Wisconsin State League in 1953 and made three appearances without a decision (but collected two hits in five at-bats) for Missoula of the Pioneer League in 1960 before eventually making it big in another line of work—country-and-western singing.

FRANK RAMSAY

The night after Bristol's Bill Bell had baffled Bluefield for his third no-hitter of the 1952 Appalachian League season, teammate Ramsay went to the mound against the Bluefield club and pitched a 1-0 no-hit game.

Ramsay's no-hitter, which came on August 26, was the Bristol staff's third of the year against Bluefield and its fifth and last of the season overall.

GARY REDUS, WILLIE AIKENS

Active Organized Baseball performers who not only cracked the stratospheric .400 batting level in a minor league season, but topped the .450 mark in the process. Redus, playing in the short-season (68 games) Pioneer League in 1978, batted .462 for Billings. In 1986, Aikens hit .454 for Puebla of the Mexican League.

JOE RELFORD

With Statesboro fans taunting the visiting Fitzgerald club with jeers of "Put in the batboy" after the hometown club built a 13-0 lead in a July 19, 1952, Georgia State League game, Fitzgerald Manager Charlie Ridgeway did just that—and the 12-year-old Relford was the youngster he summoned. Getting approval from umpire Ed Kubick, Ridgeway sent up Relford as a pinch-hitter in the eighth inning and the batboy (a black who broke the league's color barrier) grounded sharply to third base. Relford stayed in the game, taking over in center field, and sparkled defensively by making a sensational catch against the fence.

The next day, the Georgia State League fired Kubick for his role in the batboy-playing affair and slapped Ridgeway with a fine and suspension.

BOB RIESENER

New York Yankee farmhand who compiled a 20-0 record for Alexandria of the Evangeline League in 1957. Riesener led the league in victories, winning percentage (obviously), shutouts (four) and earned-run average (2.16).

Riesener was promoted to New Orleans of the Southern Association late in

Jackie Robinson gets a handshake from Montreal Royals teammate George Shuba after hitting a home run in his first game in Organized Baseball at Jersey City's Roosevelt Stadium on April 18, 1946.

the '57 season. While the switch was easy geographically (a simple move downstate), it was tough competitively. The righthander started twice for the Pelicans and suffered 12-6 and 8-2 setbacks.

Tony Napoles fashioned an 18-0 record for Peekskill of the North Atlantic League in 1946, then went 4-0 in the playoffs for the league's championship team.

JACKIE ROBINSON

The first black in modern major league baseball, he broke into Organized Baseball on April 18, 1946, at Jersey City's Roosevelt Stadium by collecting four hits—including a home run—in Montreal's 14-1 International League trouncing of the Jersey City club.

Robinson went on to lead the International League in batting, hitting .349.

Gene Rye (left) enjoyed his moment in the sun in 1930 when he walloped three home runs in one inning for Waco in a Texas League game against Beaumont. Newark outfielder Bob Seeds (right) was devastating in a 1938 game against Buffalo, homering in four consecutive innings.

GENE RYE

Playing for Waco in an August 6, 1930, Texas League game against Beaumont, he walloped three home runs—in one *inning*. Rye's cannonading came in the eighth inning, a frame in which Waco scored 18 runs.

Outfielder Rye had a cup of coffee in the major leagues in 1931, appearing in 17 games for the Boston Red Sox. He collected seven hits (all singles) in 39 at-bats.

WARREN SANDEL

The first pitcher Jackie Robinson faced in Organized Baseball. Lefthander Sandel started for Jersey City in the Giants' 1946 International League opener against the Montreal Royals and induced Robinson to ground out in the Montreal player's first at-bat in the pro ranks. But on his second trip to the plate, Robinson rifled a three-run homer off Sandel.

ROY SANNER

A combination outfielder-pitcher, Houma's Sanner won the Evangeline

League's "triple crown" in 1948 by slugging 34 home runs, knocking in 126 runs and batting .386—and, for good measure, he hung up a 21-2 pitching record that season with 251 strikeouts in 199 innings.

PETE SCHNEIDER

A pitcher for the Cincinnati Reds from 1914 through 1918 and with the New York Yankees in 1919, he became a minor league outfielder and slugged five home runs—two of them with the bases loaded—and a double in a May 11, 1923, game for the Vernon club of the Pacific Coast League. Schneider drove in 14 runs in his one-for-the-book performance, which came in a 35-11 Vernon romp against Salt Lake City.

BOB SEEDS

Newark outfielder who on May 6, 1938, against Buffalo homered in four *consecutive* innings, went 6 for 6 overall and drove in 12 runs as the Bears dismantled the Bisons by a 22-9 score. Seeds hit a bases-empty home run in the fourth inning, a two-run shot in the fifth, a bases-full homer in the sixth and two-run drive in the seventh.

Seeds continued his rampage the next day, hitting three homers as Newark thrashed Buffalo, 14-8. The former American Leaguer belted 28 homers in 59 games for Newark in '38, then was sold to the New York Giants. (In a total of 615 big-league games, coming before and after his sizzling stretch for Newark in '38, Seeds hit only 28 home runs.)

BILL SISLER

The hard-to-track minor league pitcher who broke into Organized Ball in 1923 and pitched professionally as late as 1948 (at age 44)—despite run-of-the-mill skills. Sisler, obviously able to sell his abilities regardless of his prior production, apparently signed contracts with as many as 50 professional clubs (most of them in the low minors), but often had two or fewer decisions with a team before moving on.

Sisler achieved a career-high eight victories for the Staunton club of the Virginia League in 1942.

KEVIN STOCK, BOB LOSCALZO

Modesto players who *both* hit for the cycle in their club's 23-4 California League pasting of Visalia on May 20, 1985. Second baseman Stock, who knocked in seven runs, lashed his single, double, triple and home run (a bases-loaded shot) in five at-bats, while left fielder Loscalzo went 4 for 7 with four RBIs.

BILL THOMAS

The winningest pitcher in minor league history, notching 383 victories in a pro playing career that began in 1926 and ended in 1952. He enjoyed his best season in 1946 when, at age 41, he won 35 games for Houma of the Evangeline League.

Thomas, who won 15 or more games in 15 minor league seasons, never pitched in the majors.

325

The most hits achieved by one player in one season in Organized Baseball history. Outfielder Paul Strand established the record in 1923, a year in which he played 194 games for Salt Lake City of the Pacific Coast League (extended seasons were common in the PCL) and won the league batting championship with a .394 mark.

Strand, who in 1922 had collected 289 hits for Salt Lake City while appearing in 178 games, won a return trip to the big leagues because of his lusty hitting in the PCL (he had pitched for Boston's Miracle Braves of 1914 and had seen brief outfield duty in the majors). But in 47 games for the Philadelphia A's in 1924, Strand batted only .228 (38 hits in 167 at-bats) and was back in the minor leagues to stay by midseason.

MARV THRONEBERRY

While coming to symbolize the ineptitude of the early-day New York Mets with his not-so-marvelous play for the National League club, Throneberry was, in fact, a slugging marvel as a New York Yankee farmhand. Playing for Denver, he led the American Association in home runs and runs batted in for three consecutive seasons. Throneberry hit 36 homers and drove in 117 runs for the Bears in 1955, walloped 42 homers and knocked in 145 runs in 1956 and had 40 homers and 124 RBIs in 1957.

FRED TONEY

Pitching for Winchester against Lexington in a May 10, 1909, Blue Grass League game, he threw a 17-inning, 1-0 no-hitter.

Eight years later, as a member of the Cincinnati Reds, Toney hurled a 10-inning, 1-0 no-hit game against the Chicago Cubs in a contest that also featured hitless pitching by Cubs starter Jim Vaughn through 9⅓ innings.

JOHNNY VANDER MEER

Fourteen years after pitching consecutive no-hit games for the Cincinnati Reds, he pitched another no-hitter—in the Texas League. In his first full season out of the big leagues (except for military service) since he first appeared in the majors in 1937, the 37-year-old Vander Meer pitched for Tulsa in 1952 and, on July 15, held Beaumont hitless in a 12-0 victory.

ED WALSH

Son of big-league pitching great Big Ed Walsh, he stopped Joe DiMaggio's Pacific Coast League batting streak at 61 games in 1933. Pitching for Oakland against San Francisco on July 26, he held DiMaggio hitless in five at-bats.

Eight years later, another son of a major league pitching star victimized DiMaggio. Jim Bagby Jr., pitching in relief for the Cleveland Indians on July

Marv Throneberry (left), who later won the hearts of New York Mets fans with his inept play, was a devastating slugger during his minor league days at Denver. Stan Wasiak (right), who managed 37 straight years in the Dodgers' organization, surpassed the 2,500-victory plateau in 1986.

17, 1941, got the New York Yankees' DiMaggio to ground into a double play in his last at-bat of the game, ending the Yankee Clipper's major league-record batting streak at 56 games.

STAN WASIAK

A minor league manager for a record 37 consecutive years, 1950 through 1986 (although illness limited him to a one-game stint in 1982). Guiding Vero Beach of the Florida State League in '86, he became the first manager to reach (and then surpass) 2,500 career victories in the minors.

While Wasiak piloted the Los Angeles Dodgers' Class AAA affiliate in Albuquerque from 1973 through 1976, most of his managerial career has been spent in the low minors.

JOE WILHOIT

Wichita outfielder who hit safely in 69 consecutive games in 1919, a record for Organized Baseball. Wilhoit batted .505 during his streak, collecting 151 hits in 299 at-bats, and finished the season with a Western League-leading .422 batting average.

Wilhoit, who played in the National League in 1916, 1917 and 1918, won another look in the majors after his success at Wichita. Appearing in six games for the Boston Red Sox late in the 1919 season, he went 6 for 18 at the plate. But in 1920, Wilhoit was back in the minors to stay.

Brothers Hank (above left) and Tommie Aaron combined for 768 major league home runs, Hank accounting for 755. Felipe (left, right photo) and Matty Alou are the only brother combination ever to finish 1-2 in a batting race.

HANK AARON, TOMMIE AARON

The top career homer-hitting brother combination in major league history, having slugged a total of 768 home runs. Hank, of course, is the big leagues' all-time leader; he drilled 755 homers in 23 seasons with the Milwaukee Braves, Atlanta Braves and Milwaukee Brewers. Tommy, five years younger than Hank and a major leaguer for seven years with the Braves (when they were based in both Milwaukee and Atlanta), hit 13 homers—eight of them in 1962, when he appeared in 141 games for the Milwaukee Braves.

HANK AARON, TOMMIE AARON

The only brother teammates to appear in a Championship Series, with Hank playing in all three games of the 1969 National League playoffs for Atlanta (going 5 for 14 at the plate with three home runs and seven runs batted in) and Tommie making an unsuccessful pinch-hitting appearance for the Braves against the New York Mets.

ART ALLISON, DOUG ALLISON

The first brother combination to play major league baseball. Doug Allison already was established as the starting catcher for Hartford of the newly formed National League (baseball's first "major league") when, on June 3, 1876, outfielder-first baseman Art Allison made his big-league debut as a member of the N.L.'s Louisville club. Louisville downed New York, 8-1.

Two other brother combinations played in the National League during its initial season of 1876. George, Sam and Harry Wright performed for Boston, and Fred and Pete Treacey saw duty for New York.

FELIPE ALOU, JESUS ALOU, MATTY ALOU

The brother combination amassing the most hits in one major league season, getting an aggregate of 505 in 1968. Felipe, playing for the Atlanta Braves, tied Cincinnati's Pete Rose for the National League lead with 210 hits, while Matty collected 185 hits for the Pittsburgh Pirates and Jesus contributed 110 for the San Francisco Giants.

FELIPE ALOU, JESUS ALOU, MATTY ALOU

They logged the most games played of any brother combination in big-league history, totaling 5,129. Felipe appeared in 2,082 games during his career, Matty played in 1,667 and Jesus was a participant in 1,380.

The record for most career games played by two brothers is 4,542, a figure reached by Hall of Fame outfielders Paul (2,549 games) and Lloyd (1,993) Waner.

MATTY ALOU, FELIPE ALOU

The only brothers to finish 1-2 in a major league batting race. Matty won the 1966 National League batting championship, hitting .342 for the Pittsburgh Pirates. Felipe, playing for the Atlanta Braves, was the N.L. runner-up with a .327 mark.

KEN ASPROMONTE, BOB ASPROMONTE

The only brothers to play in the first games of expansion teams. Ken played second base for the Los Angeles (now California) Angels when that American League expansion club made its debut on April 11, 1961. Bob was at third base for the Houston Colt .45s (now Astros) when that new National League team played its first game on April 10, 1962.

JIM BAGBY SR., JIM BAGBY JR.

The only father-son combination to pitch in World Series competition. Jim Sr. was the losing pitcher for the Cleveland Indians in Game 2 of the 1920 Series and the winning pitcher in Game 5; Jim Jr. worked three innings of relief for the Boston Red Sox in Game 4 of the 1946 fall classic.

The Bagbys figured prominently in two of baseball's most memorable games—one of which was the World Series contest that the elder Bagby won. In that October 10, 1920, game, Indians second baseman Bill Wambsganss turned the only unassisted triple play in Series history, Cleveland's

Elmer Smith socked the first bases-loaded homer in Series play and Bagby himself entered the record books by becoming the first pitcher to smash a Series homer. Then, on July 17, 1941, the younger Bagby, then with Cleveland and working in relief of starter Al Smith, induced New York's Joe DiMaggio to ground into an eighth-inning double play; the at-bat was DiMaggio's last on a hitless night that ended the Yankee star's 56-game hitting streak.

JIM BAILEY, ED BAILEY

The last brother battery to start a big-league game, with Jim pitching and Ed catching for the Cincinnati Reds in the second game of a September 10, 1959, doubleheader in Chicago against the Cubs. Jim, who was making his major league debut, worked 7⅔ innings and was charged with a 6-3 loss; Ed caught the entire game and went 0 for 4 at the plate.

Jim Bailey pitched in only two other major league games, both in relief, and brother Ed was his catcher both times. Ed, on the other hand, had an extensive career in the majors, playing in 1,212 games.

GUS BELL, BUDDY BELL

With Gus Bell having played for the National League in the 1953, 1954, 1956 and 1957 All-Star Games, an All-Star "first" occurred in 1973 when son Buddy played for the American League—never before had a father-son combination appeared in the midsummer classic. Gus represented the Cincinnati Reds in his four All-Star appearances, while Buddy was a member of the Cleveland Indians in '73 and an All-Star participant for the A.L. in 1980, 1981, 1982 and 1984 as a Texas Rangers player.

Only one other father-son combination has appeared in All-Star Game competition. Ray Boone, representing the Detroit Tigers, played in the 1954 and 1956 All-Star Games for the A.L.; son Bob was with the Philadelphia Phillies when he saw action for the N.L. in 1976, 1978 and 1979 and a member of the California Angels when he appeared in the game for the A.L. in 1983.

DENNIS BENNETT, DAVE BENNETT

The last lefthanded-righthanded brother combination to pitch for the same big-league team in the same game. Lefthander Dennis Bennett, who had a seven-season major league career, started for the Philadelphia Phillies against the New York Mets on June 12, 1964, and lasted 2⅓ innings in an 11-3 loss. Righthander Dave, in his only appearance in the majors, worked the ninth inning for the Phils and allowed two hits and one run.

KEN BOYER, CLETE BOYER

Brothers who each reached the 150-homer mark in the majors, a feat unmatched by any other brothers. In fact, Ken Boyer socked 282 home runs and Clete walloped 162.

Members of only one other brother twosome can claim as many as 125 homers each—Joe and Vince DiMaggio, with Joe blasting 361 and Vince

Brothers Ken and Clete Boyer (left), who played in the majors chiefly with the Cardinals and Yankees, respectively, both reached the 150-homer mark. Bert Campaneris of the A's and Jose Cardenal of the Angels (and later the Indians) were second cousins who twice finished 1-2 in A.L. stolen bases.

hitting exactly 125. And, besides the Boyers and the DiMaggios, only one other pair of brothers can boast of individual homer totals of 100 or more— Bob (156) and Emil Meusel (106).

BERT CAMPANERIS, JOSE CARDENAL

Second cousins who twice finished 1-2 in American League stolen-base competition. In 1965, Campaneris topped the A.L. with 51 steals while playing for the Kansas City A's and Cardenal, a member of the California Angels, was second with 37. Three years later, Campaneris had an A.L.-high 62 thefts for the Oakland A's and Cardenal was the league runner-up with 40 for the Cleveland Indians.

BILLY CONIGLIARO, TONY CONIGLIARO

The last brothers to slug home runs in the same big-league game as teammates. Playing for the Boston Red Sox against the Washington Senators on September 19, 1970, Billy Conigliaro smacked a three-run homer off Jim Hannan in the fourth inning and Tony hit a bases-empty shot against Joe Grzenda in the seventh. The Red Sox won, 11-3.

Brothers Billy (left) and Tony Conigliaro combined for 54 home runs while playing for the Boston Red Sox in 1970.

BILLY CONIGLIARO, TONY CONIGLIARO

The brother combination with the most home runs in one major league season as teammates. Billy Conigliaro, playing his first full season in the majors, hit 18 homers for the Boston Red Sox in 1970 and Tony walloped 36 for the American League club.

Hank and Tommy Aaron rank one behind the Conigliaros' total of 54. They established their National League-leading mark in 1962 when Hank rapped 45 homers for Milwaukee and Tommy hit eight for the Braves.

MORT COOPER, WALKER COOPER

The only brother battery in World Series history. Mort was a six-time starting pitcher for the St. Louis Cardinals in Series play, getting the call twice in each fall classic from 1942 through 1944, and brother Walker was in the Cards' lineup in all six contests.

JOSE CRUZ, HECTOR (HEITY) CRUZ

The last brothers to hit home runs in the same major league game. In the Astros-Cubs game of May 4, 1981, Houston's Jose Cruz smashed a three-run-home run against Mike Krukow in the first inning and Chicago's Hector

Cruz rapped a bases-empty homer off Joaquin Andujar in the sixth. The Astros beat the Cubs, 5-4.

HERM DOSCHER, JACK DOSCHER

The first father-son combination to play in the major leagues. Herm Doscher, a third baseman, started his big-league career with Troy of the National League in 1879 and finished with the N.L.'s Cleveland club in 1882. Son Jack, a lefthanded pitcher, made his debut in the majors on July 2, 1903, as a starter for the Chicago Cubs. He subsequently moved on to Brooklyn and wound up his big-league career with Cincinnati in 1908.

8

The number of Hall-of-Famers whose sons played in the major leagues.

Hall of Famer	Son	Son's Career Span	Years	Games	Avg. or Won-Lost
Earl Averill	Earl	1956-63	7	449	.242
Yogi Berra	Dale	1977-86	10	834	.237
Eddie Collins	Eddie	1939-42	3	132	.241
Fred Lindstrom	Charlie	1958	1	1	1.000
Connie Mack	Earle	1910-14	3	5	.125
Jim O'Rourke	Jim	1908	1	34	.231
George Sisler	Dave	1956-62	7	247	38-44
	Dick	1946-53	8	799	.276
Ed Walsh	Ed	1928-32	4	79	11-24

8, 25

The number of major league games in which brothers Felipe, Matty and Jesus Alou appeared together as teammates and the number of big-league games overall in which the three Alous appeared together. Felipe Alou, a San Francisco Giants outfield regular and a member of the National League club since June 1958, was the team's right fielder and leadoff batter in a September 10, 1963, game in New York—a major league contest in which, for the first time, he was joined by *both* Matty and Jesus (also property of the Giants). Never before had more than two brothers appeared in the same big-league game. Called up from San Francisco's Tacoma farm club and facing the Mets' Carlton Willey, Jesus made his major league debut by grounding out in the eighth inning while pinch-hitting for shortstop Jose Pagan. Matty, also just up from Tacoma but a full-season member of the Giants in 1961 and 1962, followed Jesus to the plate and struck out as a pinch-hitter for pitcher Bob Garibaldi. Felipe then grounded out against Willey, ending the historic inning. The three Alous then appeared in the same game seven more times for the '63 Giants.

After the trading of Felipe Alou to the Milwaukee Braves in December 1963, the three Alous appeared in the same Giants-Braves game six times in 1964 and nine times in 1965. And when Felipe and Matty played for the New York Yankees in 1973 and Jesus saw action for the Oakland A's that year, the three Alous appeared in the same Yanks-A's game twice.

Yankees Manager Yogi Berra, shown giving instructions to son Dale Berra in 1985, is one of eight Hall of Famers whose sons made it to the major leagues.

The Alous remain the only family to have had three brothers play in the same major league game. The only other brother threesomes to have played for the same big-league team in one season were Harry, George and Sam Wright of Boston's 1876 N.L. club and Jose, Hector (Heity) and Cirilo (Tommy) Cruz of the N.L.'s St. Louis Cardinals in 1973.

WES FERRELL

Cleveland Indians pitcher who on April 29, 1931, tossed a no-hitter in which the game's only questionable call came on a ball hit by his brother, catcher Rick Ferrell of the St. Louis Browns. Rick hit an eighth-inning smash that appeared headed to left field, but Indians shortstop Bill Hunnefield raced into the hole, snared the ground ball and whistled a throw to first base—a throw that pulled Lew Fonseca off the bag. Most observers were amazed that Hunnefield got to the ball, and thus a "hit" ruling seemed possible; by the same token, a good throw clearly would have gotten the baserunner. The decision: Error—Hunnefield. The miscue was one of three that the Cleveland infielder made that day, an afternoon on which Wes Ferrell completed a 9-0 no-hit game.

59

The most major league home runs hit in one season by a brother combination—and the figure was attained twice, both times by the DiMaggios. In

1937, Joe DiMaggio clubbed an American League-leading 46 homers for the New York Yankees and brother Vince, a rookie with the Boston Bees of the National League, socked 13. Four years later, a third DiMaggio brother, Dominic, got into the act. Joe hit 30 homers for the Yankees in 1941, Vince drilled 21 for the Pittsburgh Pirates and second-year major leaguer Dom hit eight for the Boston Red Sox.

BOB FORSCH, KEN FORSCH

Besides Gaylord and Jim Perry and Phil and Joe Niekro, the only other brother pitching twosome in major league history made up of two 100-game winners. While the Perry and Niekro combinations each boast a 300-game winner (Gaylord, Phil) and a 200-game winner, the Forsch brothers had accounted for 143 (Bob) and 114 victories (Ken) through the 1986 season.

MIKE GARBARK, BOB GARBARK

Of the 259 players who saw action in the American League in 1944, exactly two finished the season with .261 batting averages—and they were brothers. Mike Garbark, a catcher for the New York Yankees, achieved his .261 mark by collecting 78 hits in 299 at-bats; older brother Bob, also a catcher, reached that figure by going 6 for 23 as a member of the Philadelphia A's.

HEGANS, KENNEDYS

The only father-son combinations to hit safely in World Series play. Jim Hegan collected six hits in 32 at-bats for the Cleveland Indians in the 1948 and 1954 World Series; son Mike went 1 for 5 for the Oakland A's in the 1972 Series after going 0 for 1 for the New York Yankees in the 1964 fall classic. Bob Kennedy went 1 for 2 for the Indians in the '48 Series; son Terry, playing for the San Diego Padres, was 4 for 19 in the 1984 Series.

HEGANS, O'ROURKES

The fathers and sons who have come the closest to appearing in the big leagues at the same time (no father-son combination has played in the majors in the same season). Jim Hegan wound up his 17-season major league career in 1960, playing 24 games for the Chicago Cubs, while son Mike Hegan started his 12-year career in the big leagues with a late-1964 stint with the New York Yankees. The O'Rourkes also missed each other by four years, with Jim (Orator) O'Rourke playing his last big-league game in 1904 with the New York Giants and Jim (Queenie) O'Rourke reaching the majors in 1908 with the New York Highlanders. The elder O'Rourke's big-league career dated to the inception of the National League in 1876 (he played in the first game and collected the first hit in N.L. history); Queenie O'Rourke's big-time service began and ended in '08.

Special circumstances surrounded the 1904 major league appearance (one game) of the senior O'Rourke, whose big-league swan song as a player apparently had come in 1893 when he was 41 years old. While a minor league manager in '04, O'Rourke longed to play one more time for the Giants—a team he had helped to pennants in 1888 and 1889—and New York Manager John McGraw gave him that opportunity. O'Rourke, at age 52, caught the first game of a September 22, 1904, doubleheader against Cincinnati—a game in which the Giants clinched another N.L. flag.

DANE IORG, GARTH IORG

The only brothers to see action for opposing teams in a Championship Series. Dane made four pinch-hitting appearances for the Kansas City Royals against Toronto in the 1985 American League Championship Series, while Garth was used in six games by the Blue Jays as a third baseman and pinch-hitter.

FERGUSON JENKINS

The only pitcher in big-league history to surrender home runs to all three Alou brothers. Pitching in each instance for the Chicago Cubs, Jenkins yielded two homers to Jesus Alou (the first in the opening game of a July 23, 1967 doubleheader, the second on May 31, 1973) and one each to Felipe Alou (April 25, 1968) and Matty Alou (September 5, 1971). Jesus played for the San Francisco Giants when he struck his first homer off Jenkins and was a member of the Houston Astros when he walloped No. 2. Felipe connected as an Atlanta Braves player, while Matty was with the St. Louis Cardinals when he homered against Jenkins.

No pitcher gave up home runs to all three DiMaggio brothers.

JIMMY JOHNSTON, DOC JOHNSTON

The first brother combination to appear in World Series competition and the first brothers to play in the *same* Series. After Jimmy Johnston pinch-hit and played right field for Brooklyn against the Boston Red Sox in the 1916 fall classic, Doc Johnston was a participant for Cleveland in the 1920 World Series—a postseason battle in which the Indians were matched against Brooklyn and Jimmy Johnston. In the '20 Series, Doc started four games at first base for Cleveland and brother Jimmy started four times at third base for Brooklyn. The Indians' Johnston pinch-hit in another game (and stayed in that contest, taking over at first base).

Since the Johnstons went head to head in the 1920 World Series, only two other sets of brothers have been Series opponents—the Meusels in 1921, 1922 and 1923 (Bob playing for the New York Yankees and Emil for the New York Giants) and the Boyers in 1964 (Kenny playing for the St. Louis Cardinals and Clete for the Yankees).

CONNIE MACK

The first man in big-league history to manage his son in the majors. Earle Mack, a "mascot" for his father's early Philadelphia A's teams and a .135-hitting catcher in 26 minor league games in 1910 (his pro debut), was a favorite of A's players and was called upon to catch for his father's team on October 5, 1910. Earle responded by hitting a single and a triple on a day in which he caught Eddie Plank and Jack Coombs in a 7-4 loss to the New York Highlanders. In 1911, Earle saw action at third base in two late-season games for Philadelphia and in 1914 he played first base in two end-of-the-year A's contests. (Earle Mack later served his father as an A's coach for more than a quarter of a century.)

Through the 1986 season, Yogi Berra was the only other man to manage his son in the big leagues. In 1985, infielder Dale Berra played 12 games for the Yankees under his father (who subsequently was fired), going 2 for 4 in his first game (April 10) and batting .343 overall with Yogi at the helm.

Cal Ripken was in line in 1987 to become the third manager in major league history to direct a team that included his son. For Ripken, a veteran Baltimore coach who was named to manage the Orioles in '87, the father-son tieup promised to be a real plus. Cal Jr. was, after all, one of the Orioles' standout players (25 home runs in 1986) and a former Most Valuable Player selection in the American League.

CONNIE MACK, PAUL RICHARDS

The only individuals in big-league history to have managed a father-son combination. While directing the Philadelphia A's from 1901 through 1950, Mack managed Eddie Collins Sr. (1906-1914, 1927-1930) and Eddie Collins Jr. (1939, 1941-1942) and Earle Brucker Sr. (1937-1940, 1943) and Earle Brucker Jr. (1948). Richards, manager of the Chicago White Sox from 1951 through 1954 and again in 1976, had Sam Hairston on his '51 Sox squad and Jerry on his '76 Chicago club.

Technically, Mack managed a third father-son combination—*himself* and his own son. As player-manager for Pittsburgh from late in the 1894 season through 1896, pilot Mack made decisions that affected catcher-first baseman Mack; then, in 1910, 1911 and 1914, Mack was in command of the A's (and long retired as a player) when son Earle played a total of five games for Philadelphia.

MICKEY MAHLER, RICK MAHLER

The last brothers to pitch for the same team in the same major league game. On September 25, 1979, the Mahlers worked a total of three relief innings for the Atlanta Braves against the Houston Astros, with Mickey pitching the sixth and seventh innings and Rick hurling in the eighth. Tommy Boggs was Atlanta's starting and losing pitcher as the Braves fell to the Astros, 8-0.

DENNY McLAIN

Pitcher who won the American League's Most Valuable Player Award in 1968—20 years after his father-in-law had captured the same honor. McLain compiled a 31-6 record and a 1.96 earned-run average while helping the Detroit Tigers to the A.L. pennant in '68. Cheering on Denny was wife Sharon, daughter of Cleveland Indians great Lou Boudreau. In 1948, Boudreau, Cleveland's player-manager, was named the A.L.'s MVP after batting .355, hitting 18 home runs and driving in 106 runs for the pennant-winning Indians (who, like McLain's Tigers, also won the World Series).

Tigers pitcher Denny McLain (right) and Manager Mayo Smith get a good-luck greeting from former Cleveland star Lou Boudreau before the final game of the 1968 World Series. McLain, a 31-game winner, was the A.L. MVP in '68, 20 years after Boudreau, his father-in-law, had won the same honor.

JOHNNY O'BRIEN, EDDIE O'BRIEN

Twin brothers who, as rookie major league infielders in 1953, each appeared in 89 games for the Pittsburgh Pirates. By the time their big-league careers had ended (Johnny finished up in 1959, Eddie in 1958), the twins had seen pitching duty. Johnny pitched 61 innings in the majors, allowed 61 hits and won one game; Eddie pitched 16 innings, allowed 16 hits and won one game. Eddie's lone victory—and only big-league decision—came in a 3-1 complete-game triumph for Pittsburgh over the Chicago Cubs in the first game of a September 14, 1957, doubleheader. In the nightcap of that twin bill, the Pirates lost, 7-3, with the defeat being charged to brother Johnny, who worked one inning of relief. The loss was Johnny's last decision in the majors, leaving him with a cumulative 1-3 record (he posted his only victory in 1956).

The O'Briens, already well-known athletically for their basketball exploits at Seattle University (Johnny was a consensus All-America selection in 1953), played in the same major league game for the first time on May 10, 1953, when Johnny entered the second game of a doubleheader (against the New York Giants) as a defensive replacement at second base and Eddie pinch-ran in the contest.

Eddie O'Brien spent his entire big-league career with the Pirates, appearing in 231 games (primarily as a shortstop-outfielder, having pitched in only five

The O'Brien twins, Johnny (left) and Eddie, were interchangeable rookie infielders for the Pittsburgh Pirates in 1953.

games). Johnny O'Brien saw service with the Pirates, St. Louis Cardinals and Milwaukee Braves in 339 games (mostly as a second baseman, with his pitching duty limited to 25 games).

TOM PACIOREK

He appeared in the last regular-season major league game played by Julian Javier and in the first big-league contest played by Julian's son, Stan Javier. Julian Javier took part in his last regular-season game on October 1, 1972, playing second base for the Cincinnati Reds against Paciorek and the Los Angeles Dodgers. Paciorek played first base and right field for the Dodgers in that game. And when Stan Javier made his big-league debut on April 15, 1984, for the New York Yankees—he saw action in right field—Paciorek was at first base for the opposing Chicago White Sox.

GAYLORD PERRY, JIM PERRY

The first brothers to attain 20 pitching victories each in the same big-league season. In 1970, Gaylord Perry posted a 23-13 record for the San Francisco Giants and Jim compiled a 24-12 mark for the Minnesota Twins.

The only other brothers to achieve 20 victories apiece in the majors in the same year were Joe and Phil Niekro. Joe went 21-11 for the Houston Astros in 1979, while Phil was 21-20 for the Atlanta Braves that year.

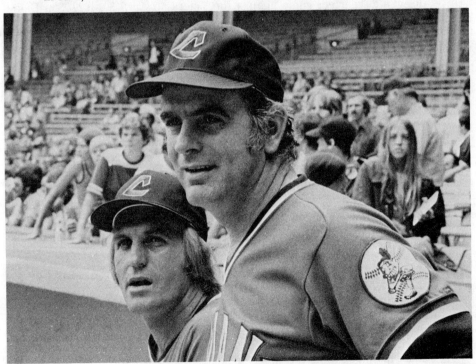

Jim (left) and Gaylord Perry, teammates with the Cleveland Indians in 1974 and part of 1975, combined for a record 529 big-league victories.

GAYLORD PERRY, JIM PERRY

The brother pitching combination with the most lifetime big-league victories, 529. Gaylord won 314 games while pitching from 1962 through 1983 for the San Francisco Giants, Cleveland Indians, Texas Rangers, San Diego Padres, New York Yankees, Atlanta Braves, Seattle Mariners and Kansas City Royals; Jim was a winner 215 times from 1959 through 1975 while a member of the Indians, Minnesota Twins, Detroit Tigers and Oakland A's. Through the 1986 season, Phil (311) and Joe Niekro (213) ranked second on the major league brothers' victory list with 524 triumphs.

The Perry brothers performed in the same major league—the American— at the same time for only four seasons, 1972 through 1975 (they were Cleveland teammates in 1974 and part of '75), and faced each other only once in a regular-season game. In the July 3, 1973, Detroit-Cleveland game, Jim started for the Tigers and Gaylord got the call for the Indians; Jim lasted 5⅔ innings but wasn't involved in the decision, while Gaylord went 6⅔ innings and was charged with the loss in a 5-4 Detroit victory.

HERMAN PILLETTE, DUANE PILLETTE

A father-son combination victimized by the Chicago White Sox in historic major league games. Herman Pillette was Detroit's losing pitcher—he tossed a complete-game seven-hitter—when Chicago's Charley Robertson threw a 2-0 perfect game against the Tigers on April 30, 1922. Son Duane went the distance for the St. Louis Browns in a 2-1, 11-inning loss in the last game in the Browns' 52-year history, a September 27, 1953, contest against the White Sox. (The Browns franchise moved to Baltimore after the '53 season and the club was renamed the Orioles.)

PETE ROSE

He appeared in the last major league game played by Ozzie Virgil Sr. and in the first big-league contest played by Ozzie Virgil Jr. In the second game of a June 27, 1969, doubleheader, Rose played right field for Cincinnati when Ozzie Sr., a member of the San Francisco Giants, bowed out of the majors as an unsuccessful pinch-hitter against the Reds. On October 5, 1980, Rose played first base for Philadelphia against the Montreal Expos when Ozzie Jr. made his big-league debut with a 1-for-5 batting performance as the Phillies' catcher.

Rose batted in the leadoff spot for his club in each game and collected two singles in each contest.

RAY SCHALK

The only player in major league history to catch a father-son combination— and he barely qualified for the distinction. Having caught the White Sox's Big Ed Walsh (a future Hall of Famer) in his early years as a big-league catcher, Schalk was midway through his second season as the Chicago club's manager when the chance developed to catch young Ed Walsh in the first game of a July 4, 1928, doubleheader. However, the opportunity to form the Sox battery with the 23-year-old Walsh came under trying circumstances: Schalk, under pressure to quit as manager, resigned on the morning of July 4, with the resignation to take effect at day's end. In his final major act as pilot of the White Sox, Schalk wrote his own name into the lineup for the opener of the doubleheader—it was his only catching appearance of the season and his 1,755th and last game as a Sox player—as Chicago faced the St. Louis Browns. Young Walsh, making his debut in the big leagues, yielded five runs in a four-inning stint and the Sox fell, 11-8.

Schalk, who removed himself from the game upon young Ed's departure, wound up his playing career in 1929 by appearing in five games for the New York Giants. Like the elder Walsh, Schalk won election to the Hall of Fame.

DICK SCHOFIELD, DICK SCHOFIELD

The only father-son combination to play in perfect games in the major leagues. The elder Schofield played shortstop for Pittsburgh on May 26, 1959, when the Pirates' Harvey Haddix fashioned a 12-inning perfect game against the Milwaukee Braves (only to lose in the 13th inning). And the younger Schofield was at shortstop for California on September 30, 1984, when the Texas Rangers failed to get a baserunner against the Angels' Mike Witt.

Eight other father-son combinations have appeared in no-hitters of nine innings or more: Earl Averill Sr. and Jr., Gus and Buddy Bell, Ray and Bob Boone, Dolf and Doug Camilli, Tito and Terry Francona, Jim and Mike Hegan, Roy Smalley II and III and Maury and Bump Wills.

NORM SHERRY, LARRY SHERRY

The last brother battery in major league history, teaming up for the Los Angeles Dodgers in a June 28, 1962, game against the New York Mets. Norm Sherry caught for the Dodgers in that contest and went hitless in four at-bats, while younger brother Larry entered the game in the eighth inning and worked two-thirds of an inning before being removed. Los Angeles won the game, 5-4, in 13 innings.

The Sherrys, big-league teammates in four seasons (all with the Dodgers), never formed a starting battery in the majors.

BILLY SULLIVAN SR., BILLY SULLIVAN JR.

The first of six father-son combinations to play in the World Series. Billy Sullivan Sr. caught for the Chicago White Sox in the 1906 Series, and Billy Jr. caught and pinch-hit for the Detroit Tigers in the 1940 fall classic. Other fathers and sons who competed in the Series:

Bagby—Jim Sr., Cleveland Indians, 1920
Bagby—Jim Jr., Boston Red Sox, 1946

Boone—Ray, Cleveland Indians, 1948
Boone—Bob, Philadelphia Phillies, 1980

Hegan—Jim, Cleveland Indians, 1948 and 1954
Hegan—Mike, New York Yankees, 1964; Oakland A's, 1972

Johnson—Ernie, New York Yankees, 1923
Johnson—Don, Chicago Cubs, 1945

Kennedy—Bob, Cleveland Indians, 1948
Kennedy—Terry, San Diego Padres, 1984

26

The number of Hall-of-Famers whose brothers played in the big leagues. The figure includes Paul and Lloyd Waner, both of whom are in the Hall of Fame, and George and Harry Wright, another pair of brothers enshrined at Cooperstown, N.Y.

Hall of Famer	Brother	Brother's Career Span	Years	Games	Avg. or Won-Lost
Hank Aaron	Tommie	1962-71	7	437	.229
Fred Clarke	Josh	1898-11	5	223	.239
John Clarkson	Arthur	1891-96	6	96	39-39
	Walter	1904-08	5	78	18-16
Roger Connor	Joe	1900-05	3	90	.205
Stan Coveleski	Harry	1907-18	9	198	81-55
Dizzy Dean	Paul	1934-43	9	159	50-34
Ed Delahanty	Frank	1905-08	4	116	.228
	Jim	1901-12	11	1095	.283
	Joe	1907-09	3	269	.238
	Tom	1894-97	3	19	.239
Bill Dickey	George	1935-47	6	226	.204
Joe DiMaggio	Dom	1940-53	11	1399	.298
	Vince	1937-46	10	1110	.249
Johnny Evers	Joe	1913	1	1	.000
Buck Ewing	John	1883-91	6	129	53-63
Rick Ferrell	Wes	1927-41	15	374	193-128
Pud Galvin	Lou	1884	1	3	0-2
George Kell	Skeeter	1952	1	75	.221
George Kelly	Ren	1923	1	1	0-0
Heinie Manush	Frank	1908	1	23	.156
Christy Mathewson	Henry	1906-07	2	3	0-1
Jim O'Rourke	John	1879-83	3	230	.295
Wilbert Robinson	Fred	1884	1	3	.231
Joe Sewell	Luke	1921-42	20	1630	.259
	Tommy	1927	1	1	.000
Honus Wagner	Albert	1898	1	74	.226
Paul Waner	Lloyd	(Lloyd also is in Hall of Fame)			
Zack Wheat	Mack	1915-21	7	231	.204
George Wright	Harry	(Harry also is in Hall of Fame)			
	Sam	1876-81	3	12	.109

PAT UNDERWOOD

Detroit Tigers pitcher who broke into the major leagues by outdueling his brother Tom of the Toronto Blue Jays in a May 31, 1979, game. Pat was a 1-0

Dom (left) and Joe were the American League representatives of the famed DiMaggio family, with brother Vince spending his entire career in the N.L.

winner in his debut, yielding only three hits in 8⅓ innings before getting relief help. Tom went the distance for Toronto and allowed only six hits— but one of them was an eighth-inning home run by Detroit right fielder Jerry Morales.

WALSH-SULLIVAN, WALSH-SULLIVAN

The battery for the Chicago White Sox in an early-October game in 1912, and again in a contest played late in the 1932 season—with the second pitcher-catcher combination being sons of the first. Big Ed Walsh and Billy Sullivan Sr. first served as a White Sox battery in 1904, gained particular attention in 1908 when Walsh won 40 games and last worked as a unit on October 4, 1912, when Walsh pitched the White Sox past the Detroit Tigers, 7-2. Then, on September 11, 1932, Walsh's son, Ed, a fourth-year major leaguer, started on the mound for the Sox and second-year man Billy Sullivan Jr. was behind the plate for the Chicago club in the second game of a doubleheader against the Washington Senators. In the only game in which young Walsh and young Sullivan teamed up as the White Sox's battery, Chicago absorbed a 9-4 defeat (loser Walsh departed after five innings, and so did Sullivan).

PAUL WANER, LLOYD WANER

The only brothers to collect 200 or more hits apiece in the same major league season—and they accomplished the feat in three consecutive years, 1927 through 1929. The Waners' highest combined hit total in one year was 460 (a record for a brother twosome), achieved in '27 when Paul amassed a major league-leading 237 hits for Pittsburgh and rookie Lloyd had 223 hits (second best in the N.L.) for the Pirates.

PAUL WANER, LLOYD WANER

The brother combination compiling the most career hits in big-league history. Paul totaled 3,152 lifetime hits in the majors and Lloyd accounted for

Hall of Fame brothers and Pittsburgh teammates Lloyd (left) and Paul Waner combined for 5,611 major league hits.

Catcher Billy Sullivan Jr. (above left) and Ed Walsh talk things over prior to a September 11, 1932, game in which both, literally, followed in their fathers' footsteps. Billy Sullivan Sr. and Big Ed Walsh had formed a battery 20 seasons earlier with the same team. The senior Walsh (left, left photo) is shown with his son in 1929.

2,459, an aggregate of 5,611.

PAUL WANER, LLOYD WANER

The first of four brother combinations to play for the same team in the same World Series. Paul was stationed in right field and Lloyd manned center field for the Pittsburgh Pirates in the 1927 Series.

Subsequent Series-playing brother teammates were: Dizzy and Paul Dean, St. Louis Cardinals, 1934; Mort and Walker Cooper, Cardinals, 1942, 1943 and 1944; Felipe and Matty Alou, San Francisco Giants, 1962. (Virgil and Jesse Barnes of the 1922 New York Giants and Ken and George Brett of the 1980 Kansas City Royals also were brother teammates on Series teams, but Virgil Barnes didn't get into the '22 fall classic and Ken Brett wasn't used in the '80 Series.)

Of the four sets of brothers to have seen action for the same team in the same World Series, only the Deans didn't appear in at least one Series game together. Dizzy pitched for St. Louis in Games 1, 5 and 7 of the 1934 Series and pinch-ran in Game 4, while Paul pitched for the Cardinals in Games 3 and 6.

GEORGE WRIGHT, HARRY WRIGHT

The first brothers to play in the same major league game. A month and a half into the initial season of the National League (considered baseball's first "big league"), Boston's N.L. team employed George Wright at shortstop and Manager Harry Wright in right field in a contest against Louisville. Boston lost by a 3-0 score in the June 6, 1876, game, which proved Manager Wright's only playing appearance of the year.

ZERO

The number of Hall of Fame members whose fathers played in the major leagues.

BILL WILSON

'ALIBI IKE'

Based on the Ring Lardner character, this 1935 film comedy starred Joe E. Brown in the title role and focused on a Cub rookie's tendency to find an excuse for virtually everything—be it an on-field foulup or an off-the-field transgression.

Also featured in the movie was 19-year-old Olivia de Havilland, a newcomer to Hollywood.

JUNE ALLYSON

Actress who was cast as Ethel Stratton in "The Stratton Story," the motion picture about big-league pitcher Monty Stratton's comeback bid after undergoing a leg amputation. Through dogged determination and aided by the support of his wife Ethel, Stratton enjoyed pitching success once more—albeit in the minor leagues.

Ethel Stratton, played by June Allyson, comforts husband Monty (James Stewart) after a hunting accident that resulted in the amputation of his leg in 'The Stratton Story.'

'THE BABE RUTH STORY'

The eagerly awaited motion picture that had its official premiere in New York on July 26, 1948—and Ruth, leaving his hospital bed, was in attendance for part of the festivities. Three weeks later, baseball's legendary Bambino was dead. The film, which starred William Bendix in the title role, received generally unfavorable reviews. Otis L. Guernsey Jr. of the New York Herald Tribune put it this way: "It would be hard to find a more colorful American figure than the Babe for motion-picture documentation, and it would be difficult to do a worse job with him than has been done here."

Bendix, reflecting on the movie 13 years later, said: "Worst picture I ever made. It could have been great, I think. But it didn't work out that way. I remember going to the previews in Los Angeles. In the early part of the picture, when I'm discovered in the orphanage, the scene was full of 16- and 17-year-old kids. Do I have a kid playing me? No, I have to do it with makeup. And I'm 38 years old (42, actually) at the time. The audience laughed. I would have laughed, too, but I felt too bad."

BAY CITY BLUEBIRDS

The fictitious minor league baseball team around which the short-lived 1983

William Bendix (above left as a teen-ager, below) was joined in his 1948 portrayal of Babe Ruth by William Frawley (above center) and Charles Bickford (above right). The Babe himself, just out of the hospital, enjoyed a moment (left) at the picture's premiere with Claire Trevor, who portrayed Mrs. Babe Ruth.

television series "The Bay City Blues" was built. The series, which lasted for less than a month in the fall of '83, focused on both the on-field exploits and off-field escapades of players striving to make the major leagues.

WILLIAM BENDIX

Television's bumbling Chester A. Riley cast as the heroic George Herman (Babe) Ruth? Say it ain't so. Well, it *wasn't* so—at least not chronologically. Bendix, you see, played the lead in "The Babe Ruth Story" (1948) five years before his visage as the well-meaning buffoon on "The Life of Riley" first appeared on TV (although he did create the Riley role on radio in 1943). And while hindsight has contributed to charges of miscasting, not everyone was upset with Bendix's portrayal of the Babe. Reviewing the "Ruth Story" in the New York Star in July 1948, Heywood Hale Broun wrote: "What saves the picture from being a solid bust is a good performance by Bendix. He looks pretty silly swinging a bat, but he has caught very well the boyish, expansive personality of the Babe, and when he is talking to kids, bargaining with Owner Jake Ruppert, or irritating Miller Huggins, well played by Fred Lightner, he makes us believe for a few moments that this is Babe Ruth himself."

In 1950, Bendix starred in another baseball movie, "Kill the Umpire," a comedy that depicted the ups and downs in the career of an umpire. Three years later, he assumed the Riley role on television.

JOHN BERARDINO

A major league infielder for 11 seasons, he has played Dr. Steve Hardy in the daytime television soap opera "General Hospital" since the highly popular show's inception in 1963. Berardino, an actor at age 6 in "Our Gang" background scenes and a bit player in motion pictures during his baseball days, played two hitches each with the St. Louis Browns, Cleveland Indians (he was a member of the 1948 World Series-champion Tribe) and Pittsburgh Pirates.

Soon after becoming entrenched as an actor in the 1960s, former ball player Berardino became actor Beradino (the "cleaner" spelling was convenient for everyone and the second "r" was silent, anyway). Before the advent of "General Hospital," he was a regular in the television series "The New Breed" and appeared in TV's "I Led Three Lives."

CHARLES BICKFORD

The actor who played Brother Matthias, George Herman Ruth's "mentor" and father figure at Baltimore's St. Mary's Industrial School, in "The Babe Ruth Story."

RAMON BIERI

The actor who portrayed Dodgers Owner Walter O'Malley in the television drama "It's Good to Be Alive" and later played Babe Ruth in TV's "A Love

John Berardino, who already had given up baseball for an acting career and dropped the second 'r' from his last name, returned to the field in 1964 for a star-studded Hollywood-style game and was double-teamed by major leaguers-turned-umpires Vic Power (left) and Jim Piersall.

Affair: The Eleanor and Lou Gehrig Story."

HARRIET BIRD

The seductress (Barbara Hershey) in "The Natural" who flirted with Roy Hobbs aboard a Chicago-bound train, invited Hobbs to her hotel room—and shot him.

JOE BOYD

The fanatical, middle-aged Washington Senators fan in the 1958 musical film "Damn Yankees," he said he'd sell his soul if it meant his lowly Senators would win the American League pennant. There was a buyer, all right

Actor Tab Hunter donned a baseball uniform in the 1958 musical 'Damn Yankees' and powered the lowly Washington Senators to dizzying heights in the baseball world in his role as power-hitting Joe Hardy, whose feats would not be accomplished without a price.

—the devil himself. Suddenly, Joe Boyd (played by Robert Shafer) was transformed into young Joe Hardy (Tab Hunter), a power hitter of staggering dimensions, and the Senators were on their way.

"Damn Yankees" was a Broadway hit in 1955, with Shafer cast as Joe Boyd and Stephen Douglass starring in the Joe Hardy role.

BROOKLYN LOONS

The name of the baseball team that was willed to a cat in the 1951 film comedy "Rhubarb." The cat not only became owner of the Loons, but served as the club's good-luck charm as well. Good luck was nothing new to Rhubarb; in addition to being bequeathed the Loons, the feline also inherited a cool $30 million.

LeVAR BURTON

More than a year and a half after portraying young Kunta Kinte in the 1977 television production "Roots," he played Ron LeFlore in TV's "One in a Million," the story of LeFlore's rise from a prison inmate to a big-name outfielder for the Detroit Tigers.

MORRIS BUTTERMAKER

The swimming-pool cleaner and former minor leaguer ball player in a 1976 film who took over as coach of a Southern California kids-league team, the Bears, that was really bad news—until, that is, the squad recruited a top-notch female pitcher, Amanda (Tatum O'Neal). Amanda, aided and abetted by her wisecracking teammates and directed by the beer-guzzling Butter-maker (Walter Matthau), helped turn "The Bad News Bears" into a surprisingly formidable unit (and a hit movie as well).

Sequels to "The Bad News Bears"—"The Bad News Bears in Breaking Training" (1977) and "The Bad News Bears Go to Japan" (1978)—were made without Matthau and O'Neal and generally were considered inferior to the original movie. "Breaking Training" told of the Bears' efforts to get to Houston's Astrodome in an attempt to win a berth against Japanese competition, and "Go to Japan" focused on the team's trip to the Orient and its adventures with promoter/con artist Marvin Lazar (Tony Curtis).

'CASEY AT THE BAT'

This 1927 film starred Wallace Beery, whose Casey character took a bottle of beer to the plate and slugged his prodigious home runs with one hand (when he wasn't striking out).

JOE CHARBONEAU

The American League's Rookie of the Year in 1980 as an outfielder with the Cleveland Indians (but a major leaguer for parts of only two other seasons), he was a member of the New York Knights in "The Natural."

'COLLEGE'

Buster Keaton starred in this 1927 movie about an athletically disinclined student who, while seeking approval from his favorite coed, tried out for the baseball team with absurd results.

GARY COOPER

Actor whose portrayal of Lou Gehrig in the 1942 film "The Pride of the Yankees" was widely hailed. The Gehrig film biography, which opened in New York about 13 months after the Iron Horse's death at age 37, also featured a sterling performance by Teresa Wright in the role of Gehrig's wife Eleanor.

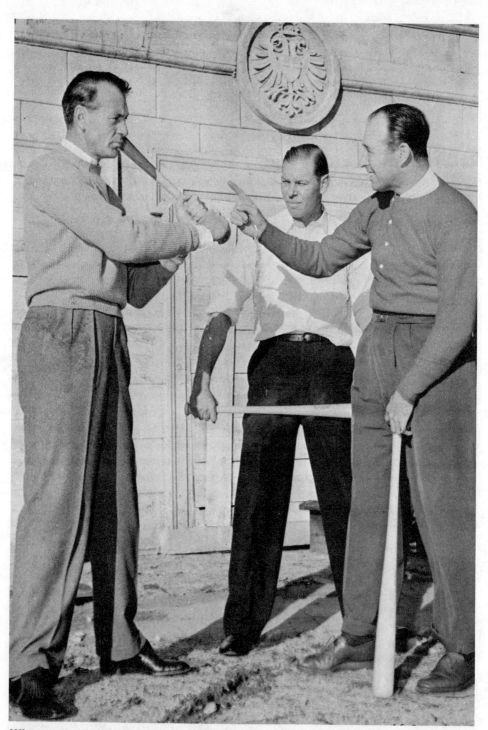

When actor Gary Cooper accepted the role of Lou Gehrig in 'The Pride of the Yankees,' former major leaguers Babe Herman (center) and Lefty O'Doul (right) were summoned to work with the natural righthander.

In a scene from the 1952 film 'The Pride of St. Louis,' a concerned Dizzy Dean (actor Dan Dailey, kneeling, right) comforts brother Paul (Richard Crenna), who has just been struck by a line drive.

RICHARD CRENNA

Still a few months away from initiating his memorable role as scatter-brained student Walter Denton in the "Our Miss Brooks" television show, he played the part of St. Louis Cardinals pitcher Paul Dean in "The Pride of St. Louis," a springtime-1952 motion picture about Paul's brother, Dizzy Dean.

DAN DAILEY

As colorful pitcher Dizzy Dean in "The Pride of St. Louis," he demonstrated how ol' Diz could master opposing batters—but not the English language. The latter shortcoming, magnified when former St. Louis Cardinals great Dean embarked on a broadcasting career, got plenty of attention in this film.

BLYTHE DANNER, EDWARD HERRMANN

They played the title roles in the 1977 television dramatization "A Love Affair: The Eleanor and Lou Gehrig Story."

DORIS DAY

Actress who portrayed Aimee Alexander, wife of pitching star Grover Cleveland Alexander, in the film "The Winning Team."

'DEATH ON THE DIAMOND'

Baseball is not a contact sport? The game is not violent? Let's see. In this 1934 motion picture, a star pitcher for the St. Louis Cardinals was shot as he rounded third base with the winning run; another Cardinal pitcher was strangled in the clubhouse; the Cards' catcher died of poisoning after consuming a hot dog, and two attempts were made on the life of a third St. Louis pitcher, one via gunfire aimed at a taxi cab in which the hurler (played by Robert Young of "Father Knows Best" and "Marcus Welby, M.D." fame) was riding, the other by a bombing device placed in the player's clothing. Obviously, this was a murder mystery, replete with the gambling crowd (a recurring element in early sports-oriented films). Despite the mayhem, there were plenty of laughs in this production.

MIKE DONLIN

A .356 hitter for the 1905 World Series-champion New York Giants and a lifetime .333 batter in the major leagues, he once left the game to tour with actress-wife Mabel Hite in vaudeville and on stage and eventually became a full-fledged stage and motion-picture actor—although he was seldom more than a "bit player."

JOANNE DRU

She appeared as Patricia Nash Dean, Dizzy's wife, in "The Pride of St. Louis."

'ELMER THE GREAT'

While Ring Lardner had created Elmer as a pitching sensation, this 1933 film made him into a slugger—in the person of Joe E. Brown. Elmer, possessing a strong swing but a weak mind, found trouble virtually everywhere he turned. But, when the big game came around, it was the Cubs' Elmer who proved troublesome (to the Yankees).

'FEAR STRIKES OUT'

The critically acclaimed 1957 film about Boston Red Sox player Jim Piersall (Anthony Perkins) and the mental illness that he suffered at the outset of his major league career. Piersall, heavily pressured to succeed by his father John (Karl Malden), was unable to cope with mounting stress—particularly the Red Sox's attempt to convert him from an outfielder into a shortstop.

Anthony Perkins donned a Boston Red Sox uniform to portray Jim Piersall in the critically acclaimed 1957 movie about a young player's struggle against mental illness.

The overall strain produced erratic behavior in Piersall, whose arguments, fights and clowning episodes alienated opponents and teammates alike and led to the ball player's hospitalization.

Norma Moore was cast as Jim Piersall's wife (Mary).

'FIREMAN, SAVE MY CHILD'

When Joe Grant (Joe E. Brown) wasn't experimenting with fire extinguishers or setting office buildings ablaze in this 1932 film, he was plying his trade as a big-league pitcher.

William Frawley (center), best known for his role as Fred Mertz in the 'I Love Lucy' show, acted in five baseball-related movies. His appearance with Yankee sluggers Roger Maris (left) and Mickey Mantle (right) was in the 1962 film 'Safe at Home.'

POP FISHER

The manager of the New York Knights in "The Natural." Pop was played by Wilford Brimley.

Assisting Pop was Knights Coach Red Blow (Richard Farnsworth).

HUCKLEBERRY FOX

Cast in "A Winner Never Quits," the television story of Pete Gray, he played the one-armed little California boy who made an inspirational trip to Memphis in 1944 to see Gray play for the minor league Chicks. The boy, devastated after his right arm had been amputated following a home accident, needed a boost and got it when he saw what amputee Gray could do on a ball field.

The real-life youngster depicted in the film, Nelson Gary Jr., became a standout outfielder and pitcher in kids-league and high school baseball in Southern California. While at one point hoping for a fling in professional baseball, Gary never advanced into the pro ranks.

WILLIAM FRAWLEY

Known to 1950s and 1960s television audiences for his portrayals of Fred Mertz on the "I Love Lucy" show and housekeeper Bub O'Casey on "My Three Sons," he had a featured role in the film "The Babe Ruth Story." Frawley played the part of Jack Dunn, owner-manager of the minor league Baltimore Orioles and the man who signed Ruth to his first professional baseball contract.

Frawley also appeared in the baseball movies "Alibi Ike," "Kill the Umpire," "Rhubarb" and "Safe at Home."

LOUIS GOSSETT JR.

He played Leroy (Satchel) Paige, famed Negro leagues pitcher who at age 42 finally got a chance in baseball's major leagues, in the 1981 made-for-television film "Don't Look Back."

'THE GREAT AMERICAN PASTIME'

A 1956 movie in which Tom Ewell managed a Little League baseball team —and managed to lose a lot of friends in the process.

'HEADIN' HOME'

A 1920 film in which Babe Ruth played a country bumpkin who apparently had no baseball skills. Apparently. Upon being angered, though, the Babe took a bat in hand and rocketed the ball for a five-block ride. His heretofore hidden talent now exposed, he soon became a big-leaguer and returned home a hero.

In 1927, Ruth appeared in a motion picture called "The Babe Comes Home," which seemingly was ignored by critics and moviegoers alike.

'THE HOT CORNER'

A 1956 Broadway comedy about the various crises that confronted a baseball manager (played by Sam Levene). Obviously not a knee-slapper, the play closed after five performances.

Eight years earlier, Levene had portrayed a newspaperman in "The Babe Ruth Story."

TAB HUNTER

The male lead in the movie version of "Damn Yankees," he also was cast as Jim Piersall in the 1955 television adaptation of the book "Fear Strikes Out." The television production of the Piersall story, presented on the program "Climax," was seen by U.S. audiences approximately 19 months before the motion picture about the Boston Red Sox player made its debut. Also starring in TV's "Fear Strikes Out" were Mona Freeman (as Jim's wife) and Robert Armstrong (as Jim's father).

Anthony Perkins might have received even more publicity for his portrayal of Jim Piersall in the movie 'Fear Strikes Out,' but Tab Hunter (above) beat him to the punch, playing Piersall in a 1955 TV adaptation of the book.

Jackie Robinson appeared on the big screen in 1950 when he portrayed himself in 'The Jackie Robinson Story,' which also featured Minor Watson (center) as Branch Rickey and Richard Lane (right) as Clay Hopper, manager of the Montreal Royals.

IRIS, MEMO

Portrayed respectively by Glenn Close and Kim Basinger, they were two key women in ball player Roy Hobbs' life in "The Natural." Iris was Hobbs' in-the-stands inspiration, while Memo was the alluring niece of the team's manager.

'THE JACKIE ROBINSON STORY'

The 1950 film biography of modern major league baseball's first black player. Cast in the title role was a 31-year-old movie newcomer who exhibited composure, timing and grace on the screen: Jack Roosevelt Robinson, the Brooklyn Dodgers' star himself.

Helpful baseball strategy tips from peanut vendor Larry (Pop) Cooper (Dan Dailey, left) to son Christy (center), a 9-year-old batboy . . .

'THE KID FROM LEFT FIELD'

A 1953 movie about a 9-year-old batboy named Christy who received insightful ball-playing tips from his father—a former player roaming the stands as a peanut vendor—and relayed the helpful hints to his struggling team. The local nine proceeded to go on a winning binge and little Christy (Billy Chapin) was managerial timber.

Christy's father, Larry (Pop) Cooper, was played by Dan Dailey, who just a year earlier had portrayed Dizzy Dean in "The Pride of St. Louis." Anne Bancroft and Lloyd Bridges also were featured in "The Kid From Left Field."

A remake of "The Kid From Left Field" came to the screen—the small screen—in 1979. The made-for-television movie featured Gary Coleman and Robert Guillaume in the Chapin and Dailey roles.

'KILL THE UMPIRE'

The 1950 film comedy in which William Bendix played an umpire-hating baseball fan (and former player) who was so obsessed with the game that he couldn't hold a job once spring training began. To confront this vocational turmoil and at the same time satisfy his yearning to be close to baseball,

... helped turn the struggling local baseball team into an instant winner in the 1953 movie 'The Kid From Left Field.'

Bendix character Bill Johnson decided to go to school. *Umpire* school. Before long, Johnson was calling 'em the way he saw 'em—and finding out that his new calling in life could be hazardous to his health (thanks to angry fans, players and gamblers).

PETE LaCOCK

A first baseman-outfielder for the Chicago Cubs (1972-1976) and Kansas City Royals (1977-1980), he is the son of longtime "Hollywood Squares" television host Peter Marshall and nephew of veteran actress Joanne Dru.

'LADIES' DAY'

A 1943 motion picture, starring Eddie Albert and Lupe Velez, that told of a young man who pitched woo and baseballs—and found it difficult to succeed with the latter when he was so wrapped up with the former.

MONK LANIGAN

The dimwitted catcher in "It Happens Every Spring" (1949). While opposing batters flailed away at the dancing pitches of Lanigan's new batterymate, Monk (Paul Douglas) had trouble catching on to the fact that his pitcher was using a special wood-resistant compound on the ball.

One constant in the history of baseball-related movies is the use of major league extras, such as pitcher Gene Bearden, who is pictured above with actress June Allyson in a scene from 'The Stratton Story.'

BINGO LONG, LEON CARTER

The star pitcher and catcher (portrayed by Billy Dee Williams and James Earl Jones, respectively) for the barnstorming black baseball team in "The Bingo Long Traveling All-Stars and Motor Kings," a 1976 film release. Primarily a comedy, the movie also was a study of survival and of American race relations of 50 years ago.

FRANK LOVEJOY

Actor who played Rogers Hornsby, a playing rival of Grover Cleveland Alexander's and then Alexander's manager, in the Alexander film biography entitled "The Winning Team."

Child actor Bryan Russell received a big assist from Yankee sluggers Roger Maris (left) and Mickey Mantle in the 1962 movie 'Safe at Home.'

PEANUTS LOWREY

One of the many real-life ball players used as extras in baseball movies. Lowrey, an infielder-outfielder for 13 seasons with the Chicago Cubs, Cincinnati Reds, St. Louis Cardinals and Philadelphia Phillies, appeared in "The Pride of the Yankees," "The Stratton Story" and "The Winning Team" (in which, as outlined by the script, he conked Ronald Reagan, playing Grover Cleveland Alexander, with a thrown ball).

Additional examples of major leaguers appearing in baseball films include the use of Gene Bearden, Bill Dickey, Jimmie Dykes and Merv Shea in "The Stratton Story" and the casting of Bob Lemon, Hank Sauer, Al Zarilla, John Berardino and George Metkovich in "The Winning Team."

Pittsburgh's Bill Mazeroski shows actor Jack Lemmon the bat he used to ground into a triple play during the 1967 filming of 'The Odd Couple.'

SAM MALONE

Presented by scriptwriters as a former pitcher for the Red Sox, Malone (Ted Danson) owns and operates a Boston bar in the hit television series "Cheers," which made its debut in September 1982.

PHIL MANKOWSKI

The former part-time infielder for the Detroit Tigers and New York Mets who produced guffaws in theaters nationwide when, as the third baseman for the New York Knights in "The Natural," he was struck in the groin by a batted ball while eyeballing a woman in the stands.

ROGER MARIS, MICKEY MANTLE

After Maris socked a major league-record 61 home runs in 1961 and Mantle walloped 54, the New York Yankee sluggers were the main attractions in a low-budget 1962 film called "Safe at Home." In the picture, a 10-year-old Florida boy named Hutch Lawton, played by Bryan Russell, bragged to friends—er, *lied* to friends—that he was an acquaintance of Maris and Mantle. What a tangled web we weave when first we practice to deceive.

BILL MAZEROSKI

Pittsburgh player who, merely following the script, hit into a game-ending triple play against the New York Mets as part of "The Odd Couple" motion picture. With the Mets leading the Pirates, 1-0, in the ninth inning of the made-for-Hollywood sequence, Mazeroski came to bat with the bases loaded and no one out and Jack Fisher pitching for New York. As sportswriter Oscar Madison (Walter Matthau) spoke on the telephone with his back to the field, Mazeroski grounded to Ken Boyer, who stepped on third base to start an around-the-horn triple play (with Jerry Buchek making the play at second base and Ed Kranepool handling the throw at first).

Roberto Clemente originally was scheduled to ground into the triple play, which was filmed at Shea Stadium in June 1967, but an impasse over film-appearance fees sent Mazeroski to the plate instead.

LUCAS McCAIN

The Old West character made familiar to television audiences by former big-league first baseman Chuck Connors in the late 1950s and early 1960s. McCain was a rifle-toting, law-preserving, marshal-helping homesteader in "The Rifleman" series.

Connors played in one game for the Brooklyn Dodgers in 1949 and appeared in 66 contests for the Chicago Cubs in 1951 (batting .239 for the Cubs with two home runs).

GUFFY McGOVERN

The blaspheming manager (Paul Douglas) of the lowly Pittsburgh Pirates in

Pirates Manager Guffy McGovern (right), played by actor Paul Douglas, chats with real-life Pittsburgh slugger Ralph Kiner during filming of the 1951 movie 'Angels in the Outfield.'

the 1951 movie "Angels in the Outfield." Guffy, a loudmouth who hated umpires and virtually every other segment of mankind, was directing his club toward a sorry finish in the National League when a messenger from above delivered some enticing news: Clean up your act, sir, and a few victories might come your way. The skipper turned over a new leaf and, sure enough, the Pirates made a turnaround in the standings. All wasn't divine, though, when an orphan girl (played by Donna Corcoran) noticed angels behind each Pittsburgh player and a newspaper reporter (Janet Leigh) tried to get to the bottom of this help from on high.

MAX MERCY

The name of the relentless and egocentric sportswriter in "The Natural." Portrayed by Robert Duvall, Mercy first met Roy Hobbs aboard a train in 1924 when a youthful Hobbs was an aspiring pitcher and then renewed acquaintances 15 years later when Hobbs, as an aging rookie outfielder, joined the New York Knights.

RAY MILLAND

Cast as the somewhat-nutty professor in "It Happens Every Spring," Milland took on a second baseball-related role in "Rhubarb," the film adaptation of H. Allen Smith's novel about a cat who owned a big-league ball club. Milland played a guardian for the cat, Rhubarb, and endured considerable travail when Rhubarb was targeted by bookies, gangsters and kidnapers.

MICHAEL MORIARTY

In the 1973 film "Bang the Drum Slowly," he portrayed pitcher Henry Wiggen, who was confronted with the to-be-kept-secret news that his roommate-batterymate was dying. The talented and intellectual Wiggen, the antithesis of his doomed friend, helped his teammate fulfill his wish of playing one more season of baseball.

GREG MULLEAVY

The son of a former big-league infielder, minor league manager and Brooklyn and Los Angeles Dodgers coach of the same name, he played the baseball cap-wearing husband (Tom) of Mary Hartman in the television show "Mary Hartman, Mary Hartman." The series, a satire of TV's soap operas, made its debut in January 1976.

'THE NATURAL'

The mystical 1952 novel by Bernard Malamud that was transformed to the screen in 1984, with Robert Redford starring as Roy Hobbs, a young man destined for major league stardom—but, because of a shooting, denied his date with baseball destiny for 15 years.

NEW YORK MAMMOTHS

The name of the baseball team managed by Dutch Schnell (Vincent Gardenia) in "Bang the Drum Slowly."

LLOYD NOLAN

Actor who played a feuding, Leo Durocher-like managerial character in "It Happened in Flatbush," a midsummer-1942 movie that attempted to depict the colorful playing style exemplified by the Brooklyn Dodgers.

MICHAEL NOURI

Perhaps best-known as the male lead opposite Jennifer Beals in the popular "Flashdance" film of 1983, he portrayed Bay City Bluebirds Manager Joe Rohner in the not-so-popular television series "The Bay City Blues" of the same year. (The show ran from October 25 through November 15, then was canceled.)

New York Yankee slugger-turned-actor Lou Gehrig (white hat) takes his lumps from the bad guys during a saloon scene in the 1938 musical Western 'Rawhide.'

BRUCE PEARSON

Name of the New York Mammoths' catcher (played by Robert De Niro) who was dying of Hodgkin's disease in "Bang the Drum Slowly," a highly praised film based on Mark Harris' mid-1950s novel.

'RAWHIDE'

A 1938 musical Western co-starring, believe it or not, Lou Gehrig. Yes, the Yankees' Iron Horse brandished a six-shooter instead of a Louisville Slugger. However, he preferred slinging to singing—he took aim at the bad guys with billiard balls in a memorable poolroom scene—and left the vocalizing to Smith Ballew, who portrayed a cowboy-lawyer.

RONALD REAGAN

In the presidential-election year of 1952, the 41-year-old Reagan was in the spotlight—because of his motion-picture portrayal of major league pitching star Grover Cleveland Alexander in "The Winning Team."

Edward G. Robinson (center) and Jeff Richards (left) receive technical advice from Hall of Fame pitcher Carl Hubbell during filming for the 1953 movie 'Big Leaguer.'

EDWARD G. ROBINSON

During a "down" period in his screen career, this noted movie tough guy played the part of a tryout-camp supervisor for the New York Giants in the 1953 movie "Big Leaguer."

BABE RUTH

He played himself in "The Pride of the Yankees," the film biography of Lou Gehrig, and was joined in the cast by noted Yankees Bill Dickey, Bob Meusel and Mark Koenig and sportscaster Bill Stern (all of whom played themselves).

VERNON SIMPSON

Name of the "It Happens Every Spring" character (portrayed by Ray Milland) who stumbled upon a chemical compound that, applied to a baseball, made the ball repulsive to wood. More effective than even a split-fingered fastball, the chemical-compound pitch transformed Vernon from a chemistry instructor at a Midwest university into a big-league pitching star.

SIBBY SISTI

A longtime infielder-outfielder for the Boston Braves who wound up his major league career with the Milwaukee Braves in 1954, he was the man managing the Pittsburgh club in "The Natural."

'THE SLUGGER'S WIFE'

A 1985 Neil Simon movie about a dual-career relationship—he (Darryl Palmer, played by Michael O'Keefe) was a ball player, she (spouse Debby, played by Rebecca de Mornay) was a singer.

ROSCOE SNOOKER

A pill-popping arbiter with a twitching eye in the William Bendix vehicle "Kill the Umpire." Snooker was played by Tom D'Andrea, familiar to Bendix fans as Chester A. Riley's sarcastic friend, Jim Gillis, in "The Life of Riley" television series.

'SOMEWHERE IN GEORGIA'

The 1916 movie in which Ty Cobb played a bank clerk/ball player who was in love with the daughter of a small-town bank president. The film, completed in about two weeks and the product of Grantland Rice's writing, featured the Cobb character's ascent to the big leagues, his return to Georgia because of homesickness, a kidnaping and the seemingly obligatory just-in-time-arrival to win the big game.

'SPEEDY'

The 1928 film comedy starring Harold Lloyd and featuring a hilarious segment in which taxi driver Lloyd took a noted passenger, one Babe Ruth, on a breakneck-speed ride to the ball park.

Also eliciting laughter from theater audiences was a scene in which Lloyd, working at a soda fountain, improvised a baseball scoreboard by fashioning numbers out of pretzels and doughnuts.

JAMES STEWART

He portrayed White Sox pitching ace Monty Stratton, whose big-league career was ended at age 26 because of a hunting accident, in the 1949 motion picture "The Stratton Story." After winning 15 games for Chicago in 1937 and again in 1938, rising star Stratton was the victim of a November 1938 hunting mishap that forced the amputation of his right leg. While he never pitched again in the majors, Stratton still staged an amazing comeback highlighted by his 18-victory season for Sherman of the Class C East Texas League in 1946.

Monty Stratton (James Stewart) shows mom (Agnes Moorehead) that baseball does indeed pay in a scene from the 1949 film 'The Stratton Story.'

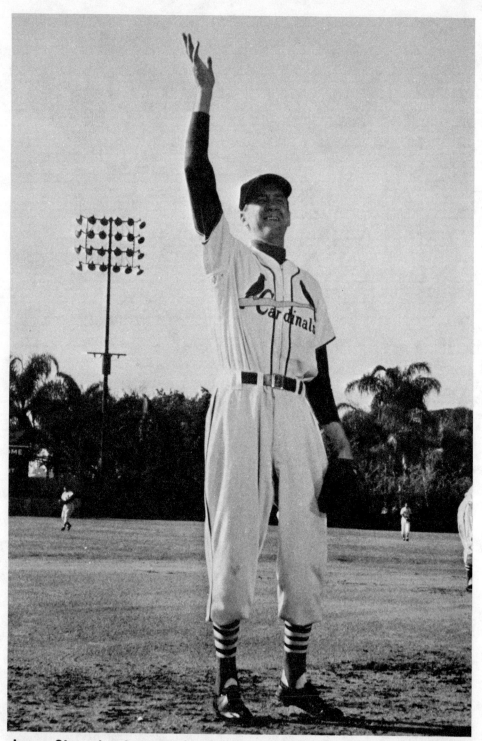

James Stewart put on another baseball uniform in 1955 when he again teamed with actress June Allyson for the movie 'Strategic Air Command.'

Actor Cary Grant and actress Doris Day joined baseball stars Roger Maris, Mickey Mantle and Yogi Berra in the Yankee dugout during filming of the 1962 comedy-romance 'That Touch of Mink.'

JAMES STEWART, JUNE ALLYSON

Six years after playing Mr. and Mrs. Monty Stratton in "The Stratton Story," Stewart and Allyson were back in a baseball-related movie. This time around it was "Strategic Air Command," a 1955 film in which Stewart played Robert (Dutch) Holland, a big-league ball player who was called back into the Air Force at a crucial time in his baseball career, and Allyson portrayed his wife.

RUSTY TAMBLYN

The wayward youth in "The Kid From Cleveland," the late-summer movie of 1949 about a sports announcer's attempt to head off a budding case of juvenile delinquency. The announcer (George Brent) received a little help from his friends—the Cleveland Indians—along the way. The film obviously tried to capitalize on the popularity of the Indians, reigning World Series champions at the time, and featured newsreel footage of the Tribe in action.

Tamblyn, who in 1952 played Grover Cleveland Alexander's young brother Willie in "The Winning Team," became known as Russ Tamblyn when he stepped into more mature movie roles later in the '50s.

'THAT TOUCH OF MINK'

A 1962 comedy-romance set in New York that starred Cary Grant and Doris Day and featured brief appearances by Yankee stars Mickey Mantle, Roger Maris and Yogi Berra.

CLAIRE TREVOR

Actress who portrayed Mrs. Babe Ruth (Claire) in the film "The Babe Ruth Story."

BOB UECKER

A .200-hitting catcher for six big-league seasons (1962-1967), his flair for comedy—evidenced in beer commercials and as a talk-show guest—landed him a major role in the television series "Mr. Belvedere," which made its debut in March 1985. Uecker was cast as George Owens, whose family benefits from the wisdom of a cultured English servant but also has to endure the servant's barbed wit.

GWEN VERDON

Playing the handmaiden of the devil in the 1958 film musical "Damn Yankees," the theme of which was delivering a pennant to the Washington Senators at the expense of a diehard fan's soul, she had the assignment of keeping Senators rookie Joe Hardy in line (or out of line, depending upon your point of view).

RAY WALSTON

As Applegate (the devil) in the movie "Damn Yankees," he hatched the plot for the doormat Senators to beat out the New York Yankees. His right-hand woman in this sizable project was Lola (as in "Whatever Lola Wants, Lola Gets"), portrayed by Gwen Verdon.

Walston and Verdon recreated the roles in which they earlier starred on Broadway.

JACK WARDEN

He was cast as Coach Morris Buttermaker in the television-series version of "The Bad News Bears," which aired in 1979 and 1980.

WAR MEMORIAL STADIUM

Home park of Buffalo's minor league baseball team and longtime home field of football's Buffalo Bills, it served as the home of the New York Knights in "The Natural" and was the principal location for most of the baseball action in the 1984 film.

MINOR WATSON

Actor who was lauded for his portrayal of Brooklyn Dodgers President Branch Rickey in "The Jackie Robinson Story."

THE WHAMMER

The Ruthian-like major league slugger (Joe Don Baker) in "The Natural" whom farmboy Roy Hobbs struck out at a carnival. The Whammer-vs.-

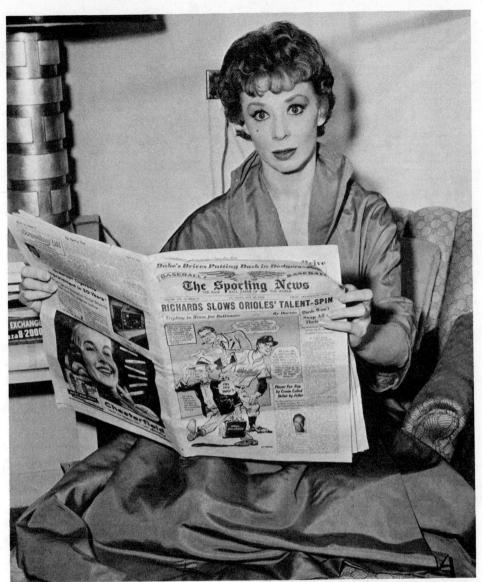

Actress Gwen Verdon played Lola, the alluring handmaiden of the devil, in the 1958 musical 'Damn Yankees.'

Hobbs matchup unfolded when a train transporting Hobbs to Chicago for a big-league tryout (the Whammer also was a passenger) made a whistle stop in a small town.

PAUL WINFIELD

He was cast as former Brooklyn catcher Roy Campanella in the 1974 television drama "It's Good to Be Alive," which focused on Campanella's fight to regain at least partial use of his limbs after a life-threatening and career-ending automobile accident in January 1958.

Frank Sinatra (left), Gene Kelly (center) and Jules Munshin sang and danced their way through the 1949 musical 'Take Me Out to the Ball Game.'

'A WINNER NEVER QUITS'

The 1986 made-for-television movie in which Keith Carradine played Pete Gray, the one-armed outfielder who overcame monumental odds and advanced to the major leagues despite his handicap. Gray appeared in 77 games for the 1945 St. Louis Browns and batted .218.

WOLVES

Name of the baseball team for which vaudeville comedians Dennis Ryan (Frank Sinatra) and Eddie O'Brien (Gene Kelly) played in the 1949 musical "Take Me Out to the Ball Game." Running the Wolves was K.C. Higgins—Esther Williams.

WONDERBOY

The name of Roy Hobbs' homemade bat in "The Natural."

WRIGLEY FIELD, LOS ANGELES

Longtime home of the Los Angeles Angels of the Pacific Coast League and home park of the American League's Los Angeles Angels expansion team in 1961, its proximity to Hollywood made it a favorite setting for baseball movies of the 1940s and 1950s.

CHAPTER 10 EXTRA BASES

CRAIG ANDERSON

New York Mets pitcher who, in relief, won both games of a May 12, 1962, doubleheader against the Milwaukee Braves—but never won another game in the major leagues, dropping his last 19 decisions. Anderson lost his final 16 decisions of '62 (and finished the year with a 3-17 record), had a 0-2 ledger in 1963 for the Mets and was 0-1 with the National League club in 1964.

Anderson, who pitched for the St. Louis Cardinals in 1961, compiled a 7-23 career record in the majors.

SPARKY ANDERSON, WHITEY HERZOG

The only managers in big-league history to have 100-victory seasons in both the American League and the National League. Anderson's Cincinnati Reds won 102 N.L. games in 1970, 108 in 1975 and 102 in 1976 and his Detroit Tigers totaled 104 A.L. victories in 1984. Herzog's Kansas City Royals won 102 A.L. games in 1977 and his St. Louis Cardinals won 101 times in the 1985 N.L. season.

ORVILLE ARMBRUST

Washington Senators pitcher whose only major league victory came against the New York Yankees on September 30, 1934—the day Babe Ruth played his last game for the Bronx Bombers. The 24-year-old Armbrust was a 5-3 winner in the season finale played at Washington, working seven-plus innings and allowing seven hits and all three Yankee runs. He walked one and struck out two. Ruth was 0 for 3 at the plate while appearing in his 2,084th and final game with the Yankees.

Ruth went on to play 28 more big-league games, all with the 1935 Boston Braves. Armbrust, whose start against the Yankees marked only his third appearance in the majors, never pitched again in the big leagues.

ERNIE BANKS

The only player to win a Most Valuable Player award in a season in which his team won fewer than half of its games—and he accomplished the feat two years in a row. In 1958, when the Chicago Cubs finished 72-82, the Cubs' Banks won National League MVP honors with a 47-homer, 129-RBI season that included a .313 batting average. A year later, the Cubs went 74-80 and Banks was an MVP repeater based on his 45 home runs, 143 runs batted in and .304 batting mark.

Hank Sauer is the only other player to win MVP selection while playing on a big-league team that failed to post a winning record. Sauer drilled 37 homers and knocked in 121 runs for the Cubs in his MVP season of 1952, a year in which Chicago compiled a 77-77 record.

DON BAYLOR

Normally the Boston Red Sox's designated hitter in 1986, he was stationed at first base on the night of April 29—and made an error that helped teammate Roger Clemens establish a big-league record of 20 strikeouts in a nine-inning game. Taking over for regular first baseman Bill Buckner (who was troubled by an elbow injury and assumed the "DH" role), Baylor camped under a fourth-inning pop foul off the bat off Seattle's Gorman Thomas—and dropped the ball. With eight strikeouts at that point, Clemens got another chance to dispose of Thomas via the strikeout route—and did just that. The Red Sox pitcher, appearing in only his 40th major league game, struck out the side in the fifth inning and fanned two batters in each of the final four innings to shatter the previous big-league mark of 19 strikeouts in a nine-inning contest.

Baylor appeared at first base only 13 times for Boston in 1986 and saw outfield duty in just three games.

BOSTON RED SOX

American League team that hit for the cycle against Chicago White Sox pitcher Orval Grove in a June 6, 1942, game—but could do nothing else against the righthander. Grove was tagged for a leadoff, first-inning home run by Boston's Dom DiMaggio and later in the game allowed a triple to Bill Conroy, a double to Jim Tabor and a single to Johnny Pesky. Grove's four-hit pitching lifted the White Sox to a 3-1 victory.

STEVE BRYE

Minnesota Twins left fielder whose misplay of a ninth-inning fly ball on the final day of the 1976 season enabled Kansas City's George Brett to win the American League batting championship—and infuriated the Royals' Hal McRae, whose own sights had been on the hitting crown. McRae wasn't upset with his Royals teammate; he was, however, enraged over the scenario that decided the title. Entering the last of the ninth inning of the game played in Kansas City, Brett trailed A.L. leader McRae by the barest of margins, .3326 to .3322. Brett proceeded to hit a high fly ball to left, on which it appeared Brye would make a routine play (thus "assuring" McRae of the batting title). However, after running toward the ball, Brye stopped abruptly and the ball fell 10 to 15 feet in front of him. The ball took a high bounce on the artificial turf and went over Brye's head—and Brett circled the bases for an inside-the-park home run. The "gift" hit boosted Brett's average to .333 and meant that McRae, who followed Brett in the batting order, would have to hit safely to win the batting crown. Facing the Twins' Jim Hughes, McRae grounded out—after which the Royals player made two gestures toward the Minnesota dugout. McRae, a black player, later implied that he thought Minnesota Manager Gene Mauch had instructed his players to help Brett, who is white, win the title. Mauch was stunned by McRae's insinuation, saying he "would never, never do anything to harm the integrity of baseball." And Brye steadfastly maintained he simply made a "mistake by playing too deep."

The game actually began as a *three-way* battle for the hitting crown, with McRae entering the contest at .33078, Brett at .33073 and Minnesota's Rod Carew at .32945. Brett had a 3-for-4 afternoon, while McRae and Carew each went 2 for 4. The final, rounded-off averages: Brett, .333; McRae, .332, and Carew .331.

Brye never played again for the Twins, winding up his career with the Milwaukee Brewers (1977) and Pittsburgh Pirates (1978); pitcher Hughes, a 5-3 complete-game winner in the controversial contest and winner of 16 games in 1975 and nine in '76, found himself back in the minor leagues in 1977 and never won another game in the majors; Brett captured a second batting crown in 1980 (winning that championship by *38* points), and McRae continued as one of the league's toughest hitters—but never again (through 1986) contended for a batting championship.

GENE CONLEY, DAVE DeBUSSCHERE

Pitchers who, when they appeared in the same 1963 major league game, were past and future members, respectively, of National Basketball Association championship teams. Conley, who played for the Boston Celtics'

1959, 1960 and 1961 NBA titlists, was the Red Sox's starting pitcher against the White Sox in an April 27, 1963, contest at Boston's Fenway Park. Ray Herbert started for Chicago, going 3⅓ innings before being relieved by DeBusschere, who went on to play for the New York Knicks' NBA champions of 1970 and 1973. The two athletes were in the '63 American League game at the same time, at least briefly, as Conley pitched four-plus innings for Boston and DeBusschere, in a two-thirds-inning stint, worked in the fourth inning for Chicago.

CHUCK COTTIER, DICK WILLIAMS

Seattle's manager on April 29, 1986, when the Mariners were victimized by Roger Clemens' record 20-strikeout performance in a nine-inning major league game, Cottier had seen duty at second base for Washington on September 12, 1962, when the Senators' Tom Cheney established the big-league record for most strikeouts in one game, regardless of length, by fanning 21 Baltimore batters in a 16-inning contest. Fired from his Seattle managerial post about a week after Clemens' masterpiece, Cottier was succeeded on a permanent basis as Mariners pilot by Williams. And, curiously, it was Williams—as a pinch-hitter for Baltimore—who had been Cheney's 21st strikeout victim in that '62 Senators-Orioles game.

TED COX

Seattle Mariners third baseman who was credited with the first official game-winning RBI in American League history. After falling behind the Toronto Blue Jays, 2-0, in the first inning of their 1980 season opener, the Mariners tied the score in the bottom half of the inning and then went ahead in the same frame when Cox slammed a two-run double off Blue Jays pitcher Dave Lemanczyk. Seattle never relinquished the lead in the April 9 night game, posting an 8-6 triumph.

SAM CRAWFORD

In his first day as a major leaguer, this Cincinnati outfielder (and future Detroit Tigers star) played against Cleveland. *And* Louisville. Competing in an era when schedules were perhaps more likely to develop occasional quirks, Cincinnati first played host to National League rival Cleveland on September 10, 1899, and then met the N.L.'s Louisville club on the Reds' home grounds later in the day. Crawford broke into the majors in the first game, rapping two singles in four at-bats against Cleveland as Cincinnati cruised to a 10-2 triumph. In the second contest, Crawford collected three hits—including the first of his major league-record 312 triples—and the Reds edged Louisville, 8-7.

BILL DAHLEN

Chicago shortstop whose 42-game batting streak was stopped in an August 7, 1894, National League contest in which teammates immediately ahead of and behind him in the batting order went 5 for 6. Second-place hitter Dahlen was hitless in six at-bats against Cincinnati, while leadoff man Jimmy Ryan

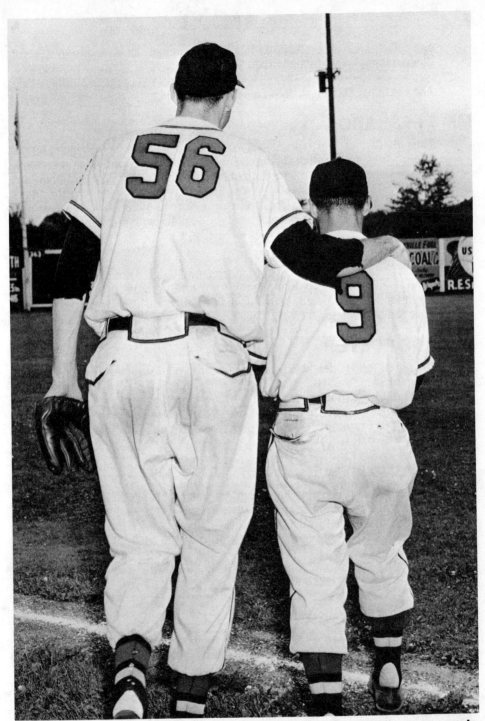

In 1951, Gene Conley, pictured above with a Hartford teammate, was en route to the major leagues and even bigger and better things in the world of professional basketball.

and third-place hitter Walt Wilmot each cracked out five hits in a 17-hit Chicago attack that helped produce a 13-11 victory.

The next day, Dahlen started on a 28-game hitting streak.

MIKE FERRARO

The only former Seattle Pilots player to advance to the major league managerial ranks, performing for the Pilots in 1969 before managing the Cleveland Indians in 1983 (100 games) and guiding the Kansas City Royals in 1986 (74 games). Ferraro appeared in five games as a pinch-hitter for the Pilots (who spent only one season in Seattle before moving to Milwaukee and becoming the Brewers), going 0 for 4 at the plate with one base on balls.

5

The uniform number that Hank Aaron first wore in the major leagues. Aaron wore number 5 while playing for the Milwaukee Braves in 1954, but asked for—and received—a double-digit number in 1955. Given "44," Aaron wore the number for the rest of his big-league career.

GEORGE FOSTER

Cincinnati left fielder who was credited with big-league baseball's first official game-winning RBI, a statistic that was adopted in 1980. Foster sent the Reds into the lead in the first inning of their April 9 season opener, drilling a two-run double off Atlanta's Phil Niekro. The Reds, behind the three-hit pitching of Frank Pastore, went on to a 9-0 triumph over the Braves in the afternoon contest.

BOB FRIEND

The last of only three pitchers in major league history to lose 200 or more games while failing to win at least 200. Friend had a lifetime 197-230 record for the Pittsburgh Pirates, New York Yankees and New York Mets in a big-league career that began in 1951 and ended in 1966.

Also losing 200 or more games in the majors without winning 200 were Chick Fraser (176-212) and Jim Whitney (193-207).

GENE GREEN

Cleveland outfielder who dropped two fly balls in the fifth inning of a 1962 game against Chicago, helping the White Sox collect a major league-record three sacrifice flies in one inning. In the second game of a July 1 doubleheader, the Sox had a runner on third base when Chicago pitcher Juan Pizarro hit a fifth-inning drive toward Green. The Indians' right fielder dropped the ball, but Pizarro was awarded a sacrifice fly because the official scorer ruled that the ball had traveled far enough to drive in the run had the catch been made. Later in the inning, Chicago's Nellie Fox hit another ball that Green dropped, with the scorer again crediting the batter with a sacrifice fly. The White Sox's Al Smith accounted for the lone "normal" sacrifice fly of the inning, with Green catching his drive (for the first out of the inning). Green's misplays contributed to a six-run White Sox inning, which Chicago rode to a 7-6 triumph.

AL GRUNWALD

Pittsburgh Pirates player who broke into the major leagues with a "cycle" performance—but, to Grunwald's dismay, he was pitching, not batting. Making his big-league debut in a fourth-inning relief role against the New York Giants in an April 18, 1955, game, Grunwald worked one-third of an inning and allowed four hits—a single by Don Mueller, a double by Monte Irvin, a triple by Willie Mays (the first man he faced) and a home run by Whitey Lockman. Grunwald was charged with four runs as the Giants, on the way to a 12-3 triumph, enjoyed an eight-run inning.

Grunwald made nine pitching appearances overall in the majors, three with the '55 Pirates and six with the 1959 Kansas City A's. His career record was 0-1.

JACK HARPER

He played for big-league baseball's losingest and winningest clubs. A two-time 20-game winner in the majors, he pitched his rookie season for the 1899 Cleveland Spiders, compiling a 1-4 record for the National League club that lost a record 134 games while winning only 20. In 1906, Harper appeared in one game for the N.L.'s Chicago Cubs, a team that won a record 116 contests. Starting for the Cubs on June 6 against the New York Giants, he was struck on the hand by a line drive and left the game after the first inning— never to perform again in the majors.

SOLLY HEMUS

The only man in modern National League history to manage at least a full season in the league and never manage against a New York team. Hemus guided the St. Louis Cardinals during his entire 384-game major league managerial career, which stretched from 1959 until July 1961 and involved years in which there was no N.L. team in New York.

The four-year period from 1958 through 1961 marked the only time in modern big-league history that New York was not represented in the N.L.

ROGERS HORNSBY

The only player in major league history to attain a .400 batting average over a five-year period. Playing for the St. Louis Cardinals, Hornsby hit a composite .402 from 1921 through 1925 by fashioning National League-leading season averages of .397, .401, .384, .424 and .403. Hornsby collected 1,078 hits in 2,679 at-bats in that period.

LaMARR HOYT

The pitcher with the highest earned-run average in a Cy Young Award-winning year. Hoyt won the American League's Cy Young honor in 1983, putting together a 24-10 season for the Chicago White Sox despite a 3.66 ERA. The earned-run figure ranked 17th in the A.L. among pitchers working enough innings to qualify for the ERA title.

Only two other Cy Young Award winners who qualified for the ERA crown failed to finish in the top 10 of their league ERA races. Both instances occurred in 1967, when Jim Lonborg of the Boston Red Sox captured the A.L. Cy Young Award with a 3.16 ERA, the 18th-best mark in the league, and Mike McCormick of the San Francisco Giants took the N.L. Cy Young trophy with a 2.85 ERA, the 16th-best figure in the league.

KEN HUNT

Cincinnati Reds hurler whose major league career consisted of one season —a year in which he was named the National League's Rookie Pitcher of the Year by The Sporting News. After logging a 16-6 record for Columbia of the South Atlantic League in 1960, Hunt went to spring training with the parent Reds as a non-roster player in 1961—and made the club. Easing into Cincinnati's starting rotation early in the season, the 22-year-old Hunt got off to a 9-4 start with the Reds before slumping to a final 9-10 record and winding up in the bullpen for the N.L. champions. Nevertheless, he captured The Sporting News' N.L. rookie pitching honor. In 1962, Hunt encountered control problems in the spring and was sent back to the minor leagues— never to return.

Hunt's last appearance in the majors was as a ninth-inning reliever in the fifth and last game of the 1961 World Series against the New York Yankees.

JERRY KOOSMAN

The only pitcher to shut out the Milwaukee Brewers in 1979—and he performed the feat on the final day of the season, thus thwarting the Brewers' bid to equal the New York Yankees' major league record, established in 1932 and never matched, of playing an entire season without being blanked. Pitching for the Minnesota Twins on September 30, Koosman shut out Milwaukee, 5-0, despite allowing nine hits.

The 1979 Brewers went 95-66 and finished second in the American League East, while the 1932 Yankees captured the A.L. pennant with a 107-47 mark (the Yanks tied one game) and then won the World Series.

SANDY KOUFAX

The only pitcher to win the Cy Young Award in his last season in the major leagues. Koufax won his third Cy Young trophy in 1966 after compiling a 27-9 record for the Los Angeles Dodgers with 317 strikeouts and a 1.73 earned-run average. Following the '66 season, Koufax, six weeks from his

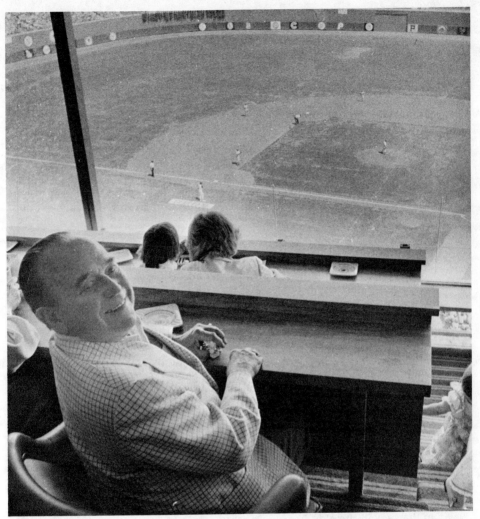

San Diego Padres Owner Ray Kroc was not so happy when he grabbed the public-address-system microphone and chastised his team during its 1974 home opener.

31st birthday, announced his retirement from baseball because of arthritic-elbow problems.

RAY KROC

San Diego Padres owner who, in the middle of the eighth inning of his fourth regular-season game as owner of a big-league club, grabbed the public-address-system microphone and, in a curt analysis of his team's performance, announced "that this is the most stupid baseball playing I've ever seen." Kroc's critique came in the Padres' 1974 home opener, an April 9 contest against the Houston Astros. That Kroc was frustrated proved no surprise; the Padres, after all, had opened the season in horrendous fashion, losing 8-0, 8-0 and 9-2 games in Los Angeles (and they were trailing 9-2 in this one against Houston). That he would share his thoughts with everyone in the stadium was a shocker; players on both clubs were angry over the public dressing-down, which they considered in extremely poor taste.

A day later, Kroc voiced his regret over the incident and said that a male streaker influenced his denunciation of the team. "The streaker just added gas to the fire," said Kroc, who had begun his previous night's remarks by saying "Ladies and gentlemen, I suffer with you" before being interrupted by the on-field streaker. After urging authorities to throw the streaker in jail, Kroc went on to offer a good-news, bad-news report to the stadium crowd—the good news being that San Diego had outdrawn Los Angeles in its home opener, the bad news being that the Padres were playing "stupid" baseball.

San Diego fell by a 9-5 score in its '74 home opener, then lost successive 9-1 games to Houston (meaning that the Padres had been outscored 52-9 while opening the season with six straight defeats). The club, managed by John McNamara, finished the season with a 60-102 record and finished last in the National League West.

JOHNNIE LeMASTER

Shortstop who in 1985 played for three major league clubs—all of whom finished in last place and lost at least 100 games. Perhaps fittingly, LeMaster's batting statistics reflected the company he was keeping (although, it should be pointed out, the infielder spent 2½ months on the disabled list in '85 and had only 94 at-bats overall). LeMaster began the season with San Francisco and was hitless in 16 at-bats for the Giants, who wound up 62-100 and in the basement of the National League West. Traded to Cleveland in early May, he batted .150 for the Indians. Cleveland, on the way to a 60-102 record and a cellar finish in the American League East, dealt LeMaster to Pittsburgh before the month was out. Spending the balance of the season with the Pirates, LeMaster hit .155 for a team that went 57-104 and brought up the rear in the N.L. East.

LOS ANGELES ANGELS

Of the 10 modern big-league expansion franchises, the team that posted the best record in its first season of play. The Angels entered the American League in 1961 and compiled a 70-91 mark (.435 winning percentage) that year.

After playing surprisingly well in their first season, the Angels were just short of amazing in their second year. Eighth-place finishers in the A.L. in '61, the Angels leaped to third place in 1962 with an 86-76 record (.531) and finished only 10 games out of first place.

HEINIE MANUSH

From the inception of The Sporting News' end-of-season major league All-

Star Team (1925) through the publication's 29th year of choosing the combined American League-National League "dream club" (1953, the St. Louis Browns' last season), the lone Browns player to win a spot on the select unit. Manush made it as an outfielder—along with Babe Ruth of the New York Yankees and Paul Waner of the Pittsburgh Pirates—on the 1928 team.

MAY 2, 1939

A notable day in Detroit baseball history, with Lou Gehrig, Fred Hutchinson and little William James Brown figuring in the goings-on. This was the afternoon on which New York's Gehrig ended his record consecutive-game playing streak, asking that he be scratched from the lineup for the Yankees-Tigers clash at Briggs Stadium after appearing in 2,130 straight major league contests. As Gehrig watched the proceedings (he would never play again in the majors), the Yanks crushed Detroit, 22-2. Among the victimized Tiger pitchers was Hutchinson, a 19-year-old righthander who was making his big-league debut. Hutchinson, a standout Detroit pitcher after World War II and eventually the Tigers' manager, yielded four hits, five walks and eight runs in two-thirds of an inning. And, on this day, young Mr. Brown also made his debut. Born on May 2, 1939, in Crestline, O., William James (Gates) Brown became a 13-year Tiger player (1963-1975), a pinch-hitter deluxe and one of the most popular players in Detroit history.

MILWAUKEE BREWERS

The only team to play in both the West Division and East Division of a major league. When the American League West's Seattle Pilots abruptly moved to Milwaukee and became the Brewers prior to the 1970 season, the A.L. kept the franchise in the West Division for '70 and 1971. But when the second Washington Senators franchise, an A.L. East club, relocated in Texas after the '71 season and became the Rangers, the Brewers were switched to the East in 1972 and the Rangers were placed in the West.

JOHN MOHARDT

A college football teammate of George Gipp at Notre Dame from 1918 through 1920, a major league teammate of Ty Cobb with the Detroit Tigers in 1922 and a National Football League teammate of Red Grange with the Chicago Bears in 1925. Mohardt, a halfback with the Fighting Irish and the Bears, was an outfielder with the Tigers but played in only five big-league games. In his lone official at-bat in the majors, which came on April 21, 1922, Mohardt singled off Cleveland's Charlie Jamieson (an outfielder who was called upon to pitch in a lopsided game).

RICK MONDAY

Chicago Cubs center fielder who in the fourth inning of an April 25, 1976, game at Dodger Stadium snatched an American flag from two persons who were about to set the banner on fire. Los Angeles' Ted Sizemore was at the plate when a man and a youth ran onto the field and stopped in front of Cubs left fielder Jose Cardenal. Noticing that the flag-carrying intruders were

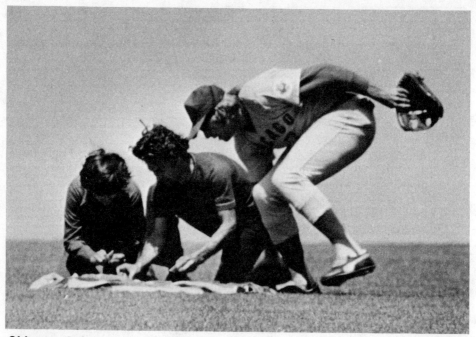

Chicago Cubs center fielder Rick Monday reaches down to snatch an American flag that two persons were trying to set afire during a 1976 game at Dodger Stadium.

fumbling with lighter fluid, Monday raced over, scooped up the flag and delivered it safely to a security guard. When Monday went to bat in the next inning, the crowd gave him a standing ovation.

"If you're going to burn the flag, don't do it in front of me," Monday said. "I've been to too many veterans hospitals and seen too many broken bodies of guys who tried to protect it. . . ."

TERRY MULHOLLAND

San Francisco pitcher who had an undistinguished rookie season (1-7 record) in the major leagues in 1986—but didn't go unnoticed. Case in point: September 3, third inning, Giants vs. the New York Mets. Mulholland fielded a hard smash off the bat of Keith Hernandez and wheeled to throw to first base. However, the ball stuck in the webbing of Mulholland's glove and the 23-year-old lefthander couldn't pry it loose. What to do? Improvise, that's what. Mulholland kept his cool, ran toward first base and, when about seven feet from the bag, pitched his glove (with ball firmly embedded) to Giants first baseman Bob Brenly. Hernandez was out. . .and Mulholland was headed for the week's television highlight films.

NEW YORK METS

The last of only 10 big-league teams to post 100 or more victories in a season without having a pitcher win 20 games. The Mets, paced by Bob Ojeda's 18 victories, won 108 regular-season games in their World Series-championship season of 1986. Dwight Gooden won 17 games, Sid Fernandez collected 16 victories and Ron Darling was a 15-game winner for New York.

Year	Club	Won	Lost	Leading Winner on Staff
1915	Boston Red Sox	101	50	Rube Foster, Ernie Shore, 19
1931	St. Louis Cardinals	101	53	Bill Hallahan, 19
1941	New York Yankees	101	53	Lefty Gomez, Red Ruffing, 15
1942	Brooklyn Dodgers	104	50	Whitlow Wyatt, 19
1967	St. Louis Cardinals	101	60	Dick Hughes, 16
1975	Cincinnati Reds	108	54	Billingham, Gullett, Nolan, 15
1976	Cincinnati Reds	102	60	Gary Nolan, 15
1977	New York Yankees	100	62	Ed Figueroa, Ron Guidry, 16
1984	Detroit Tigers	104	58	Jack Morris, 19
1986	New York Mets	108	54	Bob Ojeda, 18

Of the 10 teams to win 100 games without benefit of a 20-game winner, only the 1942 Brooklyn Dodgers did not win the World Series. And those Dodgers didn't even win the pennant, finishing second to the National League-champion Cardinals (who won 106 games).

PHIL NIEKRO

The last pitcher in the majors to win and lose 20 or more games in the same season. Niekro went 21-20 for the Atlanta Braves in 1979, sharing the National League lead in victories with brother Joe of the Houston Astros and leading the major leagues in defeats.

1942

The last year in which there were no managerial changes in either the National League or the American League. Both circuits had eight clubs at the time.

The last year in which one league went an entire season without a managerial casualty was 1963, when each of the 10 N.L. pilots completed a 162-game schedule. (The A.L.'s last turnover-free season was 1962, a year in which the junior league also had 10 teams.)

96

The most hits gathered by any New York Met in 1972, marking the only time in modern big-league history that a team playing 150 or more games in a season failed to have a player reach the 100-hit plateau. The Mets' hits leader in '72 was Tommie Agee, who batted .227, two points higher than the club's National League-low .225 mark.

Injury problems contributed heavily to the Mets' low individual hit totals in 1972, with only two New York players managing 400 or more official at-bats (Agee was tops with the modest total of 422). Despite the batting woes, the '72 Mets finished third in the N.L. East race with an 83-73 record (six beginning-of-the-season games were canceled because of a players strike).

SPIKE OWEN

A former teammate of Boston's Roger Clemens at the University of Texas and a soon-to-be Red Sox teammate of the standout pitcher (Owen was traded to Boston during the stretch run of the 1986 season), he was at shortstop for the Seattle Mariners in the April 29, 1986, contest in which Clemens struck out a major league-record 20 batters in a nine-inning game. Owen, in fact, was Clemens' record-tying 19th strikeout victim as Seattle's leadoff batter in the ninth inning. (After Owen's final-inning strikeout, the Mariners' Phil Bradley fanned for the fourth time in the game as Clemens rang up No. 20. Ken Phelps then grounded out to end the game, which the Red Sox won by a 3-1 score.)

Dave Henderson, part of the August 1986 trade that sent Owen to Boston and a postseason hitting star for the Red Sox in '86, played center field for the Mariners in the April 29 game at Fenway Park and struck out three times against Clemens.

MILT PAPPAS

The winning pitcher in the last game played by the original Washington Senators American League club, the losing pitcher in the first game played in the Los Angeles Angels' A.L. history and the loser in the last major league game played at Pittsburgh's Forbes Field. Pitching for the Baltimore Orioles on October 2, 1960, Pappas defeated Washington, 2-1, in the final game preceding the Senator franchise's move to Minnesota. On April 11, 1961, he was a loser against Los Angeles when the Angels made their A.L. debut with a 7-2 triumph over the Orioles, and on June 28, 1970, Pappas, then with the Chicago Cubs, fell to the Pirates, 4-1, in the Forbes Field finale.

REGGIE PATTERSON

Chicago Cubs pitcher who, during Pete Rose's quest to attain a major league-record 4,192 career hits, allowed Rose's 4,189th, 4,190th and 4,191st hits. Working in relief for Chicago in a September 6, 1985, game, righthander Patterson yielded a sixth-inning single to Cincinnati's Rose, who earlier in the day had homered off Cubs starter Derek Botelho for hit No. 4,188. Then, on September 8, Patterson, serving as a short-notice starter after scheduled pitcher Steve Trout had been injured in a bicycle mishap, was nicked for No. 4,190, a first-inning single by Rose. In the fifth inning, Rose, the Reds' manager-first baseman, tied Ty Cobb's lifetime mark of 4,191 hits by singling to right off Patterson.

Rose, with the baseball world watching his every move, was not expected to start in the September 8 contest because he had been sitting out against lefthanders all season and lefthander Trout was the anticipated starter for Chicago. Accordingly, fans nationwide were stunned to hear or see that Rose was indeed in the lineup on that Sunday afternoon at Wrigley Field (because of the Cubs' switch from a lefthanded to a righthanded starter). Also adding to the drama was the fact that Rose had thrust himself into a position of perhaps tying or even breaking Cobb's record away from his hometown fans—and doing so one day before the Reds would return to Cincinnati to open a home stand. (While Rose did tie Cobb on September 8, he then was retired on his final two at-bats of the day.)

GAYLORD PERRY, DON SUTTON

Of big-league baseball's 10 pitchers with 3,000 career strikeouts, the only two who never posted a league-leading season strikeout total in the majors. Perry, fourth in lifetime strikeouts with 3,534, achieved his strikeout high of 238 in 1973 for the Cleveland Indians; however, Perry's '73 total was only fourth best in the American League. In 1975, Perry had his highest seasonal ranking, tying for second place in the A.L. with 233 strikeouts while pitching for the Indians and the Texas Rangers. Sutton, sixth in career strikeouts with 3,431, had a high of 217 for the Los Angeles Dodgers in 1969, the seventh-best figure in the National League that year. Sutton's best ranking in one season was fourth, which he attained in 1972 and 1973 when he fanned 207 and 200 batters for the Dodgers.

MARINO PIERETTI

Of Washington's five principal starting pitchers in 1945 (each made 25 or more starts), the only non-knuckleballer. Pieretti, a rookie, compiled a 14-13 record for the '45 Senators. The knuckleball brigade was led by Roger Wolff (20-10), followed by Emil (Dutch) Leonard (17-7), Mickey Haefner (16-14) and Johnny Niggeling (7-12).

JUAN PIZARRO

He earned the first save in American League history. The pitching statistic for protecting a lead was introduced in the major leagues in 1969, and Boston's Pizarro netted the initial A.L. save in support of winning pitcher Bill Landis (who also had worked in relief) by hurling the final inning of a season-opening 5-4 Red Sox triumph over the Baltimore Orioles in a 12-inning game played on the afternoon of April 8.

CY RIGLER

Umpire who was wired for sound for an August 25, 1929, game at the Polo Grounds so his behind-the-plate calls could be heard in the stands. Wires from a microphone inserted into Rigler's mask were strung down the inside of his uniform and connected to metal plates on a shoe. Rigler stood on a metal sheet behind the catcher and once the umpire made contact with the sheet, his voice could be heard via stadium amplifiers. While the innovation clearly was in the spotlight that day at the New York Giants' home park, the Giants themselves attracted some attention by pounding the Pittsburgh Pirates, 10-5.

ROBIN ROBERTS

The only pitcher in major league history to defeat the Boston Braves, Milwaukee Braves and Atlanta Braves. Roberts was 12-6 against the Braves when the franchise was based in Boston, 21-24 against the club when it operated in Milwaukee and 1-0 against the team after it moved to Atlanta.

Only four big-league pitchers suffered losses to all three "versions" of the Braves: Ron Kline, Vernon Law, Joe Nuxhall and Curt Simmons.

SAN FRANCISCO GIANTS

National League club whose 1981 pitching staff became the first in major league history to notch more shutouts than complete games in a season. The Giants, getting six shutouts that involved more than one pitcher, blanked opponents nine times overall in '81 but had only eight complete games.

Only four other big-league teams have had more shutouts than complete games in a season. The Chicago Cubs recorded 10 shutouts and nine complete games in 1983, the New York Mets had 15 shutouts and 12 complete games in 1984, the San Diego Padres totaled 17 shutouts and 13 complete games in '84 and the Houston Astros had 19 shutouts and 18 complete games in 1986.

Two clubs have had an equal number of shutouts and complete games in one year—the 1985 Montreal Expos (13 of each) and the '85 Atlanta Braves (nine of each).

ERIC SHOW

San Diego pitcher off whom Cincinnati's Pete Rose collected his record-breaking 4,192nd major league hit in the first inning of a September 11, 1985, game. Rose, who had matched Ty Cobb's total of 4,191 hits on September 8 in Chicago, had not played against the Padres on September 9 in the opening game of a Reds home stand and had gone 0 for 4 in a September 10 contest against San Diego.

Supporting Cast:

● **Bruce Bochy.** Show's batterymate in the game played at Riverfront Stadium.

● **Tom Browning.** Cincinnati's starting and winning pitcher, yielding no runs and five hits over 8⅓ innings. John Franco and Ted Power each pitched one-third inning of relief to nail down a 2-0 victory.

● **Nick Esasky.** Cincinnati left fielder who drove in both of the game's runs, scoring Rose with a fielder's-choice grounder in the third inning and driving home the Reds' player-manager (who had tripled) with a sacrifice fly in the seventh inning.

● **Eddie Milner.** Cincinnati's leadoff batter, he fouled out in the first inning. Rose followed Milner to the plate, worked the count to 2-1 against Show and then lined what he called "the big knock"—lifetime hit No. 4,192 in the majors—into left-center field, and the crowd of 47,237 cheered wildly. Padres left fielder Carmelo Martinez fielded the ball, threw it in and one of baseball's great chases—if not the game's greatest chase—was over.

Show allowed seven Reds hits and two runs before leaving the game in the eighth inning for a pinch-hitter.

BILL SINGER

Los Angeles Dodgers pitcher who was credited with the major leagues' first save, which became an official relief-pitching statistic in 1969. Singer earned the save on April 7, 1969, in a season-opening National League game at Cincinnati, working three scoreless innings after taking over for Los Angeles starter and winner Don Drysdale. Singer did not allow a hit, walked one batter and struck out one as the Dodgers beat the Reds, 3-2.

JOHN SIPIN

San Diego Padres second baseman who belted triples in his first two big-league at-bats—but never collected another three-base hit in the majors. Breaking into the big leagues on May 24, 1969, Sipin rapped first- and fourth-inning triples off Ken Holtzman of the Chicago Cubs. Sipin had 227 more at-bats in the majors, all for the '69 Padres, and connected for 14 additional extra-base hits (12 doubles and two homers) while winding up with a .223 batting average.

The only other players to hit two triples in their first major league games were Ed Irwin of the Detroit Tigers in 1912, Roy Weatherly of the Cleveland Indians in 1936 and Willie McCovey of the San Francisco Giants in 1959. (Irwin, in fact, played in only one major league game. He was one of the amateur players whom the Tigers recruited to fill their ranks for a 1912 game against the Philadelphia A's when teammates of Detroit great Ty Cobb staged a walkout in the wake of Cobb's suspension for going into the stands in New York to confront a heckler. Irwin, who played third base and caught against the A's, was the only sandlotter to hit safely in the contest.)

WARREN SPAHN

The only big-league pitcher to win earned-run-average titles in three decades. Spahn captured National League ERA crowns with the Boston Braves in 1947 (2.33) and with the Milwaukee Braves in 1953 (2.10) and 1961 (3.01.).

GIL TORRES

Washington Senators player who in less than a year's time hit into two triple plays at Griffith Stadium, with Detroit second baseman Eddie Mayo making the initial putout each time. In the seventh inning of the second game of a July 20, 1945, doubleheader, Torres smashed a line drive that a leaping Mayo snared and turned into a triple killing. Then, on May 8, 1946, Torres hit a third-inning liner that deflected off the bare hand of Tigers pitcher Hal Newhouser. Mayo caught the ball before it hit the ground and again was the triggerman on a triple play.

AL TRAVERS

A righthanded pitcher who surrendered 24 runs in his only major league

Al Travers, who allowed 26 hits and 24 runs during his one-game fling as a major league pitcher, later became a Catholic priest.

appearance. A 20-year-old college student at St. Joseph's in Philadelphia, Travers was thrust into the big-league spotlight on May 18, 1912, despite the fact he wasn't good enough to make his college varsity baseball team. The scenario: Detroit superstar Ty Cobb had been suspended for going into the stands on May 15 in New York in pursuit of a heckler. Cobb's teammates decided to protest the suspension, which had been imposed by American League President Ban Johnson, by going on strike May 18 in Philadelphia (where the Tigers were to play the A's). To avoid a fine, forfeiture and possible loss of the Detroit franchise, Tigers Manager Hugh Jennings rounded up a quorum of Philadelphia-area sandlot players to play for his club. Nine locals, including Travers, performed in the game—although not all were starters. The 42-year-old Jennings and Tiger coaches James (Deacon) McGuire (46) and Joe Sugden (41) also appeared in the game, with Jennings failing in a pinch-hitting role, McGuire beginning the game as Travers' batterymate and Sugden playing first base. McGuire and Sugden each singled and scored a run. As for Travers, he pitched the entire game and allowed 26 hits in a 24-2 setback to the A's.

After his fling in the big leagues, Travers returned to his studies and later became a priest.

The Tigers ended their walkout after one game, and Cobb was back in

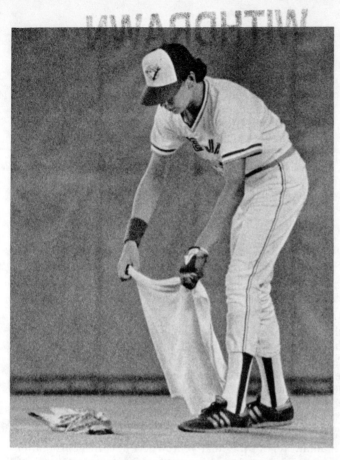

A Toronto ball boy drops a towel over a sea gull that was accidentally killed when struck by a between-innings throw from New York Yankees outfielder Dave Winfield in a 1983 game.

action a short time later after completing his suspension.

ELMER VALO

Outfielder whose big-league playing career was affected by three franchise relocations. Valo spent his first 13 seasons in the majors with the Philadelphia A's, then accompanied the team to Kansas City when the American League club changed home bases after the 1954 season. A member of the Brooklyn Dodgers in 1957, he moved with the National League team to Los Angeles after the season when major league baseball made its historic double switch to the West Coast (with the New York Giants defecting to San Francisco). And after playing for the Washington Senators in 1960, Valo found himself in Minnesota the following year when the Senators franchise moved to the Minneapolis-St. Paul area and was named the Twins.

DAVE WINFIELD

New York Yankees outfielder who accidentally killed a sea gull with a between-innings throw toward the bullpen during an August 4, 1983, game in Toronto and subsequently was charged with cruelty to animals. As Toronto prepared to bat in the fifth inning, Winfield, having just finished outfield warmups, winged a ball in the direction of a ball boy—but it struck a sea gull that had been lolling around on the outfield grass. After the deceased bird had been removed—Winfield stood with cap held over his heart—the game continued and the Yankees, paced by Winfield's two runs batted in, won, 3-1. Canadian fans, particularly respectful of wildlife, let fly with verbal blasts at Winfield, who was met after the game by several plainclothes officers and taken to a Toronto stationhouse. Charged with the crime and advised of his rights, Winfield posted a $500 bond.

A day later, Canadian officials, assured there was no criminal intent involved in the incident, announced that the case would be dropped.

WILBUR WOOD

The last pitcher in American League history to win and lose 20 or more games in the same season. Wood posted an A.L.-leading 24 victories for the Chicago White Sox in 1973 and dropped 20 decisions that year.

BILLY WYNNE

Chicago pitcher who won his first major league game at Milwaukee's County Stadium—but he didn't beat either the Braves or the Brewers while ringing up victory No. 1. Pitching for the White Sox in a June 16, 1969, game in Milwaukee—the Sox played a total of 20 "home games" in the Wisconsin city in 1968 and 1969—Wynne defeated the Seattle Pilots, 8-3.

Although Wynne didn't beat a Milwaukee team while winning his first big-league game at County Stadium, his victory did come against a club that became a County Stadium tenant the next year. The Pilots franchise, after one year in Seattle, was transferred to Milwaukee in '70.

TOM ZACHARY

Having suffered a "low" in 1927 when, as a Washington Senators pitcher, he allowed Babe Ruth's 60th home run, Zachary enjoyed a "high" just two years later when, as Ruth's teammate with the New York Yankees, he compiled a 12-0 record that ranks as the best single-season mark by an undefeated pitcher in big-league history.

AL ZARILLA, GUS ZERNIAL

The only players whose last names started with "Z" to play together in the same outfield. Zarilla and Zernial teamed up in April 1951, playing right and left field, respectively, as part of a Chicago White Sox outfield unit in four games. At the end of the month, Zernial was traded to the Philadelphia A's.

FRANK ZUPO, GEORGE ZUVERINK

The only "Z" battery in major league history. Zupo and Zuverink twice formed a one-inning battery for the Baltimore Orioles in 1957, the first time coming on July 1, 1957, when Zupo made his big-league debut with a 10th-inning catching appearance against the New York Yankees.